D1728065

Simple
Treasures

Simple Treasures

Myles Sweeney

XULON PRESS

Xulon Press
2301 Lucien Way #415
Maitland, FL 32751
407.339.4217
www.xulonpress.com

Unless otherwise indicated, Scripture quotations taken from the Holy Bible, New International Version (NIV). Copyright © 1973, 1978, 1984, 2011 by Biblica, Inc.™. Used by permission. All rights reserved.

Scripture quotations taken from the King James Version (KJV)–*public domain.*

Scripture quotations taken from the New King James Version (NKJV). Copyright © 1982 by Thomas Nelson, Inc. Used by permission. All rights reserved.

Scripture quotations taken from the New American Standard Bible (NASB). Copyright © 1960, 1962, 1963, 1968, 1971, 1972, 1973, 1975, 1977, 1995 by The Lockman Foundation. Used by permission. All rights reserved.

Scripture quotations taken from the Holy Bible, New Living Translation (NLT). Copyright ©1996, 2004, 2007 by Tyndale House Foundation. Used by permission of Tyndale House Publishers, Inc.

Scripture quotations taken from the English Standard Version (ESV). Copyright © 2001 by Crossway, a publishing ministry of Good News Publishers. Used by permission. All rights reserved.

Scripture quotations taken from the Christian Standard Bible. (CSB). Copyright © 2017 by Holman Bible Publishers. Used by permission. All rights reserved.

Scripture quotations taken from the Gods Word Translation copyright ©1995 by Baker Publishing Group.

Scripture quotations taken from The Message (MSG). Copyright © 1993, 1994, 1995, 1996, 2000, 2001, 2002. Used by permission of NavPress Publishing Group. Used by permission. All rights reserved.

Printed in the United States of America.

Paperback ISBN-13: 978-1-6312-9923-0
Hardcover ISBN-13: 978-1-6312-9924-7
Dust Jacket ISBN-13: 978-1-6628-0632-2
eBook ISBN-13: 978-1-6312-9925-4

To my wife, Sallie,
for her constant encouragement,
amazing kindness,
and overwhelming love.

I'm a much better person
because of you.

TABLE OF CONTENTS

Part I

Set the Vision

INTRODUCTION

Proverbs 3:13-15 says, "How blessed is the man who finds wisdom, and the man who gains understanding. For her profit is better than the profit of silver, and her gain better than fine gold. She is more precious than jewels, and nothing you desire compares with her" (NASB).

Through the years, God has revealed some wonderful treasures to me in the form of specific truths from His Word. He showed me truths about what it means to walk out an empowered Christian life. He showed me truths about the destiny He has for each one of us. He showed me truths about how to reach that destiny, and about the pitfalls and obstacles standing in the way. These priceless treasures are buried and forgotten in much of the modern Church, but they are essential.

That is not to say that I am someone special. Jesus says in Luke 10 that God delights in hiding things from those who think themselves wise and clever, and in revealing them to the childlike. The ordinary. The simple.

I have been a pastor and conference speaker for over thirty years. When God first showed me these truths, I immediately wanted to shout them to the world. At first, God wouldn't let me. He walked me through many years of personal practice and application before He ever let me take them to the pulpit, and for that I am grateful.

Since then, I have had the joy and privilege of speaking about the simple treasures God revealed to me in church after church and nation after nation. And I've seen the life-changing power of these truths first-hand. This book is a collection of some of those teachings.

The New Testament Greek word *kairos* means God's perfect time. Since you are holding this book and reading these words, this is *kairos* for you. It's God's perfect time for you to receive these treasures.

Here's the first treasure: God wants you to be truly successful.

A lot of Christians from many different denominations would take issue with that statement, but it is absolutely biblical and absolutely true. That's what God's Word says in 3 John 1:2, "I pray that in all respects you may prosper . . . just as your soul prospers" (NASB). Jesus Himself said the more fruit you produce in your life, the more God is glorified (John 15:8).

God wants you to be successful. He wants you to be successful in your career, in your marriage, in raising your children, and in every single area of your life. That is His heart's desire, but success is not going to happen automatically. If you sit around and wait for it to fall from heaven, you're going to be waiting forever. That's not how it works.

Because God wants you to be successful, He gave you the path to success. That path is called His Word. It is a handbook for life. If you walk in the paths lined out by the Word, you will walk into success. If you build the characteristics described in the Word into your life, you will walk into success. 2 Peter 1:3 tells us that God's divine power has "given us everything we need for life and godliness." As a born-again child of God, He's given you everything you need to be successful, but you have to get up and participate with Him in the process, in order to experience that success in your life.

I want you to reach the success and significance that God Himself wants you to have. Don't take your God-given potential with you to the grave. A passionate pursuit of your divine potential will radically, wonderfully change your life.

This is not hollow, Christianized self-help. This is powerful and real. And this is not some temporary high. It is lasting change that will stand the tests of trials and time. In Jesus' words, it is "fruit that remains" (John 15:16). I vouch for the truth in these messages because I've seen the results in my own life, and in the lives of literally thousands of others. There is more blessing in the pathways of God than anyone could ever imagine.

God's life-changing truths are for the simple. For those who will freely receive them and walk in them. And His truths are simple in that they are not complicated. They are not densely theological. They are straightforward and practical. That's by His design, because He wants us to get them.

These truths are more precious to me than just about anything. I hope you find the same value within these pages. May God open your eyes and your heart to His simple treasures.

PROPHETIC VISION

Why did God create you? What is His created purpose for you? These are important questions, and your answers will change the way you live and cause you to press forward into the things that God has for you.

In Proverbs 29:18, God says, "Where there is no vision, the people perish," (KJV). This verse was not God speaking to the heathen or the lost. It was Him speaking to His very own people and saying, "If you don't have vision for your life, you are going to perish. You are going to miss what I have for you. You are going to miss the blessings I intend for you to have in your life." It is imperative that you and I have a vision for our lives.

This verse in Proverbs reads very differently in each English translation. The New King James Version says, "Where *there is* no revelation, the people cast off restraint." The New Living Translation says it this way: "When people do not accept divine guidance, they run wild." Even though they use different words, they are all saying the same thing.

Vision can come from many places. It can come from things God has spoken to you through His word, from prophetic words given to you by others, or from the Lord speaking to you directly and saying, "This is what I have for you." When those words of prophetic vision come to us, they give us direction for our lives. When we lose our grasp on those prophetic utterances or lose focus, we begin to cast off the restraints they provided for us.

Prophetic words come to us from God like guardrails that keep us on the road. They are boundaries that keep us moving in the right direction. When we cast those barriers off, we cast off the restraint of God's words upon our lives and we begin to live carelessly. We live over here, then we jump and live over there. We don't have any boundaries anymore. When we do that, saints, this is what happens: we flounder around, we become easy targets for the devil, and we perish. We miss what God has for us in our lives. We miss God's best, His destiny, and His created purpose for us.

The word translated as *vision* in Proverbs 29:18 could also be translated into this term: *progressive revelation*. It is very important that we understand the extra meaning in those two words. So many people spend their lives sitting and waiting, saying, "One day God is going speak to me. He's going to tell me what He has for me in my life. When He does that, I'm going to get up, and I'm going to go do it." Those people are still going to be sitting there when Jesus comes back because God doesn't work that way.

When God gives us vision, He gives it to us progressively, in bits and pieces. He doesn't show us the end; He just shows us the next couple of steps. When we walk those steps out, He shows us more steps.

I live in Wharton, Texas. Wharton is about an hour's drive from Houston. If I were going to drive to Houston one night, I would pull to the end of the driveway at my house and look for Houston, right? Except Houston is too far away. The lights of the city are impossible to see from the end of my driveway.

"Well, I guess I can't go to Houston, then. I'll just have to sit here and wait until I can see Houston, then I will be able to go there."

That's crazy. What do I have to do? I simply have to turn on my headlights and drive the twenty or thirty yards of road they light up. As I drive those twenty or thirty yards, I start to see another twenty or thirty yards. As I drive those, I see another twenty or thirty yards. The next thing you know, I start to see Houston.

God's vision for our lives works the same way. It is progressive. God just shows us the next step or two, and we have to begin to walk those steps out in faith. Just take the next step.

Without this kind of progressive revelation or prophetic vision, people perish. Another way to say prophetic vision is a forward-looking vision in God. What does God have for me? Why did He create me?

Those questions bring us to Psalm 139. This chapter is, I think, the most beautiful passage in all of the Bible. I know everybody has their own favorite chapter of the Bible, the one they think is the best or the most beautiful. To me, Psalm 139 is just hard to beat. Some of the most beautiful words in the Bible are in that chapter.

Psalm 139 is King David getting a revelation of how much God loves him, how much God cares about him, and how great God's plans and purposes are for him. This is a wonderful, beautiful, and very exciting chapter to study. Grab your Bible, open it up, and read here with me.

Psalm 139:1-2 says, "You have searched me, Lord, and you know me. You know when I sit and when I rise; you perceive my thoughts from afar." God knows everything about you.

Psalm 139:3-4 says, "You discern my going out and my lying down; you are familiar with all my ways. Before a word is on my tongue you, Lord, know it completely." That is amazing. Before each and every single one of us speak a word, God already knows what's going to come out of our mouths. He is that intimately involved with our lives. He is that concerned about us. He has that much care for us. Isn't that beautiful?

David goes on to say, "You hem me in, behind and before. You laid your hand upon me. Such knowledge is too wonderful for me," (Psalm 139:5-6). This revelation from the Lord is frying some of the fuses in David's brain. It's information overload for him. It's so wonderful and big and great that he has a hard time believing God loves him that much.

Psalm 139:7 starts the beautiful passage so many of us know: "Where can I go from your Spirit? Where can I flee from your presence? If I go up into the heavens, you are there; if I make my bed in the depths, you are there. If I rise on the wings of the dawn, if I settle on the far side of the sea, even there your hand will guide me. Your right hand will hold me fast." God is revealing to David how much He cares about him, and it is so exciting to David.

There is a powerful truth later in the chapter. Psalm 139:17 says, "How precious to me are your thoughts, God!" That is the way the NIV translates this statement, but it can also be translated, "How precious are your thoughts concerning me, O God!" (GOD'S WORD Translation). Looking at the context of Psalm 139, it's clear this is a better translation. This is David getting a revelation about how much God thinks about him, cares about him, and watches over him. So David was essentially saying this: "Wow, it blows my mind that you think about me as much as you do, God!"

David goes on to say, "How vast is the sum of them! Were I to count them, they would outnumber the grains of sand," (Psalm 139:17-18). What a statement, saints. Have you ever thought about this passage of Scripture? Ever pondered it for a minute? This is not just a happy thought for the day. This is wonderful, powerful truth from God's Word.

Do you know what God spends the bulk of His day doing? Thinking about you. David said God's thoughts for you in a single day are like the grains of sand on a seashore. Have you ever been to a beach? I've been down to South Padre Island, which is about as good as beaches get in Texas. I know South Padre doesn't compare to Florida and other places in the world, obviously, but for Texas it's pretty good.

Imagine this with me. Imagine you are standing on a beach. It's early in the morning, and nobody else is there. Look to your left and your right. As far as you can see out into the horizon is sand and more sand and more sand. Halfway to the waves, just pick up a handful of that sand. Let those many, many grains slip through your fingers slowly. Let them drop to the beach until you finally end up with only one tiny grain of sand left.

That one grain of sand represents one thought God has for you. All the rest of those billions and billions of grains of sand on that beach, to the right and left as far as you can see, represent the rest of God's thoughts about you in just one day. In Psalm 139, this revelation is exploding inside King David's head. He's floored. You can see why it's too wonderful for him.

This is incredible stuff, but there is even more here. Psalm 139:13 says, "For you created my inmost being; you knit me together in my mother's womb." David is understanding something that he never understood before. He is realizing this: I am handmade by God.

Every single one of us was handmade by God. You were created through a God-ordained biological process going on inside your mom, but this verse tells us there was more going on while you were developing inside your mother's womb. Through Psalm 139, God is saying, "I was there. I was personally involved while you were being formed in your mother's womb. I took an active part in your creation."

You might have been an accident to your parents, but you were not an accident to God. You might have been born in the backseat of a car, but you were born in the very providence of God. God was very active and involved in the process. You were handmade by God.

I am handmade by God. Do you know what that means to me? Before I was one day old, God knew my hair would be just this color. He knew my eyes would be this color and this shape. He knew my smile would be the way it is. He knew my nose would be this big.

This isn't just an interesting little Bible study. This truth can change the way you think and live. I know from experience. When I really got a hold of this truth from Psalm 139, it changed me. I don't drive the highway anymore and look at billboards and think, "Oh, I wish I looked like him. I wish my nose weren't so ... I wish ... I wish ... I wish."

I am handmade by God. I am special. I am unique. I am valuable.

My wife, Sallie, likes to shop. I—like most men—am not much of a shopper. Men and women have different ideas of shopping. When women think of shopping, they think of something like a bee pollinating flowers. They walk through the store, going from thing to thing and touching everything in there. When men think of shopping, we think hunting expedition. We pick out the game, shoot it, bag it, and get it to the car as quickly as we can. Even though shopping is not my favorite thing to do, I like being with my wife. I go shopping with her often just to hang out with her.

I remember one time Sallie went shopping and I tagged along. She was going from store to store and having a great time. As we were walking along, she saw one of those little craft and gift stores. If you're a guy, you probably know the kind I'm talking about. Those are the worst, aren't they?

"Oh, let's go over here!" she said.

"Wait, honey!" I said. "Look at that store over there. Or that one. Or any store other than one like this."

"No, I want to go in this one," she said.

"All right, fine."

We went in, and she started walking around the store, looking at different things. I was just killing time, wandering around the store. I remember walking over and looking at one little thing they had for sale. It caught my attention because I had seen objects like it in many other stores that day—similar design, similar purpose. But I looked at this one and thought, "Man alive, what is wrong with these people? Look at the price on that thing!" It was many times more expensive than any of the other objects I had seen that day.

My first thought was, "Where's Sallie? I need to find her quick and get her out of here. These people have jacked up their prices to astronomical levels. They're gonna rip us off." But then I began to look at the object. I started wondering what was so different about it. It was

9

designed to do the same thing as all the other ones I had seen. Why was it so much more expensive? I picked it up and rolled it around in my hand. Then I turned it upside down and saw one word on the bottom of it. I knew instantly why it cost so much more. On the bottom someone had written the word *handmade*.

That changes everything. It wasn't something churned out by some machine manufacturing thousands of the same thing, one after another. It was handmade by somebody. That made it much more valuable.

You were handmade by God Almighty. We are talking about the same God who put all the stars in the sky and calls them all by name. We are talking about the same God who designed and crafted every part of this earth and all the living things on it. You were handmade by Him. You are valuable. You are unique. You are special. You are handmade. There has never been anybody else like you, and there never will be in the future. Even identical twins have different fingerprints.

Think about this one: scientists have been studying snowflakes for decades and decades and decades, and they have not found even two snowflakes exactly alike. Out of billions and billions of snowflakes, every single one has a different design. That just barely starts to give us an idea of how vast and infinite and creative God truly is, and it shows us this: God loves variety. God made each of us different. He made each of us special. That's part of why we are each so valuable to Him. You are valuable because you are one of a kind.

It is so important that we take hold of this truth. If you are a young person, you especially need to get a hold of this thing. Young people are even more susceptible to the desire to be more like other people. But God made you by hand according to His perfect will. To not like the way God made you is the ultimate act of rebellion against Him.

In Psalm 139:14, David says, "I praise you because I am fearfully and wonderfully made; your works are wonderful, I know that full well." David got it. God does everything wonderfully, and David knew it. Do you understand that? God doesn't make junk. Everything God makes is perfect, and that includes you and me. We are handmade by God, and all the works of His hands are wonderful.

David got a hold of this truth, and his response was praise. We read Psalm 139:14 in the English translation and think David just got a little excited. We think David just gave God a little, "Lord, I praise you." But that's not what the word translated as *praise* here means in the Hebrew. This is the Hebrew word *hallel*. That's an interesting word that literally means to act clamorously foolish or to rave as if a madman. David wasn't quietly saying, "God, I praise you. I thank you that you made me wonderfully." He was shouting and running and jumping and twirling all over the place in joy and gratitude to God. He was going so wild in praise that people thought he was going nuts! That's what *hallel* means.

When was the last time you woke up, walked into the bathroom, looked in the mirror, and went crazy with joy because of how well God made you? It might do you good to set this book down, take ten minutes, and go get a little practice doing that. It is good and healthy for us to celebrate the way God made us. This truth needs to explode for us, and we need to get it deep down inside. Only after we get it will we come into what God has for us.

The Bible is not talking about just the way you are made physically. God knit your physical features together in your mother's womb, yes. But, perhaps even more importantly, God was also weaving into you different giftings, talents, abilities, and callings. He was preparing you.

God looked out into the future and said, "On these days and in these places, I need somebody who can do this, this, this, and this." Then He turned and began to put you together inside your mother's womb. He made you with the giftings, the abilities, and the talents you would need to accomplish those things in the times and places you would be existing in. That's what God is after. He made each one of us by hand with a purpose and destiny for life. Each and every one of us has a created purpose. And—I hope you get this loud and clear—you will never find fulfillment in your life apart from doing that which God created you to do.

God created you with a destiny and purpose. As you walk in that, you will find fulfillment. If you don't walk in that, you won't find fulfillment. So many, many people are not experiencing fulfillment in life. Even many people who love God and are born again, baptized in the Spirit, and involved in church don't have fulfillment in their lives. What's wrong? God created a slot for them, and they are not living in the slot.

You have every bit of gifting and talent you need to fulfill your created purposes already inside you. God didn't set any person up for frustration. He is not like that. He is a good father. He would not say, "I want you to do this," and then not give you the ability to do it. Why is that so important? Because, even in the Church, people look around and say, "Well, I wish I had her gift. I wish I could do that like he does." When we do that, we demean our own gifts. Everything we need to accomplish God's created purpose is in us.

So if we are not fulfilled in life, what's the problem?

"Well, I know. I need a new boat. You know, if I could just get a different car. Maybe a different house. Hey, maybe a new wife!"

Think that last one is harsh? There's a 50 percent divorce rate in the Church. Something's going on here.

Most unfulfilled people don't understand why they aren't fulfilled. Everything is good, everything should be happy, but they know there's still something missing. What's the problem? It has nothing to do with how much stuff they have or don't have. That's not the issue. The issue is that God created a slot for them to function in, and they are far, far from it.

People like that need prophetic vision for their lives. They need to realize and believe God created them with a destiny and a purpose. And as they begin to move forward into that destiny, God will show them the next step. They won't see it all, just one or two steps. As they take those steps and begin to move closer and closer to the slot God created them for, fulfillment will begin to well up within them. They will start to say, "Man, I'm enjoying life!" As they keep moving in that direction, more and more fulfillment will come. Then they will finally drop into the slot God created them for, and—Pow!—it will explode inside of them and they will say, "Man, I love living! I just love life! I can't wait for tomorrow! I am so excited for this week!" Oh, I know there will always be hassles and problems. There will be challenges at work and at home. But despite those things, there will be fulfillment. Fulfillment always comes from walking in God's created purpose.

For many years, when I led young people in particular to the Lord, so many times I would walk with them to the point where they were ready to give their lives to the Lord, then they would all say the same thing. It was almost like there was some conspiracy out there. Maybe they were all talking on the internet together.

"Well, I want to give my life to God, but I'm just scared."

"What are you afraid of?" I would say.

"Well, I understand what you're saying, Myles. If I give my life to Him, then He is the Lord of my life. I have to be obedient to Him."

"That's right. What are you afraid of?"

"What if God called me to be a missionary in Africa? You know, sleep in a grass hut on a dirt floor. I don't know if I could do that or not."

I have had that conversation many times. This is how I used to answer: "Oh, don't worry about that. Only a tiny percentage of Christians actually get called to go as missionaries to Africa. Don't even worry." That was a wimpy answer. It really was. Once I saw the truth about destiny and fulfillment from God's Word, I changed my answer. Now, in those situations, I say this: "You need to understand something. It is all about your created purpose and destiny. If God created you to be a missionary in Africa, you could sleep in Buckingham Palace for the rest of your life and never find the fulfillment you would have found sleeping in that grass hut on that dirt floor. And, on the other hand, if He didn't create you to be a missionary in Africa, then you could go there to 'serve God' and be absolutely miserable. It is all about what God created you to do."

Have you seen the movie Chariots of Fire? The beginning may be slow, but it's a powerful movie and an incredible story. One of the main characters is a guy by the name of Eric Liddell, "The Flying Scotsman." He was of the fastest men who ever lived. The guy was so fast he could just about outrun a jackrabbit.

Eric was a missionary with his sister in China. Once, when they returned to England on furlough, there happened to be a big race with some of the fastest runners in all of England right where they were. All the people around Eric tried to talk him into running the race, saying, "Oh come on, Eric. Run!"

"I don't even have my track shoes with me. I've just got my boots on," he said.

"Oh, that's all right. Just run!" they said. "It'll be fun. You were really fast back when you played soccer. Why not run in the race?"

He finally agreed and entered the race. All the runners lined up, and they fired the gun. He took off running and left them all behind. All the people watching were stunned. He just had boots on, and he still smoked some of the fastest runners in all of England.

After that race, many people gathered around him and said, "Eric, you've got to stay here. You've got to train. You've got to run in the Olympics. Run for England and win a gold medal!"

"No, no, no," he said, "I'm called to the mission field in China."

But they kept pressing him. He decided to pray and seek God about it, and he ended up feeling that God wanted him to stay in England, train, and run in the Olympics.

You would think the people in his life would be excited about that and happy for him, but that's not the case. They weren't happy about it. They didn't understand. His sister, Jenny, was especially upset with him. She felt that Eric was selling out his calling from God in exchange for fame, fortune, and a gold medal. She couldn't believe his decision, and she gave him such a hard time over and over and over. In the movie, Jenny tries to talk him out it in the middle of a church service, and Eric finally has enough. He grabs her hand and they walk straight out of the church service. He takes her to a nearby field and tries to explain himself to her there on a hillside. He says, "Jenny, you've got to understand. I believe that God made me for a purpose. For China, but He also made me fast. And when I run, I feel His pleasure."[1]

Jenny never understood, but Eric went on to train for the Olympics in obedience to God. When he got to the Olympics, everyone was dying to see him run. They had all heard how fast he was. But the preliminaries for his race, the 100 m, were on a Sunday, and Eric said, "I never run on Sunday." Everyone tried to pressure him into running, but he wouldn't do it. Newspaper reporters from around the world wrote big stories about the man who gave up a certain gold medal in order to honor God. Eric Liddell got a platform to preach to the world.

The story doesn't end there. Later that week, one of the other British runners, who had already won a medal, came to Eric and said, "Eric, I want you to take my spot in the 400 m race." Eric tried to refuse, but the other runner insisted. So Eric entered the 400 m. He got there in the blocks, they fired the gun, and all the runners took off together. Eric was running in his familiar style—head back, arms flailing. He left all the other runners in the dust.

In the movie, the entire crowd stands up. A roar rises as he runs away from the rest of the pack. All of a sudden, the race goes into slow motion and the iconic music cuts in. The crowd's roar fades, and his words from the hillside play as he runs toward the finish. "Jenny, I believe God made me for a purpose. He also made me fast. And when I run, I feel His pleasure."[1]

If the Church of the Lord Jesus Christ could just get hold of that one truth, it would transform us, individually and corporately. What has God created you to do? What gifts has He given you? What is your prophetic purpose and destiny? As you walk in those things, you will feel God's pleasure in your life.

My favorite passage in all the Bible is not John 3:16. I love that verse, so don't send me any nasty emails. I love a lot of different verses, but my favorite verse in the Bible actually comes out of Acts. Acts 13:36 says, "When David had served God's purpose in his own generation, he fell asleep; he was buried with his ancestors." David served God's purpose in his generation. What a statement. I can't think of any better epitaph. I want those who outlive me to be able to put this on my tombstone in truth: "Myles Sweeney fulfilled God's purpose for his generation." What about you? Do you want that to be true for your life? Do you want to fulfill what God has for you to do in your generation?

Jeremiah 29:11 is a very familiar verse to so many Christians. This is God speaking to us, His children: "'For I know the plans I have for you,' declares the Lord, 'plans to prosper you and not to harm you, plans to give you hope and a future.'" We quote that verse a lot. Do we actually believe it? The truth is many of us don't. We read it. We hear it. We know it. But something deep down inside of us says, "That's just not true. It hasn't been true for me in my life."

If that's where you are, let me ask you a couple of questions. The first one is this: Whose fault is it?

Can we talk and be candid about this? If you feel like your life has not gone well thus far and you have not really been blessed, then whose fault is it? Did God mess up? Or did you?

There is a heretical teaching and belief that is widespread in the Church today. I see this one all the time. A lot of Christians seem to believe that, somehow or another, the more mature they become, the closer and closer to the world they can get. They think really mature Christians can get really close to the world, and the world won't bother them or affect them. That is crazy thinking. It's non-biblical, and it's just flat-out crazy.

You may or may not know this, but these days the National Park Service offers mule rides down the side of the Grand Canyon. I have heard many people say it's an incredible thing to do. They say the views are phenomenal. The path they go down is just about six feet across, no guard rails. But these mules have been down the same path hundreds and hundreds of times, and they just follow one after another, back and forth down the side of the canyon. Cliff wall on one side, sheer drop-off on the other.

I would think twice about making that trip. But let's say you and I make plans to go there tomorrow and ride the mules down the side of the Grand Canyon. When we get there, you can just run up and jump on any old mule you please. I'm going to sort through those babies very carefully.

"What are you going to be looking for, Myles?"

I'm looking for a sure mule.

"Well, how will you know when you've found one?"

Because all the hair on one side will be rubbed off! I want a mule that stays so far away from the edge that he has rubbed all his hair off on the side closest to the cliff.

That's maturity, saints. Don't fall into the trap of foolish thinking that says maturity leads you closer and closer to the world. Maturity means walking further and further into God, His purposes, and His calling on your life.

If you have trouble believing Jeremiah 29:11 is true for you and your life, then here is my second question for you: Have you closed your book?

I'm talking about the book of your life. Have you closed your book? God isn't finished writing yet. He's got new sentences, paragraphs, and entire chapters He wants to add. Don't close the book of your life.

We have to journey to our destinies. We don't go from here to there in one big step. I know most of us wish it worked like that. I wish it worked like that. Especially when I was a young Christian, I wanted to just take one big step and be exactly where God was taking me. But it doesn't work that way. We journey there, step by step. And along the journey we will climb some mountains, go through some valleys, ford some streams, and traverse some deserts. But we always need to keep moving forward because God is never finished with us in our lives.

Many years ago, Sallie and I went on a wonderful trip. We were in Denver, Colorado, and we planned to take a train from there all the way to Glenwood Springs, Colorado. We had our little brochures all about Glenwood Springs. It looked like an incredible, beautiful place with mountains and steam baths and natural hot springs. A gorgeous, gorgeous setting. We couldn't wait to get there.

We went down and bought our train tickets. They had "Glenwood Springs" printed right on them. Then we got on the train. It was one of those glass-top trains, so we had a great view of all the beautiful scenery. Snow-covered mountains, green valleys, rushing rivers—the ride was wonderful.

Then, in an instant, everything went black. We said, "What happened? It's just black. Where'd all the scenery go?" We got out our brochures, looked at them, and said, "Well, this doesn't look like Glenwood Springs." It stayed black and stayed black and stayed black. We finally realized something must be wrong, so we tore up our brochures and train tickets. Then we jumped off the train.

No we didn't. That would have been idiotic. We were just in a tunnel. That's it. Can I tell you something right now? Your brochure is real. Your tickets are good. If you are going through a tunnel, don't lose heart. Don't faint. Don't give up. Don't close the book of your life. Let God take you forward into the plans and purposes He has for you.

Let's go back to Jeremiah 29:11, "'For I know the plans I have for you,' declares the Lord, 'plans to prosper you and not to harm you, plans to give you hope and a future.'" The Hebrew word translated there as *future* is translated in other places in the Bible as *destiny*. So

God is saying this: "I want to give you your future. I want to give you your destiny."

We get so many crazy ideas in the Church today. I have seen so many Christians who think, somehow or another, they are going to do the right things and put pressure on God. Through religious acts, they plan to twist God's arm and make Him cough up their destinies. Right here in Jeremiah, God is saying, "Look, I want to give it to you! What are you talking about? I created you for this very purpose. Why would I be the one blocking it?"

God wants to give you your destiny. But you have to learn how to have prophetic vision for your life and walk out that destiny one step at a time.

The word translated as "future" or "destiny" is the Hebrew word *acharit*. That is a fascinating Hebrew word with a fascinating meaning. It doesn't mean what we normally think of when we hear the word "future" or "destiny." *Acharit* literally means the hinder part, or the back end. Jewish scholars believe this passage is speaking of the back end or the hinder part of our lives, which would be the future. But as the rabbinical scholars studied that word and this passage in even more depth, they understood a further and more interesting meaning from it. Jeremiah 29:11 describes us backing into our future.

We tend to think we are all marching straight forward into our future. The truth is so many times we move into the future falling backwards, one step at a time. But this is where we need the wonderful truth God has for us in Jeremiah 29:11. God loves us so much. He cares about us so much. He has put so much of Himself in us, and He has a stake in us reaching our potential and fulfilling our created purposes in life. That's why God says, "You know what? If you have a heart to do this thing, even when you are falling backwards, I will make sure you end up in the right place."

That is our Father's love for us. We need to have prophetic vision for our lives. Ask God what He has for you. Don't expect the next twenty steps in your life because that is not the way God usually reveals His plan for us. Just ask for the next step or two, and be faithful to take those steps, knowing in faith that God will show you the next one. Then put one foot in front of the other just like that until you walk into purpose, destiny, and fulfillment in your life.

THE PURPOSE OF VISION

Why is vision so important? What does it do in your life?
I want to address these questions and give you some truths about vision that are critically important for every single one of us to understand. This chapter will be very simple and practical, which is perfect because vision itself is very simple and practical.

We don't tend to think of vision as practical, but it is. Too often, when we think of vision, it calls to mind a concept of some big, vague, cloud-like thing far off in the sky. Ooooh. Aaaah. Maybe thinking about it gives you goosebumps. Whatever. That's not vision. Vision is very, very practical in our lives. I love this quote from Fred Pryor, "Vision is a process that allows you to think ahead to where you want to be and what you want to be doing, and to create workable plans to lead you there." Vision is not clouds in the sky or simply thinking ahead. Vision is creating workable plans to reach the future.

If you are a born-again believer today, then you are on a pathway of discovery. Every single one of us is on the pathway of discovering who God created us to be. Why did He put the gifts and talents that He did inside of me? Why did He shape me, form me, and wire me the way He did? Why am I the way I am? You were created to ask questions like those and live on a pathway of discovering who you are supposed to be and what you are supposed to do. Then, somewhere along that pathway, God gives you vision.

Vision is a picture we get inside of us, a picture that comes from God. It is a picture of our future—who we are meant to be and what we are meant to do. That vision will always be practical. Why? Because if it's truly a vision from God, you will be able to create plans to get from where you are to that picture inside of you. Lots of people like to use the word "vision" without understanding this truth.

"Pastor Myles, I have a vision."

When did you get that vision?

"Well, I got that vision fifteen years ago."

What have you done about it?

"Nothing. But I got that vision."

You don't have a vision. You have a fantasy. Vision and fantasy start out the same; they start out as a picture of something that could be out in the future, whether that picture is from God or from eating too much spicy food before bed. But there is a big difference between vision and fantasy. If you have a vision, then you are willing to do what it takes to make that picture of the future a reality in your life. If you have a fantasy, you are not willing to do what it takes. You just like to think about it.

Every single one of us needs to have vision for life. What is your vision for life? If we are being honest, that is a bit of an overwhelming question for most. A lot of people, particularly men, default to thinking and talking about their careers when asked that kind of question. But that was not the full question. Career is just one aspect of life. Yes, you should have a vision for where you are going in your career. But you should also have more than that. That is why I say *a* vision. I am not really talking about just one vision for your whole life. I am talking about the multiple visions you should have within the overall vision that God has given you for your life. You should have a vision for your marriage. You should have a vision for your family. You should have a vision for your career. You should have a vision for your ministry. You should have a vision for your finances. You need vision in every area of your life.

But what is the purpose? Why is it important to have vision in your life? What does vision do for us when we have it?

1. Vision provides boundaries.

In Proverbs 29:18, God says, "Where there is no vision, the people perish," (KJV). This verse was not God addressing the heathen nations; God was speaking directly to His own people and saying they would perish if they did not have a vision for their lives. So you and I need a vision for our lives, or else we are going to perish.

What does the word *perish* mean? It can mean several different things. It can mean death. It can mean an entire life falling apart. But many times it simply means coming up short. If we don't have vision, we will perish—always come up short of what God intended for us. We will miss God's best for us in all the different areas of our life; we will miss what we wanted down in our heart of hearts. We never got there simply because we never had a vision.

"Where there is no vision, the people perish." The English Standard Version of Proverbs 29:18 doesn't use the word *perish*; it says where there is no vision, the people "cast off restraint." Another one, the New Living Translation, says the people "run wild." Without vision, there is no discipline or restraint. So where does discipline come from? It comes from vision. Vision creates discipline in our lives.

So many times we look at ourselves and say things like, "Well, I'm just lazy," or, "I'm just not a persevering person." You know what? Those can be true. Those things can be parts of the problem; they can be pieces to the puzzle, if you will. But if you focus on those pieces, it becomes easy to miss the biggest piece of the puzzle—you just don't have vision. That is why you are lazy in some situations. That is why you struggle to persevere. You don't really have a vision. You don't believe you can actually have the future you want to go for. And when there is no vision, what happens? The boundaries come off. You live in a lazy way, meandering through life instead of going for the things that God has for you.

If you truly have vision for something, then you will say no to anything that gets in the way of that vision. You are going to say no because you want the vision to come to pass in your life. If it is something that will help you go forward into the vision, then you will do it. If it is something that will keep you from going forward into the vision, then you will not do it. It is that simple.

There are a lot of different examples of this. How about a common one? Many, many men in the world have vision to be godly husbands. That goes for men who are married, and it also goes for men who are not married, but want to be someday. What does that vision mean? It means they believe it can be real for them. They believe they can become godly husbands. Because they believe that, they are going to do things that help them become godly husbands and not do things that would keep them from becoming godly husbands.

I have two daughters, both happily married now. Before either daughter was proposed to, each future husband came to me first to ask my blessing for the marriage. I take those kinds of things very seriously. Nowadays, most people treat asking for the father's blessing as a kind of little game. It used to mean something and be really important, but now people just go through the motions of it, if that. The guy comes in and asks for the daughter's hand in marriage, and of course the father has to say yes because they are just doing a little dance and playing a little game. Well, I don't do little dances, and I don't play little games. Especially not with things as important as this.

So my two sons-in-law, whom I love greatly, each came to me to ask for each daughter's hand in marriage. The conversations went very similarly. I told the son-in-law, "There's gonna be several things that you're going to have to do in order for me to say yes."

Once they recovered from the surprise, each of them asked, "Well, what do you mean?"

"The Bible says Jacob worked for Rachel's father for seven years in order to marry her. Then Rachel's father tricked him and gave him the sister, so he had to work for another seven years in order to marry Rachel. That was fourteen years of basically slave labor, but after he finally married Rachel the Bible says those fourteen years were as a few days to him (Genesis 29:20). That's a biblical story right there. So if you're not a guy who's willing to work on areas of your life and change things in them, then you're not the guy we're looking for."

"Well, okay. This is different, but explain the program to me."

"Here's number one: I'm looking for a guy who can convince me—look me in the eye and assure me—that he absolutely will be a godly husband."

"Oh, I'll be a go—"

"No, stop. Don't finish that sentence. I don't want to hear that right now. I want you to think about that. Pray about that. And then I want you to come back, look me in the eye, and tell me that in such a way that I know you mean it. Then you're going to have to explain to me what you're going to do in order to actually become a godly husband."

"What do you mean by that?"

"Come on. Do you really believe that one day you're just going to wake up and say, 'Oh my God. What happened overnight? I became a godly husband.' No. There is going to be a path that you're going to walk, and I want to know what that path is going to look like for you."

Both of them gave me blank looks on that one.

"Okay," I said, "Let me help you out. How about this one? 'Mr. Sweeney, I guarantee you right now that under no circumstances, no matter what happens in my life, will you ever look at me, ask me what great book I have read on marriage this year, and hear me answer "Not one." That will never happen. I will read at least one good book on marriage every year.' That is one good step toward becoming a godly husband."

This is real life. Do you understand why I asked those things of the men that were going to become the husbands of my daughters? I wanted to make sure each of them had a vision for becoming a godly husband. What do you have a vision for?

Many, many ladies have vision to be incredible mothers. Again, you may not be married or have children yet, but you can still have vision for being a godly mother and believe you can become one in God. It does not matter what kind of mother you had or how many times you have messed up before now. Today you can change the vision, begin to walk in it, and believe that it will become true. What steps are you going to take to get there?

If you really have a vision for something, it changes your life. Vision is not just a kind of nice thought. Vision changes your life. Vision is saying, "I believe that's real. I believe that's true for me. I believe I can become that. How do I get there?" Then you start living differently.

I really believe that without a vision, people perish. Without a vision, people come up short of what they could be and should be in God. They miss so much of what God has for them simply because they don't have a real vision for an area of their lives.

As a very young believer, just a month or two after I was born again, I heard a message that changed my life. I'll be honest with you and tell you I wasn't really listening very well. I can't remember the message. I can't even remember who taught the message. But I do remember this: somewhere in the middle of that message the speaker read a quote from D. L. Moody. I don't remember anything that came before or after, but this quote rang my bell: "The world has yet to see what God can do through a man that's totally yielded to him."[1] That hit me. Everything else was a blur, but something rose up inside me in response to that statement. I wanted to be that man. That was a vision for me, and it began to change the way I lived.

About two months after that happened, a friend of mine from the Dallas-Fort Worth area called me. He said, "Myles, there's a guy speaking in Houston this week. He's going to be there for five nights. You need to go and hear him. He's incredible." The speaker was a guy by the name of Milton Green. I had never heard of him, but I called Sallie, we lined up a babysitter, and we drove in to hear him.

We got to the church. We sat down. Worship started. It was pretty good, but it freaked us out a little bit. People around us were raising their hands, and I was thinking, *What's up with this? Wow. If that's good for them, I guess that's cool. I'll never do it.* That's where I was at the time.

Then Milton got up to speak. As soon he started speaking, Sallie and I turned to look at each other. We thought it was a bad joke. He wasn't just country. This man was *hick.* I was having a hard time even understanding him. The first thing that went through my mind? *That sorry jerk of a friend. He jacked us around. He pulled a trick on us and made us pay for a babysitter and drive all the way down here.* But Sallie and I held in there for a little while, and that's when this man started talking about how God had changed his life.

For Milton, everything started one day at work. He owned a big carpet cleaning business in Fort Worth. One morning a guy came into his office and told Milton a story about how he had lost his job and hadn't been able to find another for months. This man had lost his home. He and his wife were living out of their car. The man had heard Milton was a Christian businessman, so he thought he would take his chances and come ask for a job.

Under normal circumstances, the man would have been hired on the spot. But Milton knew he was overstaffed at the time, and he was already looking at firing someone to compensate for it. He knew he couldn't add another employee, so he told the guy to come back in a couple of months and ask again. The guy accepted it and walked out dejectedly. As soon as the door shut, Milton heard the Lord speak to him very clearly. "I want you to hire him. Go get him. Go hire him."

"Lord, I don't need any—"

"Milton, I want you to hire him."

He could not escape that strong impression from God. So he went out to the parking lot, caught the guy, brought him back in, and hired him. Then Milton gave him the address of a home that somebody had just moved out of. The carpet needed to be cleaned before anyone moved in. He sent the guy there to clean the house and told him he would be there at about four o'clock to check his work.

As it turned out, he happened to be close to the house earlier in the day, at about two, so he decided to swing by and see how the guy was doing. Pulling up in the driveway, Milton was surprised to see the guy sitting in a rocking chair on the front porch. He was thinking, *This isn't good.* "What are you doing? You taking a break?"

"Oh, no sir. I'm finished. I'm a fast worker."

"Really? Well, let's go inside and see what kind of worker you are."

Milton walked through the house, checking the guy's work. Honestly, it wasn't too bad of a job. For the most part the house was pretty clean. He had done a decent job with the carpet. But there were still a couple of spots. He had left some stains along the baseboards and in a couple of closets. Milton walked back out of the house, stood on the porch, and got into a quiet, ugly argument with God right there.

"God, I didn't need to hire this man. You told me to hire him. He does sloppy work. You know the only reason my business is successful is because we do everything with so much excellence. People know that. We have a reputation. Now I hire this guy I don't need because you told me to, and he does sloppy work."

So Milton was standing there on the porch, going off on God to himself. The guy was standing next to him the entire time. He finally started wondering what was going on and interrupted the argument with God, "Hey, is there a problem here?"

That was all it took. Milton wheeled on him.

"Is there a problem here? Are you kidding me? Man, that is just awful work in there. That's not excellence. My business exists because of the excellence in the work we do. We get referrals because of the great work we do. You didn't finish that job, and that's not going to work. Let me explain something to you, young man. Until you start calling dirt what I call dirt, our relationship can't go any further. Do you understand me?"

"Yes sir. I got it, sir. I understand," he said.

"I'm going to give you a second chance," Milton said. "I'm going to go check on another job. I'll be back here in two hours. This is your last chance to do a better job."

After that, Milton got into his car and drove off. He only got about two blocks away from the house before he pulled over on the side of the road and cried for two hours. God spoke to him.

"Milton, that's the same thing I've been trying to tell you for months. Until you call dirt what I call dirt, our relationship can't go any further."

Milton Green told that entire story the night we drove down to listen to him. I felt like I was sitting in the car with him. That night I got another piece of the vision. God said to me, "You want to be a man fully surrendered to Me? You hear Me calling you? You're hearing right. I want that to happen in your life. That is what I have for you. But this is what you're going to need to do. Here's another step in the process of becoming that."

Are you struggling with the problem of discipline in your life? Are you lazy? Are you out of control? Have you stopped persevering down the path you started on? If the answer to any of those questions is yes, it doesn't mean that you are worse than anybody else around you. You are just a person who lacks vision.

"Oh, I'm just a lazy person."

There are lazy people. There are people who don't persevere. But usually laziness is more of a symptom than a root. And most of the time the root is simply this: you don't have a vision. That's why you won't stay on the path. That's why you are not motivated to get up and go after it. You have mislabeled yourself because of a lack of vision.

I did not say you weren't saved. I just said you lacked vision. I did not say you aren't going to heaven, but I am saying that you are not going to go very far between here and there unless you get more vision in your life.

I expect a lack of vision from people outside the Church, but I am amazed at how many people I meet inside the Church who are as confused as a pill bug on a yo-yo. They don't know why God made them. They have no purpose in life. Sometimes they had a glimmer of vision earlier in life, but somewhere along the way they abandoned it. They saw pieces of their purpose and began to move toward them, but then things happened—things like disappointment, failure, and other people's actions. At some point they just stopped believing the vision could really become true in their lives.

Anyone who is not living with vision will cast off the restraints of God's Word in their lives. They will get rid of the boundary lines and guard rails designed to keep them going down the path towards who God has called them to be and what God has called them to do. Because of that, they come up short. They miss the blessings that God Himself wants them to have. That is not because they are bad people. It is simply because they need more vision. They need to believe the things God has said to them.

"Oh, that would be so nice if it really came to pass. It just would be so wonderful. I would really like to believe—"

No, no. You have to actually believe it. Is it from God or not? It is critical to press in to God, receive what He has for you, and believe it. Once you get that, it changes everything.

Newsflash: God is smarter than we are. He realizes that we need vision for the areas of our lives. We need goals. We need purpose. We need a reason to get up in the morning, excited about the day. We need a reason to wake up on Monday and say, "Woo hoo! Another week!" Think that's unrealistic? It may be unrealistic for you, but not for someone who has vision. People who have vision wake up every day excited about what God is going to do. Monday, Tuesday, Wednesday—it doesn't matter what day it is. There is no "Hump Day." Every day is a great day. Listen, that's real. If you don't think that's possible, just ask my wife and my children about me. I'm not just different. That's not just my personality. I got a vision, and it changed everything.

You need a purpose, a goal, a vision, a reason to do what you do. You need something in your life like that. Why? So that you can know when to say no to some things and say yes to others. When you get a real vision from God, you will start saying, "No, that ain't gonna help me. No, that won't work. Yes, I want that in my life." Having a vision changes things in you. I don't care how many times you have heard Nike tell you to "Just do it." You know what? That doesn't work. It's a nice saying. It's a great slogan. It sells shoes and clothing really well. But it doesn't work in the real living of life, where the rubber meets the road. First there has to be a vision. If there is not, you won't be able to stay on the path consistently over a long period of time.

"Myles, honey, will you stop eating ice cream?"

"Why?"

"Just do it."

Nah. Mrs. Sweeney tried that one on me. It doesn't work. I'm still eating the ice cream. You need something more than, "Just do it." You need something more than, "Just don't do it." You have to have a vision to change things. And if you really believe you can have that vision, you will do what it takes to get there.

"Honey, why don't we read a book together? Let's get a good book on marriage and read it together over the next month or two. Every few nights let's read a chapter together and talk about it."

"Nah. Not going to do that."

Are you kidding me? Why would that ever be the answer? I can tell you one possibility. You might answer like that if you didn't have a vision for the marriage. You might answer like that if you did not believe your relationship to your spouse could ever be any different. I am sure you would like for your marriage to be a little bit better. I am sure you would like for there to be some changes, especially in your spouse. But if you don't really have a vision for a better marriage, you will not do what it takes to improve it.

There has to be a vision of winning. There has to be a vision of achieving some goals. And please get this: the payoff has to be bigger than the pain you will go through to get to it. There is going to be pain in the process. There is almost always pain. So if you are not willing to go through pain to get to the payoff, guess what. You will not get there.

I use marriage as an example so much because it is easy to see the principles of vision at work in that area, even for people who are not married. It is also a very relatable example. Almost everyone who is married has some kind of desire for a better, improved marriage. So let's imagine something. Imagine someone who is not happy with the marriage that he or she is in. It's not where it could be and should be. Here's the deal: changing a marriage involves a painful process called counseling, repentance, and hard work. No one is willing to go through that process without the belief that they can really have the marriage they desire. Why go through all of the mess if it is not going to result in any real change? But if someone believes in the possibility of having a gorgeous picture of a marriage, you know what? That someone will do anything to get there.

Sallie and I did marriage counseling with other couples for over thirty years. One of the first things we did with every couple was sit down together and ask them to describe their marriage in single words. The couple would list some off—disappointment, hurt, pain. I would fill up a page of white copy paper writing down all of the words they would give us. Once the page was full, I would set it to the side and get out a blank piece of paper. Then Sallie and I would ask the couple to forget their marriage as it was for a minute and describe the perfect marriage in single words. The couple would list off some very different words—happiness, joy, fulfillment, peace. I would sit there and cover the new page writing these words. Then Sallie and I would set those two different pieces of paper on the table in front of the couple and lay a ruler between the two pages. Then one of us would ask them this: "What if I could promise that we can get you from this page, the way you described your marriage right now, to that page, the way you described the perfect marriage? What would you be willing to do?"

"That's impossible."

"I didn't ask whether or not you think it's possible. I'm not really interested in your opinion right now. I'm just asking you a simple question. What would you be willing to do to get from here to there?"

Every single person, through thirty years of counseling, gave the same answer: "Anything."

That's a big word, but it was always true. Once they truly believed they could have the good marriage they wanted, they were willing to do anything. That applies to everyone for any and every area of life. We could be talking about career or finances or parenthood. It doesn't matter. What are you willing to do? If you have a real vision, you will do whatever it takes. You will pay whatever price, you will go through whatever pain, and you will make whatever sacrifice you need to in order to get there.

If you do not persevere, it is because you don't have a real vision that you honestly believe can be true for you. If your mind wanders off, it is because you don't have vision. If you don't stay within the boundary lines, it is because you don't have vision. Sometimes those boundary lines are the lines between righteousness and sin. Crossing would be sin, so you don't cross because sin would keep you from your vision. Sometimes those boundary lines are simply the lines between who you actually are and who you are not.

Vision tells you who you are so that you can know who you are not. And that is so freeing. Once you discover who you are, how God wired you, and what you are supposed to do, all of the other stuff just starts falling off. I don't have to be this. I don't have to act like her. I don't have to be like him. I don't have to do what that person does. I know who I am called to be, so I don't have to be all that other junk. That is freedom. It is wonderful to get a vision and discover who you are because it gives you the power to say no.

"Will you help us with this?"

No, that's not who I am.

"Can you do that?"

No, that's not what I'm called to do.

This is who I am. This is what I'm called to do. I got it. I understand it. I'm going for it, so I can drop everything else.

This is so important. One of the reasons why it is so important is because there has been a perversion of the first of the four spiritual laws. The four spiritual laws used to be a very common thing; they are just four basic truths of life and relationship with God written by Dr. Bill Bright. The first law is this: "God loves you and offers a wonderful plan for your life."[2] That is a very true and wonderful statement, but it has been perverted without anyone even noticing. What we actually tend to believe these days is something like this: God loves you and everyone around you has a wonderful plan for your life. Everybody wants to tell you how to live your life, what you need to do and not do. If you let others make you into something that you are not, do you know what is going to happen? You are going to be miserable and frustrated and unusable to God.

This is true for individuals, but it is also true for churches. It is important for each individual church to recognize the church identity God has called it to. That has nothing to do with comparison to other churches.

I always make sure the members of the Grace churches understand this. Operating as the type of church God has called us to be does not somehow make us better than any other church in the community, region, or state. It's not about what we are doing that they aren't doing or what they are doing that we aren't doing. What matters is being the kind of church God has called us to be and doing the things He has called us to do. That is the only thing that matters. A church cannot be all things to all people. We are who we are because this is what God has called us to do where He has called us to be. We are just trying to be faithful and obedient to walk the path God has called us to walk. Yes, we are different. It's not better or worse. It's just different.

"Well, I just really wish the pastors would wear robes."

I'm sorry, but you're in the wrong church. Robes ain't happening. Love you, but we're not going to do that.

"All the songs need to be at least two hundred years old because that's where the anointing was."

No, that's not what we do at our church. We are just simply trying to be who God has called us to be.

"Why do you do this? Why don't you do that?"

I teach at pastors' conferences often here in the U.S. and abroad. So many times pastors absolutely freak out when I tell them we do things in our church that I don't like.

"What? Aren't you the head of the church?"

Oh yeah. I love our worship, but if I were choosing, I would do different songs. It is not a problem because I can worship to anything, but there are types of songs that I prefer over others. Good thing it really isn't about that. It is about what God calls us to do to reach the people we are called by God to reach.

Now, there are biblical principles I make sure the churches I lead adhere to. I can tell you this: any church I am a pastor of will not sing songs of escapism. You will not walk in and hear the worship leader start singing "I'll Fly Away." Not going to happen. That song is all about getting out of here. The vast majority of Christians, especially those in America, are just trying to catch the first Rapture bus out. Not in my church. We are about people who want to change their own lives and change the world. We are going to be singing songs full of victory, triumph, and the expanding of God's Kingdom on this earth. That is who we are. That is who God has called us to be.

2. Vision tests character.

This is the second purpose of vision. You can see this clearly in Psalm 105:16-19.

> *"When he summoned a famine on the land and broke all supply of bread, he had sent a man ahead of them, Joseph, who was sold as a slave. His feet were hurt with fetters; his neck was put in a collar of iron; until what he had said came to pass, the word of the Lord tested him."*

As God begins to reveal to us different aspects of His vision for our lives, we will be faced with tests. We will be faced with test after test and decision after decision. Am I going to move forward or not? Am I going to continue to believe the vision is attainable or not? Am I going to persevere or am I going to come up with a list of excuses detailing why the vision cannot become true for me? Am I going to believe the truth of the vision God has given me? Am I going to wilt? Am I going to fade when the heat comes on? Or am I going to hang in there, no matter how bad everything looks, until I actually possess what God told me is mine?

Joseph hung in there. Many times it looked really bad for him and bad for the word God had given him. It looked like there was absolutely, positively no way the word was going to come to pass in his life. But he didn't let go of the vision. Now we have a great vantage point for looking at Joseph's story. We can see the whole picture. It is easy for us to see that God was using the nasty stuff in his life to bring him into his destiny. It looked like Joseph was hitting wall after wall, setback after setback, but God used every one of them to bring Joseph into a place where he could accomplish a great purpose.

God will use all kinds of circumstances, situations, and people to push you where you need to go. It does not always mean that He came up with those things. Sometimes yes, sometimes no. Bad things happen. They don't always come from God. But God will use even the worst things the devil can throw at you and the world can dish up to you for good in your life.

Joseph was a good Jewish boy. Go to Egypt tomorrow? No way! He wasn't ever going to leave Canaan. God understood that, so he took Joseph to Egypt against his will. How else was Joseph going to meet Pharaoh? That was not going to happen back in Canaan. How else was he going to become second-in-command of the most powerful kingdom on earth at that time? Also not going to happen in Canaan. God used negative circumstances in Joseph's life to bring him into his destiny.

We can sit here and say, "Boy, I can really see that in Joseph's life." Big deal. Until you and I can see it in our own lives, that truth does us no good. When are you going to look at your life and believe this? You have to come to a place where you can say, "You know what? This looks ugly. This looks nasty. But I believe God's hand is in this. I can't see it. I don't understand why these things are going on. I don't like them. They are painful. They are unpleasant. But you know what? Somehow or another, I know that I know that I know God is in this thing, and He is going to bring me through. He's actually going to use these things to help me be who He has called me to be and accomplish what He has called me to accomplish."

If we are going to go after the vision God gives us for the areas of our life, we need to understand that we are likely to take a few trips our travel agent doesn't have a brochure for. The Word of God says, "The truth will set you free," (John 8:32). Here is the other part of that concept: sometimes the truth will make you miserable before it sets you free.

That verse applies in a lot of ways. The truth of who Jesus is will set you free when you receive salvation and accept Him as your Savior and Lord. That is an excellent application of the verse, but there are many other applications. One of them is what we're talking about today. God will give you truth about who you really are, who you are created to be, and what you are supposed to do with your life. Then, as you move towards that truth, you very well may move into misery before you move into rejoicing. Sometimes that is part of what happens along the way, and we have to be able to hang in there and push through in order to actually live the vision.

In John 16:33, Jesus said it this way: "In this world you will have trouble." That may sound like a threat, but it is actually a promise. You have probably never seen that one on a refrigerator magnet, but it is a promise. Jesus added to those words, saying, "But take heart! I have overcome the world." Amen. You may be going through something nasty and ugly. We live in a fallen, sin-soaked world. It is not the one God designed. It is the one that we messed up. That is why bad things happen to us and are going to continue to happen to us. Curveballs are going to come our way. That is just part of life. There is going to be trouble, but you know what? In Christ, you can overcome those things. It is fine to whine and cry for a short time, but you need to snap out of it and believe God. Get into the Word of God and believe what He says is the truth. Say, "You know what? That's true for my life too. I'm going to keep going forward. I'm not gonna quit because I believe I will do the things He showed me."

We have to get this. Jesus is telling us we are going to have trouble. But He's also telling us to chill out. Relax. Even rejoice in the midst of the problems because He has overcome the world. If you will put your hand in His hand and continue to walk forward with Him in obedience to the things He tells you to do, then you are not going to be underneath the trouble you are facing. Instead, you will be on top of it. You are going to put a saddle on that puppy and ride it before the day is done. The trouble is not going to get the better of you, you are going to get the better of the trouble.

Joseph was seventeen years of age when his brothers sold him into slavery. Think about that. It was thirteen years before he got the final promotion from God into his true destiny, his created purpose. Thirteen years of one misery after another, one roadblock after another, and one awful thing after another. He got his hopes up . . . life dashed them against the rocks. He got his hopes up again . . . dash. High hopes yet again . . . dash. Thirteen years of that. Those years would have killed somebody with less vision than Joseph. But this man held on to the vision God had given to him. Remember what that vision was? The sun and the moon, representing his parents, and eleven stars, representing his brothers, bowing down to him. Joseph saw that he was going to come to a place of great power and influence, and he held on to that vision despite all of the things that made it look impossible.

Speaking about Joseph, Psalm 105;19 says, "Until what he had said came to pass, the word of the Lord tested him." All along the way, Joseph could have focused on the situations he found himself in, but he didn't. He could have been staring at the bars of the prison he was in, but instead he was looking at the stars in the vision God had given him. He didn't see bars. He saw stars.

How about you? What do you see? What do you see when you look at things you have gone through and the things you are going through right now? Do you see bars? Does life look like a prison cell to you? Does it seem like something is always boxing you in and holding you back? Or are you looking at stars?

Abraham could have seen the bars of his old age, but instead he saw the stars of God's promise of a son. Joshua could have seen the bars of the fortified city called Jericho. Instead, he saw the stars of God's promise to him of his inheritance. David could have seen the bars of the giant Goliath, but instead he saw the stars of God's faithfulness to him in battle. Because of that, Goliath ended up seeing stars just before he blacked out completely. Saul looked at Goliath and said, "Man, that guy is too big to kill." David looked at the same giant and said, "Man, that guy is too big to miss." Saul and David looked at the same thing, but they saw it differently. Saul saw bars. David saw stars.

What do you see when you look at the different areas of your life today? When you look at your marriage, your family, your ministry, your career, and your finances, what do you see? Do you see a lot of bars, or do you see the stars? Have you received vision from God? Are you locked in on that, believing it is God's will and created purpose for you? If you are, then nothing will keep you from realizing that vision in your life.

Sometimes when God speaks, the best thing for us to do is meditate on what he said—chew on it a bit, roll it around, and get hold of it. But there are other times when God speaks and the best thing that you and I can do is respond.

Have you been looking at your life and your circumstances and seeing absolutely nothing but a bunch of bars? Now is the time to choose to see stars. Did anything in all of these thoughts and truths about vision stand out to you? Did God speak something to you? Now is the time to respond. Make a decision today—not just a decision for the moment, but for life. Make the choice today to walk the path of God's vision for your life. Receive the vision that God has for you, and believe it is a promise for you. Today is the day to choose to believe. Believe you can become everything God has called you to be and do everything that He has called you to do. Believe you can reach the vision, and don't settle for anything less. Make the choice today to not settle. Do what it takes. Set your feet on the path and walk it until you reach the destination the Lord has prepared for you.

QUITTER, CAMPER, CLIMBER

H abakkuk 3:19 says, "The Lord GOD is my strength, And He has made my feet like hinds' feet, And makes me walk on my high places," (NASB).

If you have been born again, then you need to understand something. God has empowered you to walk on high places. That's what He says, right there. He is your strength, and he has empowered you to walk on high places with feet like hinds' feet. Hinds are deer in the mountains that are able to climb up to places that look impossible. So God has empowered you, as a believer, to walk on high places.

But this verse is not referring to just any high places. Did you catch that in the last part? It says that God "makes me walk on *my* high places," ([Italics added]). In other words, God did not just create you to walk on any high places; He created you to walk on your high places. God empowers you and me to walk in the high places He created us for. He created us to live at that level—to fulfill everything He has put inside of each one of us to fulfill. Because of what He has done for you and me, we can live in high places, we can walk into everything He has called us to be, and we can do everything He has called us to do.

Have you heard of Mount Everest? Thought so. Everest is the tallest mountain in the world. It's almost six miles high. Think about that. That is above the jet stream, which means the peak is higher than most planes fly. Very few people even attempt the climb to the top of Everest. Those that do enter what is called the death zone in the very last part of the climb. When they hit twenty-six thousand feet and go above it, their bodies are actually dying every minute they are up there. That is why the last assault has to be done in one day. Climbers run up there and run back because if they stay there too long, they die. At that height, the human body literally degrades. It tangibly weakens and wears down. Cuts will not heal. If you cough too hard, you crack a rib.

Think about the height of Everest, the death zone, and all of the other challenges that come with the ascent. The first question that comes to many people is this: Why? Why would anybody want do that? Paul G. Stoltz, a great climber, once answered that question.

> *Scaling the mountain is an indescribable experience, one only fellow climbers can understand and share. Amid the relief, satisfaction and exhaustion is a sense of joy and peace as rarified as the mountain air. Only the climber tastes this sweet success. Those who stay encamped may be justified, as well as warmer and safer, but never will they feel "on purpose," as alive, as proud and as joyful.[1]*

Life is like mountain climbing. Oh, it really is. There are so many similarities between the life that you and I are called to in Christ and climbing a mountain. All of us are called to be mountain climbers. Every one of us is called to an ascent, and I want to give you this up front: true fulfillment is achieved by relentless dedication to the ascent.

Now I'm going to share some gold nuggets with you. I want to give you some truths that changed my life and my trajectory many years ago. If you'll take hold of these things, you can literally change the direction of your life and end up in a very different and much better place months or years from now. Take notes. Write these things down. Put them on a piece of paper and stick that paper to your bathroom mirror or the dashboard of your car. These things, if they get down inside of you, will literally change your thinking, change where you are headed, and change where you end up in life.

We all want fulfillment in life. What is fulfillment? It is waking up and saying, "I love life! I love living! I'm excited about this day! I'm excited about this week and—oh my God—this month! And can you imagine what next year is going to be like?"

"Well that sounds like somebody who has no problems."

Nope. Problems have nothing to do with it. Fulfillment is an internal thing that has nothing to do with what is going on externally in your life. You can have lots of problems or no problems and have a tremendous amount of fulfillment either way. True fulfillment does not move one way or the other based on whether the problems in your life increase or decrease. Fulfillment is not tied to anything external; it is a totally different deal.

Please listen to me on this. Fulfillment does not come by finding a comfortable place to lie down. Fulfillment is achieved by relentless dedication to the climb. Do you want to live a fulfilled life? Then climb! Be dedicated. Be relentless about climbing. Ascend into everything God has called you to be and do. That is where you are going to find fulfillment.

"Well, I thought that—"

"But if I—"

No, don't go there. Don't believe in the excuses; they come from lies. American culture today is selling lots and lots of lies, and way too many people—inside the church as well as outside—have bought into those lies and ended up anything but fulfilled. How do you achieve fulfillment? Relentless dedication to the ascent.

Imagine you are climbing a mountain—a literal, physical mountain. As you climb that mountain, you are going to hit some spots where it is kind of flat, kind of smooth, kind of easy. Not even all of Everest is straight up. When we hit those easy spots, we tend to say, "Wow, this is nice. I could use a little bit of a breather here. I'm still working. I'm still walking. I'm still burning energy and oxygen, but you know what? It's not like it has been, and this feels nice." But then you hit other patches where the climb becomes very steep, very difficult, and very, very dangerous. Spots like those come a whole lot more frequently than the level ones where you get to stroll. Climbing in these sections is one slow, painful step after another.

It is the same way in life. We hit weeks or months or seasons where there are no big problems and everything seems to be going pretty well. You know what? Those times are nice. It's nice to experience them. But you know that is not life. If you have been around for any time at all and have been paying attention, you know the easy spots do not last forever. Life doesn't work that way. You are going to hit another steep patch, and that's just life. For a while it will be one slow, painful step after another. But you have got to keep climbing. When you hit a tough spot, it is so easy to just stop and camp. It is even easier to just back up, throw in the towel, and say, "You know what? I'm done. I can't do this." And then you miss what God has for you. You miss fulfillment in life.

The story of how Jesus called His disciples has always fascinated me, even when I was a young Christian. Not everybody sees it like I do, but I think it is absolutely phenomenal. Jesus just walked up to these people. He engaged with them very, very briefly, and then He said, "Come, follow me," (Matt. 4:19). Then He turned around and walked off. It's decision time. He's gone; He's moving. No time to think. He said, "Come, follow me," but I really believe He was telling them, "Come, climb a mountain with me."

"Well, that's a stretch."

Not really. That is a great picture of exactly what He called the disciples to do. They climbed an impossible mountain with Him.

"What's the plan?"

"Well, I'm going to be here just a little while longer. Then I'm going to turn everything over to you guys."

"What are we supposed to do then?"

"You're going to change the world."

Climb an impossible mountain with me. I want to tell you, those guys dropped everything and went climbing. It looked impossible, but those guys did it. They climbed and they climbed and they kept on climbing to their very last breath.

In 2 Timothy 4:7 the Apostle Paul says, "I have fought the good fight. I have finished the race. I have kept the faith." Those are incredible words that become even more incredible when you look at Paul's life and what he did. He goes on in 2 Timothy 4:8, "Now there is in store for me the crown of righteousness, which the Lord, the righteous Judge, will reward to me on that day—and not only to me, but also to all who have longed for his appearing."

I believe God has put within each and every single one of us an inner drive to ascend. I believe He hardwired every human being with the strong desire to climb and keep climbing. Sometimes we let life get in the way of that. You may have faced a hurt that cut too deeply, a specific circumstance that overwhelmed you, or a multitude of little things that piled up until it just felt like too much. It may have happened when you were growing up or not come along until later in life, but somewhere along the way you buried the drive to climb deep down inside.

I ran across this quote from Sir Edmund Hillary some time ago. Hillary was the first person to climb Mount Everest. He did it when everybody called it an impossible task. Everybody but Hillary believed no human being could climb Everest. Then he did it. Afterward, near the end of his life, he said this, "Despite all I have seen and experienced, I still get the same simple thrill out of glimpsing a tiny patch of snow in a high mountain gully and feel the same urge to climb towards it."

Some people, like Sir Edmund Hillary, respond to that inner drive inside of them by climbing literal mountains. Others climb mountains of career success. Others climb mountains of knowledge or education. People climb mountains of all kinds of different things. Some people just want to climb up into the American dream. Here is the truth: there is not one single thing wrong with any of those mountains. As long as they are balanced, climbing those mountains can be very, very good and healthy. But not a single one of those comes even a little bit close to touching the whole reason why God put that inner drive to climb in us.

God put that drive in you and me because He wants us to climb into everything He created us to be. He wants you to come into the fullness of your potential and into everything that you can and should be in God. There is something in us that wants to climb, to get to the summit; God hardwired that into us so that we would climb, climb, climb. He wants us to say, "I will not stop. I will not be content. I am content with natural things, but internally I have a Holy Ghost discontentment that says there is more for me. God has called more out of me. I can walk into more things. I can be more things to His glory, to His honor, and to the effectiveness of His Kingdom on this planet.

In Ephesians 4:15, Paul says our goal is to "grow up in every way into him who is the head, into Christ," (ESV). That is our goal. To grow up in all respects into Christ. Is that your goal? Are you pressing towards that? Are you absolutely dedicated to climbing up into all that God has called you to be? Are you relentlessly ascending into the fullness of the potential that God put within you? If you can say yes, that's great. Let this be an encouragement to you. If not, then pay attention to this chapter because it is for you.

If it is true that God has put the drive to climb in every single person, then there is one big problem. Why are there so few people on the mountaintop? If that is everyone's desire, why is it not overcrowded up there? And if everyone has the drive to climb hardwired inside of them, why is base camp full of so many people? To answer these questions, it is important to understand that there are three groups of people in this world. There are quitters, there are campers, and there are climbers. Every single person alive fits into one of these categories.

Before we get into the description of these three groups, it is incredibly important to understand two things. First: no one was born into any of these groups. It is neither your destiny to be a quitter, nor were you predetermined to be a climber. The group you are in was not set for you; it is set by you. Second: no matter how long you have been in one of these groups, you can always change. It does not matter if you have been in a group for an hour or if you have been there for your whole life up to now. You do not have to stay in that group a single moment more. At any point in time, you can choose a different group to be a part of. That is an important truth, an "Amen, praise God!" truth.

Quitters

There are a great number of people who opt out, cop out, back out, and drop out. Those are the quitters. Quitters abandon the climb. They refuse the opportunity that the mountain presents.

"Well, I thought mountains were kind of, you know, one of those negative deals. I've been praying that I wouldn't have any mountains in my life."

Well, if you don't have any mountains, then you are going to just be a big bowl of Jell-O. You will never come into a fraction of the potential inside of you because the mountains are what draw your potential out.

Quitters never become who they were made to be. God makes this so clear in Scripture. The trials we go through produce Christ-like character in us. In other words, they draw out the things that Christ put in us. Mountains present incredible opportunity for us, and we need to change the way we think about them.

Quitters have the exact same internal drive that campers and climbers do, but quitters have taken that drive and stuffed it down. They have shoved it deep within them and covered it up with other stuff. They don't realize when they stuff down the drive, they also stuff down real fulfillment in life.

Quitters lead compromised lives. They have abandoned their dreams. This is how they make decisions: they look at all their options, and then they select the flattest and easiest path. They think finding the easy path is how to make good choices in life. The great irony of that is this: they think—by choosing the flatter, easier path—they are avoiding the hardship and pain of the climb. But they actually end up experiencing even more hardship and even more pain during their lives. Then the pain gets even worse when they approach life's end because they look back and see a life poorly lived, and that's the most painful moment a person can face. John Greenleaf Whittier said it this way: "Of all sad words of tongue or pen, the saddest are these, 'It might have been.'"[2]

Others out there are going to pick up and go for it, but the quitter just says, "Nah, I think I'll just stay here." And you'll see this with quitters: quitters become resentful. Typically not in the beginning, but, as life goes on around them and others go by them, bitterness and resentment build up. Even depression can sometimes settle in. So many times you will see them strike out at people around them just because of the hurt and resentment inside of them. You will especially see them striking out at people who are ascending.

Quitters are often involved with substance abuse. Maybe alcohol, maybe drugs. Maybe Nintendo and Xbox or binge-watching TV shows.

"What are you talking about, Myles?"

I'm talking about anything that has a numbing effect on life. Quitters look for something that will numb them and allow them to escape. They have given up on their dreams. They have buried their God-given drive to climb, so they need some sort of anesthetic to dull the loss.

Do you identify with any of this? It doesn't even have to be your entire life overall; maybe it is just in one specific area. If you feel that you are operating as a quitter in any way, shape, or form and you want to know how to change, let me give you three words right now: recognize, repent, and envision.

The first word is recognize. How do you get out of this place? Recognize where you are. Recognize that you have been a quitter in your life or in a specific area of it. You cannot get from A to B until you first recognize that you are at A. What is the first thing you look for on the map when you are trying to find a store in the mall? You look for the little red dot that says, "You are here." You are not going to be able to get to where you want to be until you own up to where you are.

The second word is repent. When I use this word, I do not mean to conjure up any kind of ceremonial or convoluted religious concept. The word repent is a very simple word in the Bible. It is the Greek word *metanoia*. *Metanoia* means a change in mind; it is a change in the way you think that brings a corresponding change in the direction you walk. After you recognize where you are, the next step is to believe God has something more for you than what you are living now. Declare that God has something better for you; that is changing the way you think. And when you change the way you think, that is going to change the direction you are going. You will begin to walk a completely different way.

The last word is envision. Lock in on what you believe is God's best for you. Get missile lock on that thing. Don't take your eyes off it. Do not allow other things in life—disappointment, hurt, setbacks, and failures—to distract you or take you away from it. Do not allow those things to cause you to lose sight of the peak. Denis Waitley said, "When you are in the valley, keep your goal firmly in view and you will get the renewed energy to continue the climb." Where do I get the renewed energy to get up and make that climb? I recognize where I am. I repent. I stay focused on what God has for me, and I believe it for myself.

Campers

Like quitters, campers live compromised lives. The difference is in the degree of compromise. Campers usually feel very justified in telling themselves, "Hey, you know what? It's time for me to just stop and relax and enjoy the fruits of my labor." Sounds good, doesn't it? But the truth is they want to stop, relax, and enjoy the things they have received from their partial ascent. They climbed up to a certain point, they got some things from it, and now they are just going to enjoy those things. That is the way a camper thinks.

I have been around a lot of different people in my life—Christians and non-Christians in this nation and other nations of the world. Never ever in my life have I met a single person that, when asked to define success, would answer with the word comfort. Yet when you look at so many people's lives, you would think that comfort is the ultimate goal! Culture is selling that lie today.

Campers redirect all of the energy that brought them to their place on the mountain. That place may be fairly low on the mountain or halfway up or even close to the top, but wherever they are, they tend to devote all of their energy toward setting up their campsite. They want this cozy little campground setup. They hang strings of lights in the trees. Oh, wouldn't this be a good place for a fire pit over here? All of their energy starts going towards developing the camp.

That is the difference between camping and taking a break. Resting is important; we all need rest. When you are climbing, you need to take breaks. But campers go way beyond that. They may have started out taking a break, but the next thing you know their focus is no longer getting to the top. Their focus is on the campsite.

Most campers also trick themselves. They fool themselves into believing they have already reached success.

"You don't think I'm a success? Look at my campground! Let me turn on the lights in the trees. Come over here. Let me show you the incredible view. Wow, I'm a success. I could stay here forever."

Yeah, that's the problem. They foolishly consider themselves successful because they have a misconception about what success is. Campers tend to think of success as a destination, but in reality success is a journey. That major shift needs to happen in many people's thinking. If you start thinking correctly, biblically, and truthfully about success, it will change the way you live. Western culture has sold us on this idea that somehow or another we get to this one place called success, and then we can stop and settle down. Can you show me a verse in the Bible for that? Feel free to look, but you are not going to find one. Success is not the destination, it is the climb itself.

I have met many people who were and are incredibly successful in the conventional sense of the word. I know people who built very successful businesses, people who reached the net worth they always dreamed of, and even people who achieved things in ministry that were outwardly impressive. Every single one of those people worked incredibly hard to get to a place or a destination that he or she thought was going to be success. Every single one of them got to that place, then started looking for what was missing because it didn't feel like success.

Actual mountain climbers describe a similar experience. It is amazing how many people climb gigantic mountains—Everest, Annapurna, the Matterhorn. If you read about those mountain climbers and their experiences, you will notice some similarities in their stories. When they start to climb, they are so excited to get to the top. Then they make it to the peak, incredible view and everything. You know what a lot of them experience? They get to the top and realize there is nothing there. It was never really about the top. It was about the climb.

Can you relate that to your life? Don't buy into the lie that there is a destination point called success. Success is the climb itself.

Climbers take breaks. I said that earlier, but there is another thing that climbers have to do. Before going for a really high peak, climbers have to acclimatize. Camping is not the same thing as acclimatizing. When you come into a higher altitude, your body has to adjust. It is not possible to show up and climb Everest in a week. It takes a minimum of seven to eight weeks, assuming perfect weather, to climb Everest. Why? Because you have to acclimatize. You climb up to base camp number one, then you stay there for days. While you are at camp one, do you know what you do during the day? You climb up, almost to camp two, and then you come back down and spend another night at camp one. Then the next day you climb up and you come back down. Then the next day you do it again. That is the way you acclimatize. Then you finally make your assault on camp two and spend the night there. Then you wake up the next morning, climb almost to camp three before you come back down to camp two. You do this day after day until you acclimatize. There are four different camps on Everest, and you have to stay at each one for a period of time before you can go on.

Acclimatization is an incredible picture of life and the way Jesus calls us to climb into the high places He has for us. As we reach new levels in life, we need to stay in one place long enough to get established. Have you reached a new place in life? Good, get established there. Have you received a new truth or new understanding? In 2 Peter 1:12, the Apostle Peter tells us that we need to "be established in the present truth," (KJV).Don't just say "Wow!" and move on to the next thing. Build that truth into your life.

I have met hundreds and hundreds of people who wanted to race to the top. I have never seen one of them get there. The people who are racing do not take time to stop, develop, and acclimatize. They do not establish things in their lives; they just take off after the next thing at a dead sprint. As I have continued climbing, most of the time I end up climbing past the corpses of their careers and their ministries. That is not the way to go. I am thankful that I paid attention early on, looked at what the Word of God had to say, and understood this truth about life. The goal is never about speed. Life is about steady growth that proceeds from a rock-solid foundation. Build that truth into your life, and it will take you to a different place.

Hebrews 6:11-12 says, "We desire that each one of you show the same diligence so as to realize the full assurance of hope until the end." (NASB). So often we take this verse and verses like it and make them all about getting out of here and getting to heaven. That is not what Paul meant when he used the word *end*. In this verse, Paul is talking about the hope of glory that is in us. He is saying that he wants us to show the same diligence to come into the hope that God has for us, which is God's glory fully and completely in us.

The rest of that passage says this: "Show the same diligence so as to realize the full assurance of hope until the end so that you will not be sluggish, but imitators of those who through faith and patience inherit the promises," (NASB). How do you inherit the promises? How do you reach those high places that are your high places to walk in? Through faith and patience.

That verse makes me wonder why Christianity has such a large faith movement, but not a single whisper of a patience movement. Does that strike you as odd like it strikes me? It is good to be all about faith, but you better be all about patience too. The Bible says it is through faith *and* patience that you inherit the promises.

If you have been camping, you need to do two things. You need to fix your vision on the peak in faith. At the very same time, you need to patiently build a sure foundation in your life. Focus your vision and strengthen your foundation. The key is to do both; one or the other will not work. So many, many believers fall into one of two camps; they do not seem to be able to put these things together. It concerns me greatly every time I see it.

The first camp is full of those who have a strong foundation, but no vision to go higher. These believers are strongly grounded in the Word.

They are strongly grounded in their beliefs. They are strongly grounded in who God says they are. The trouble is they really have no plan to go much higher than where they are right now. Maybe someday they will move their camp up another twenty yards. Maybe.

Then there is the second camp. This one is full of people who have vision for going much, much higher, but they have a weak foundation because of their own impatience. They have the vision. Boy, they are going to hit the summit. Oh, God has all these things for them. They believe in the promises of God. Hallelujah! But they do not have a strong foundation of God's Word in their lives. Therefore, their climbs are going to be brief round trips that do not include the top of the mountain. They will be limping back into base camp very soon.

You need to have a solid foundation *and* a vision for the top. You may be camping because you have one or the other, just not both. If you are in the first camp—you have a strong foundation, but you do not have a vision—you are going to be content to camp. Maybe you want to move your camp a little bit, but you are pretty content. If you are content to camp, you will not go for all the promises of God and the things He has for you. And if you do not go for them, you will not get them. What about the second camp? If you have all kinds of vision and faith, but you do not have a strong foundation, look out. Pain—coming soon to a life near you. You are not prepared. You do not have the foundation you need to make the climb. Either one of those things, without the other, will cause you to become a camper.

Climbers

Of the three types of people, only the climbers live life fully. Climbers and climbers alone receive fulfillment. The climber Endicott Peabody once said this:

For life—which is in any way worthy—is like ascending a mountain. When you have climbed to the first shoulder of the hill, you find another rise above you, and that achieved there is another, and another still, and yet another peak, and then height to be achieved seems infinity: but, you find as you ascend that the air becomes purer and more bracing, that the clouds gather more frequently below than above, that the sun is warmer than before and that you not only get a clearer view of Heaven, but that you gain a wider and wider view of earth, and that your horizon is perpetually growing larger.[3]

That is the truth of our lives and our climbs. As we climb up into what God called us to be and do, the air gets purer, the sun gets warmer, the clouds seem to be below us more than above us, and not only do we have a clear view of heaven, but we have a much, much more expanded view of what is happening here on Planet Earth.

Climbers have a deep sense of purpose in everything they do. It does not matter what they are doing. Whether they are doing something huge or something other people would consider absolutely minuscule and meaningless, it is all purposeful to them. They could be frying burgers at McDonald's and see a grand purpose in it the entire time. Does that mean they want to be frying burgers at McDonald's forever? Heavens no. Not a climber. But they always see a purpose in what they are doing. It is not wasting time. They are not just hanging out, wasting their days and months, and waiting for something big to come along in life. No, what they are doing is always the big thing in life. If we do not see what we are doing that way and embrace it, we will never get to the bigger things in life.

Climbers are purposeful. They are intentional in what they do. They do not stumble around and happen to come upon something. They are not blind hogs finding acorns every now and then; climbers go on acorn hunts. They map the thing out. They do their homework. They know when and where to go. And they do not just go for one acorn, they go for a whole bushel full of them.

Climbers are intentional about life. I love this quote from Mark Udall: "You don't climb mountains without a team, you don't climb mountains without being fit, you don't climb mountains without being prepared and you don't climb mountains without balancing the risks and rewards. And you never climb a mountain on accident—it has to be intentional." That is great advice for climbing a literal mountain and great advice for life.

If you want to be a climber, you need people around you. Don't you dare be a lone ranger; you will pay a steep price if you try to go it alone.

If you want to be a climber, you need to be fit. Better hit the spiritual gym and work out.

If you want to be a climber, you need to prepare yourself. Prepare yourself internally by building godly, Christ-like character within you. Prepare yourself externally too. If you want a promotion at work, prepare for it spiritually by building character into your life, but also prepare for it naturally by learning everything there is to know about the job. Do whatever work you need to do, get whatever education you need to get, and generally do whatever you need to do in order to reach your destination. Don't be a Charismatic squirrel—not building any character into your life, not doing any hard work or preparation, but applying for the promotion, praying about it, and getting angry at God when you don't get it.

If you want to be a climber, you need to be intentional. You will never become a climber on accident. You will never climb a mountain on accident

"How did I end up here? I was just out for a stroll and now, next thing you know, here I am on top of Everest."

You have to be intentional from the very start. Make an intentional choice to start the climb, saying, "In this area of my life, I believe God has showed me this. This is God's best for me. This is His plan and purpose for me, and—by God—I'm starting this climb." But it does not stop there. You have to be intentional about climbing every single day of the climb.

In Philippians 3:12, Paul says, "Not that I have already obtained all this, or have already arrived at my goal, but I press on to take hold of that for which Christ Jesus took hold of me." To paraphrase, Paul is saying, "I don't even understand it. I don't know why, but Jesus saw something in me that I couldn't see. He looked at me and said 'Wow! I want you! I see incredible potential in you. Come over here! I need you.'"

This was why Paul struggled, strived, and climbed for the many years of his life. He spent his life relentlessly dedicated to climbing into that which Christ saw in him. Paul was shocked that Jesus saw something in him. He was still struggling to believe it, but he knew it was true, and he was determined to find out exactly what Jesus saw. He pursued that; he climbed and climbed and climbed to reach the point where he could discover for himself what Jesus saw in him.

Paul was intentional. Climbers are intentional. They choose not to live life by default. They live life by design. Living by default is letting everybody else script your life for you. What am I going to do this week? What am I going to do this year? Well, I'll just have to wait and see what everybody else tells me. Living life by default is getting pulled and pushed by all the people and circumstances around you. Living life by design is receiving the revelation of God about what He has for you, then designing your life around that.

I understand the idea of designing your own life might offend the hyper-religious. You might be thinking it is only the place of God to design our lives. A wise person will, of course, seek God's input into the design. But you and I are given free will. We either choose to script our lives the way we want, or we let other people script it for us. We either design our lives, or we wake up every morning and ask for the notes. What is my script for the day? What am I supposed to do? Climbers don't do that. Climbers are intentional. Climbers have a passion for what they do. They have a zest for life itself. They have a zest for the climb.

In life there are quitters, there are campers, and there are climbers. Every single person on earth fits into one of these categories—you, your family members, people you work with, people at church, and everyone else. Every single person on earth faces a mountain; we all have the opportunity to climb. Quitters, campers, and climbers respond to that opportunity very differently. As a result, they have very, very different levels of joy and fulfillment in life.

John Muir, one of the most famous naturalists and mountaineers in America, sums up the climb in one single, powerful sentence. He said this: "The mountains are calling and I must go."[4] Is there a mountain calling you? Oh, you bet there is.

Challenge the mountain.

Start the climb.

Part 2

Get Started

FROM SIMON TO PETER

T here is a powerful moment in Matthew 16:13-18.

> *When Jesus came to the region of Caesarea Philippi, he asked his disciples, "Who do people say the Son of Man is?"*
>
> *They replied, "Some say John the Baptist; others say Elijah; and still others, Jeremiah or one of the prophets."*
>
> *"But what about you?" he asked. "Who do you say I am?"*
>
> *Simon Peter answered, "You are the Messiah, the Son of the living God."*
>
> *Jesus replied, "Blessed are you, Simon son of Jonah, for this was not revealed to you by flesh and blood, but by my Father in heaven. And I tell you that you are Peter, and on this rock I will build my church, and the gates of Hades will not overcome it."*

Most Christians have read this story before, but almost everyone misses the deeper story playing out. On the surface it is a good story, sure. But there is something going on here that a quick reading of the English translation will never give you. There is a play on words in this passage directly connected to the name "Simon Peter." At this point in time, Peter's name was Simon. In this moment, Jesus gives him a new name—the name that everyone knows him by now.

Here's an important tip for studying the Word: names in the Bible are meaningful. This pattern is evident again and again. Throughout the Old Testament and into the New Testament, names have great significance. When you run across the name of a person or a place in the Bible, it is never a bad idea to look up the name's meaning. I can give you a lot of different examples from Scripture. Perhaps one of the best is when Jacob's wife, Rachel, gave birth to her last child. She realized she was going to die, so with one of her last breaths she named the new baby boy in her dying arms Ben-Oni, which means son of my sorrow. Immediately after she died, Jacob took his son and quickly renamed him Benjamin, which means son of my strength.

The descendants of Benjamin, Jacob's son, became a tribe of great warriors. That is what they were known for throughout biblical times. These guys were masters of the sword and the bow, and every one of them could use weapons with their right and left hands equally. They were mighty, fierce, skilled warriors. They were sons of strength.

Let me make something clear. There are men all across this world that have been misnamed and mislabeled in the arms of a dying church—a church that is dead already and doesn't know it. So many men are desperately in need of other fatherly men who can hear the voice of God and say, "No, that is not who you are. This is who you are."

We need to understand this: God wants to name us correctly. That is exactly what is going on between Jesus and Simon in Matthew 16. The name Simon means a reed or a tall blade of grass. When the wind blows one way, a reed goes with it all the way to the extreme. Then the wind changes, and the reed follows it again to the extreme. That is exactly who Simon was. Have you read the stories about him?

Here is one of his best moments. He was in a boat with the disciples during a storm. They saw Jesus walking on water toward them. Simon Peter said, "Jesus! Can I walk on the water out there with you?"

"Come on!" Jesus said.

So he got out. He walked on the water. Then he panicked. "I'm drowning!"

You can see this play out again and again in the Gospels. Even after Jesus gave him a new name, it didn't entirely change things. A few chapters later, Jesus and His disciples are in the upper room, and Jesus begins washing the feet of each of the disciples. He gets to Peter, and Peter says, "No! You aren't washing my feet."

Jesus says, "Okay, then you won't have anything to do with Me. You won't have any part of Me."

Then Peter jumps up. "Wash all of me then!"

That is the Simon nature. He was a reed, blown around to extremes. His parents labeled him that from birth. Everybody else knew that he was Simon. He had two cousins and a brother in the twelve disciples, and they all knew that he was Simon. That is who he had always been. He proved it regularly. Everybody knew it. He knew it. But Jesus said, "No. That's not who you are. Let Me tell you who you really are. You are Peter."

Peter comes from the Greek word *petros*, which means a large boulder or rock. Stable, immovable, not blown here and there. Simon thought he was a reed. Jesus told him that he was actually just the opposite.

Just like Simon, we need to hear the voice of God and realize that we are not who we think we are. It does not even matter if others have affirmed that identity in us, we are actually something very, very different. God sees the truth of who we really are even when we don't. Our concept of identity is simply based on all we currently know about ourselves.

We say, "This is who I am."

God frowns, thinking, "No, that's not who he is."

Then we get saved. We become a part of a church that preaches and teaches the Word of God, and that helps us begin to understand. Then we say, "Oh! I'm not who I thought I was. I'm nothing like I thought I was. I'm a different person than that."

We gain some of the truth about ourselves, and that is exciting. But many of us get too excited at the very beginning.

"Oh, now I have discovered all of who I am!"

No, you haven't. You have discovered just a small part of it. There is still more you need to discover before you know who you really are. Not a single person on the planet fully knows the real identity God sees in him or her. Not fully. We are all on a pathway of self-discovery.

It doesn't matter if you are at the beginning of the journey or near the very end; there is still more to go. God wants to reveal more to you today, this week, next week, next month, next year, in the next five years, in the next ten years, and so on. God wants to reveal to you more of who you really are every day.

The problem is we believe lies. And the biggest and most powerful lies we believe are the ones about ourselves.

"Well, I'm just not very good at this. And I'm not good at that."

Well, that *might* be true. There are things that we just aren't good at. But a lot of the things that we believe we can't do are lies. Proverbs 23:7 tells us this: "For as he thinks within himself, so he is," (NASB).

"I'm just shy."

Are you really?

"I am. I'm just not an outgoing person."

Well, I know that is the way you act. You are operating that way right now, for sure. But does that have anything to do with who you really are? Almost certainly not. You chose to believe it, maybe even from a young age. I imagine it has been reinforced by parents, family members, teachers, and peers. So now you have taken it on as your identity, but it is not who you are.

"Well, I'm just a hothead. I have a short temper."

Well, I don't doubt that you act that way, but is that who you really are?

"Well, I'm just a little slow."

Are you really? Or have you just believed another lie about who you are? Believe this instead: God alone knows who you are. Nobody else. Spiritually mature people can hear from God about who you are and impart the truth to you, but that is still coming from God. God alone knows who you are. Every single one of us needs to walk the pathway of discovery. God wants every single one of us to move from Simon to Peter. He wants you to move from who you believed you were to who you really are in him.

How do we go from Simon to Peter? It is evidently not just a word from Jesus. We have already seen Simon Peter operating in his old identity in the upper room chapters after he received his new name from Jesus. Peter was still struggling to step into his new identity. There is a process to walking from Simon to Peter. How do we get to Peter?

I have studied this for years, and I have found three keys that are important in the process of going from Simon to Peter.

1. Pursue your destiny.

Take a look at the interaction between Jesus and Simon Peter in Luke 5:1-3.

> *"One day as Jesus was standing by the Lake of Gennesaret, the people were crowding around him and listening to the word of God. He saw at the water's edge two boats, left there by the fishermen, who were washing their nets. He got into one of the boats, the one belonging to Simon, and asked him to put out a little from shore. Then he sat down and taught the people from the boat."*

It is important for us to understand that this is not the first time Jesus encountered Simon Peter. The events of John 1 and Mark 1—when Jesus first called Peter to follow Him—happened roughly nine months before. Those chapters tell us that when Jesus called Simon, he dropped his nets and followed Jesus. That was nine months before this. Why is he back to fishing in his boat again? What happened?

We don't know for sure. The Bible doesn't go through the details, but it was likely for one of the same two reasons that people today go back to their old lives after encountering Jesus.

Reason number one: it is easier to do what you are used to than it is to step forward into your destiny.

"I'm comfortable here. I've done this for a while. I can manage this. This works for me."

Then God calls us to a place way out there, and it is difficult for us to see ourselves reaching that destination successfully. So what do we do? We drift back to what we are comfortable with.

Many people are familiar with the Peter principle; it is all over our culture today, especially in the business world. The Peter principle is the idea that the next promotion will put you in a place of incompetence. It is the idea that if you go too far or make too much progress, you will go beyond what you can handle and inevitably fail. A lot of us carry that mindset out of the business world and into other areas of life.

The name of that principle does not come from the Peter of the Bible. Peter, for all of his mistakes, was always the first one to go for it. On two separate occasions, he jumped out of a boat in the middle of a lake, headed straight for Jesus. He was not interested in waiting around or playing it safe. I love that about him, and I know that Jesus and the Father loved that about him too. God has called you and I to be like the biblical Peter; He has not called us to be worried about the Peter principle in our lives.

There is an opposite extreme. God has not called you and I to climb the ladder on our own either. There are a lot of people who land in a business or in a church and immediately begin climbing. How is this church structured? How do I climb the ladder to get to a place of leadership? Life is not about climbing the ladder in ministry, in the corporate world, or in any other area of life.

We are not meant to climb ladders or operate in the Peter principle; we are meant to talk to God. God, where do you want me to be? What do you want me to do? God has gifted and called you to be somewhere and do something. Find that spot and flourish there. Hear from God and do what he tells you to do. That is all you have to think about.

Reason number two: you don't really believe that you are who God says you are. You doubt that you can do what God called you to do.

We need to recognize that we are handmade, created by God for a purpose. There is a verse in the Bible—quoted endlessly by pastors, speakers, and leaders—that says, "The gifts . . . of God are without repentance," (Rom. 11:29, KJV). What does that mean? It means you can screw up in every way you could possibly think of, but the gifts that God put in you will still be there. God doesn't change His mind.

"Well, you screwed up. I'm gonna take that gift of preaching away from you. You just messed up way too many times."

It does not work that way. Those gifts are going to stay there no matter what you do. That is the verse and the concept that is quoted so often, but that is only part of the verse and part of the picture. The verse in its entirety says this: "For the gifts *and calling* of God are without repentance,"([italics added]). No matter how many times you screw up, no matter how many wrong turns you take, and no matter how many ugly, nasty things you do, God's calling will still be on your life. It is not just God's gifts that are without repentance, it is God's call.

So many of us are so fearful that we cannot do what God has called us to do. We have to shake that off. We have to press through it.

"Well, I'll get in line for prayer again today. Somebody pray that the fear leaves me."

No, just step out of it. Make a decision. Stop looking for prayer and choose to step forward.

Another reason so many of us are missing what God has for us is because we are so afraid of giving it 100 percent.

It is a common practice, especially for men, to do things half-heartedly out of a fear of failure. Many people choose to give only 60-80 percent effort so that if they fail, they can say, "Well, I didn't really give it my all anyway." This is an especially common tactic for students in school. Students like this believe they are not really good at math, so they don't study very hard. They give some effort, but nowhere near all they could give. Then, when they get a C, they have an excuse.

"I didn't really give it my all."

That phrase is a protective measure. Some people live life that way so they have an easy excuse in their back pockets at all times. In the end that is not going to work well for anyone.

We have to go for this thing. Turn it loose. Go all in. Get after it. Lamentations 1:9 speaks about the people of God in the Old Testament, saying, "She (the people of God) did not consider her future. Therefore she has fallen astonishingly . . . " (KJV, parentheses added). Oh Lord. Don't ever let that be written about my life.

If only you knew what God had in store for you. If only you realized what you could have been and what you could have done. If you don't consider your future, your fall will be astounding.

If you want to go from Simon to Peter, you need to pursue your destiny. Have a passion for something that burns inside of you and says, "I've got to get from here to there. I'm not sure how far 'there' is, but I'm all in. I'm going after this thing."

When what later became all of Grace Ministries International first started in Wharton, Texas, we were just a few families meeting in a rundown old building on the square. The wood floor of that building was built up about four or five feet above the subfloor below, but there was an area of it that was so rotten it caved in and opened up a big hole.

We took metal folding chairs, put them in a circle around the area, and put police tape through them. We had to ask parents to keep their kids away from the hole.

That is where we started. At that point we weren't even trying to start a church. We were just a small group of people who wanted to meet together and learn and grow. We wanted something different than the dead churches we had been in. But as people kept coming and we kept growing, everyone started telling me, "You're supposed to lead this."

"Get your finger out of my face. I will serve and work, but I—"

"No, you are supposed to pastor this."

"Get your dadgum finger out of my face. I'm not doing this. I can do counseling. I can speak at different events and things; I'm comfortable with that. But I'm not pastoring."

They didn't let up. They told me that I needed to pastor again and again and again. Then God started speaking to me. If that sounds a little weird or strange, I don't mean for it to. I'm not talking about God speaking audibly. It wasn't like that at all. Some people have the gift or the ability to hear God with their physical ears. I don't. But God will speak to my heart, and it's always just as clear to me as hearing someone speak to me out loud.

But this time I was thinking, "No, that can't be God. That's you, Satan. Get away from me. God loves me. He wouldn't make me do that." I kept struggling. Then my wife started telling me. "Honey, I think God's saying that you're supposed to pastor this."

This is the true story. I am really not embellishing at all. I spent most of my Saturday nights at the church building. Sometimes I would stay there until one or two in the morning. At first I was preparing my message for the next day, but most weeks I ended up just sitting on the steps of the stage and weeping.

"God, why are You doing this to me? I hate this. I have served You faithfully all these years. I have tithed. I have done all these things. I have been faithful to You. Why are You punishing me? Why are You making me preach? I hate preaching. It's not who I am."

This didn't happen just two or three times. I spent about fifty to eighty Saturday nights on those steps, crying my eyes out and asking God why He was making me preach and pastor.

So many times we don't believe in ourselves. I have now been a pastor and a preacher for many, many years. Do I love what I do? Yeah, now I do. But back then I hated it. I was convinced that it wasn't me. Many times the very thing that you have been most fearful of and you have most pushed back against is the very thing that God is calling you to do.

The devil is damned. He is going to hell. There is no doubt about that. But let me tell you this: he may be damned, but he is not stupid. Sometimes he is even smarter than we are. Once he gets a sense of God's calling on your life, he runs out ahead of you and builds a big obstacle right in your path. Why? Because if you fulfill your destiny, his kingdom will suffer greatly. He wants you to stop. And if he can convince you, through fear and lies and obstacles, that your destiny is not achievable or not a part of who you really are, then he will succeed. You will stop pursuing your destiny, and you will never make it from Simon to Peter.

Peter understood this. It took him two tries, but he got it. He understood that he needed to pursue his destiny, and that is one of the key reasons he moved from Simon to Peter.

2. Receive correction.

You're going to love this one. This part of the story starts in Matthew 16:21-23.

> *From that time on Jesus began to explain to his disciples*
> *that he must go to Jerusalem and suffer many things at*

*the hands of the elders, the chief priests and the teachers
of the law, and that he must be killed and on the third
day be raised to life.*

*Peter took him aside and began to rebuke him. "Never,
Lord!" he said. "This shall never happen to you!"*

*Jesus turned and said to Peter, "Get behind me, Satan!
You are a stumbling block to me; you do not have in mind
the concerns of God, but merely human concerns."*

This is just a few verses after Peter received his revelation about the identity of Jesus. The next thing you know, Peter starts rebuking Jesus and trying to give Him prophetic direction. Jesus turns to Peter and says, "You know, that's an interesting thought. I want to be open-minded about these things, but I think you're a little mistaken here. I appreciate your heart, but I think you're off a little bit."

No, that's not what He says. Jesus doesn't even say, "Peter, you're just flat wrong." No. He looks Peter straight in the face and says, "You devil."

There are so many people that respond to correction from others with, "Oh, poor me. How could you be so harsh to me? That was such a hard word." Jesus told Peter, "Get behind me, Satan!" (Matt. 16:23). What did Peter do? How did he respond to correction? He didn't sulk. He didn't pout. He didn't call 911 or Child Protective Services. He didn't change churches. He didn't go talk to his buddies about how harsh Jesus was. He took his correction and hung in there. He manned up and took his medicine. He owned that puppy and said, "You're right, Jesus." If he had, he never would have made the transition from Simon to Peter.

"Well, how do you know for sure that he hung in there, Myles?"

Because he is still there in Matthew 17. But Jesus wasn't finished with him yet. In fact, God the Father now wanted a piece of him. This is the story in Matthew 17, "After six days Jesus took with him Peter, James and John the brother of James, and led them up a high mountain by themselves," (Matt. 17:1).

We are talking about the Mount of Transfiguration here; you know where this is going. But I want to pause the story to make sure you understand something about this passage. Sometimes we read this first verse and think, "Isn't that nice of Jesus? Even after Peter screwed up, Jesus took him up the mountain along with James and John."

Jesus was not taking them up there for a picnic. They were going to partake of a glorious moment, yes. But don't miss what else was going on there. This was designed by God to be a woodshed experience. This was a moment of correction.

Jesus did not take these three specific disciples with him because they were the most deserving. Jesus took Peter, James, and John because they were the ones giving him the most trouble. Peter tried to tell Jesus to not do what God had called Him to do. One minute James and John were fighting over who gets the positions of honor in Jesus' future kingdom, and the next minute they were trying to call down fire from heaven to burn up a whole village. These three were the problem cases. Jesus brought them up the mountain with him for a little daddy time.

> *There he was transfigured before them. His face shone like the sun, and his clothes became as white as the light. Just then there appeared before them Moses and Elijah, talking with Jesus.*
>
> *Peter said to Jesus, "Lord, it is good for us to be here. If you wish, I will put up three shelters—one for you, one for Moses and one for Elijah."*
>
> *While he was still speaking, a bright cloud covered them, and a voice from the cloud said, "This is my Son, whom*

I love; with him I am well pleased. Listen to him!"
(Matthew 17:2-5).

Jesus takes these three guys up the mountain with him. He reveals himself in the fullness of his glory. Up to this point his glory has always been wrapped in flesh, but here he unzips. It appears that at least James and John kind of clue in to what is going on at this point, but poor Peter is still clueless. Here is Moses. Here is Elijah. Here is Jesus in all his glory. And here is little nobody Peter, still trying to organize the whole thing. That is what's going on here. So God yells to them.

"Well, God wouldn't yell like that."

I see an exclamation point that says differently. Look at this passage in any translation you want; God's words have an exclamation point. They are translated that way because, in the original Greek language, those words are in the emphatic. God was not speaking to them. God was yelling at them. "This is my Son, whom I love! LISTEN TO HIM! Shut your mouth! Open your ears! Stop running and barking out ahead of everybody! Slow down, get in step, and listen!"

If Peter hadn't received that correction from Jesus and from Father God, he never would have made it from Simon to Peter. He never would have found or walked in his true identity.

There are many verses in Proverbs that speak about correction and people who won't receive correction. Proverbs 5 says if you won't receive correction, then you will come to utter ruin (13-14, ESV). Anybody in here want to sign up for that one?

Proverbs 10:17 says if you won't receive correction, you will lead others astray. You should receive correction yourself. But if you are even hanging around people who won't receive correction, be careful. Watch out for people who get corrected and whine about it to you. Those people will lead you astray. That is what the Word of God says. Be careful.

"Well, I'm ministering to him."

Then make sure there is only one-way traffic on that bridge.

Proverbs 12:1 really brings it home: "Whoever hates correction is stupid." Do I need to break that down in the Hebrew for you?

Proverbs 15:5, "whoever heeds correction shows prudence."

Don't listen to everybody around you. Listening to everyone is one of the biggest mistakes you can make. Stop doing that. Listen to those who genuinely love you and have a track record of hearing from God and walking in obedience to Him. Those people have your best interest at heart. If somebody like that comes to you and tells you that you are a donkey, you need to stop and think about it. You need to get on your face before God and pray about it. If two people like that come to you and tell you that you're a donkey, then you *really* need to pray about it. You may even need to fast and make sure you hear what God is saying to you. If three or more people like that come to you and tell you that you're a donkey, then you need to go buy a saddle because you are one. You don't have to overthink this thing.

Proverbs 13:18, "Whoever disregards discipline comes to poverty and shame."

Proverbs 15:31-32, "One who listens to life-giving rebukes will be at home among the wise. Anyone who ignores discipline despises himself, but whoever listens to correction acquires good sense," (Christian Standard Bible).

I want to highlight a couple things from that last reference. Here is the first thing: God says if you won't receive correction, you despise yourself. If you won't receive correction, you despise who you really are. You despise the Peter that God has called you to be.

Here is the second thing: God uses the words "life-giving rebukes." Those are powerful words. This verse isn't just talking about correction. It is not talking about addressing problems kindly, nicely, and with the right words. Rebukes are harsh. Rebukes are strong. But godly rebukes are life-giving. If you want to stay Simon, feel free to dismiss them. If you want to walk in the real life that God has called you to, you're going to need to drink them in.

If you want to go from Simon to Peter, then you must receive correction.

3. Get back up from failure.

Then seizing him, they led him away and took him into the house of the high priest. Peter followed at a distance. And when some there had kindled a fire in the middle of the courtyard and had sat down together, Peter sat down with them. A servant girl saw him seated there in the firelight. She looked closely at him and said, "This man was with him."

But he denied it. "Woman, I don't know him," he said.

A little later someone else saw him and said, "You also are one of them."

"Man, I am not!" Peter replied.

About an hour later another asserted, "Certainly this fellow was with him, for he is a Galilean."

Peter replied, "Man, I don't know what you're talking about!" Just as he was speaking, the rooster crowed. The Lord turned and looked straight at Peter. Then Peter remembered the word the Lord had spoken to him: "Before the rooster crows today, you will disown me three times." And he went outside and wept bitterly, (Luke 22:54-62).

Think back to the Lord's Supper. During that meal, Jesus told his disciples that all of them were going to run. Do you remember how Peter responded? He basically said, "Oh no, no, no. I mean, I don't know about these other guys. They'll probably run, but let me tell you something. I'm the man. I got your back, Jesus. I'm not going anywhere." What was he really saying there? Peter was saying, "I'm not gonna fail! I'm not going to experience personal failure in my life."

Personal failure is something that every single person will deal with.

"Oh yeah. Glad I got that stuff over with a few years ago."

Nope, sorry. You are going to deal with it again and again and again. Personal failure: coming soon to a life near you. It happens. It is a part of life. None of us have arrived yet. We are going to mess up. We are going to screw up. We are going to drop the ball. We are going to flake out. We are going to do things we will wish we had not done. We are going to mess up, so we have to learn how to deal with failure the right way.

Life is not all about avoiding failure. Avoiding failure is a good thing, and we want to do as much of that as we can. But since we haven't arrived yet, we need to be prepared to deal with failure when it comes. Sometimes the failure will be thrust upon us when we did nothing to bring it on. Sometimes the failure will come directly from our own bad decisions and stupid mistakes. But no matter the reason for it, we have to learn how to look at failure differently.

Are you familiar with the name Dr. Seuss? Yeah, I thought you might be. Do you have any idea how long it took Dr. Seuss to get his first book published? He took his book to twenty-seven different publishers over the course of many years before a single one said yes. It was hard work to even get a meeting with a single publisher to present his book. He managed to get twenty-seven meetings, but every single publisher said no and told him to get out. After twenty-seven rejections, what kind of man goes to number twenty-eight? I'll tell you what kind—not a Simon, but a Peter.

You have to learn how to deal with failure. You have to learn how to deal with setbacks. Henry Ford went bankrupt two times in less than three years. His name is a big deal now, but he would have been a nobody if he had not dealt with those failures in his life. What about Michael Jordan? Did you know that he got cut from his high school basketball team? The coach told him to try track because he was no good at basketball.

These are true stories. The problem is this: we hear these stories of people who succeeded after failure and say, "Yeah, amen!" But then we fail in our own lives and totally give up because, "I failed."

Most of us have heard of Thomas Edison's thousands of failed lightbulb experiments. A friend of Edison's once recounted a conversation he had with the inventor in the midst of his nearly endless trial and error.

> *In view of this immense amount of thought and labor, my sympathy got the better of my judgment, and I said: "Isn't it a shame that with the tremendous amount of work you have done you haven't been able to get any results?" Edison turned on me like a flash, and with a smile replied: "Results! Why, man, I have gotten a lot of results! I know several thousand things that won't work."[1]*

Instead of considering fruitless experiments as failures, Edison just thought of them as discovering ways that don't work. When I first read that story, I thought, "That's cool." Then I read it again years later and thought, "Oh, that's really cool." But I didn't understand how it applied to my life for a long time after that. It *is* a cool quote, but when are we going to start looking at personal failures in our lives simply as discovering ways of doing life that don't work? Can we look at failure differently?

Charles Kettering, one of America's greatest inventors, said, "It is not a disgrace to fail."[2] He encouraged everyone to "analyze every failure to find its cause. . . . For failing is one of the greatest arts in the world."

Look at yourself and say this: "My failure is not a disgrace." This doesn't mean you should gloss over failure. Don't act like it didn't happen. Don't put some happy little spin on it. Own your failure, but learn from it.

Kettering also emphasized that everybody must learn how to fail intelligently. If you don't get anything else from this message, get those two words. Fail intelligently. I used to repeat those words out loud and in my head over and over and over for months. When I fail, my tendency is to beat myself up. But I knew I needed to learn to fail intelligently, so I kept repeating those words until they got down to my spirit. That is who I want to be. I want to be somebody who fails intelligently.

Henry Ford said failure is just the opportunity to begin again more intelligently.[3] Thomas J. Watson, Sr., one of the greatest and most-revered CEOs in the history of America, once said, "If you want to increase your success rate, double your rate of failure."[4] How many people naturally want to be successful? Everyone. How many people naturally want to double the rate at which they fail? Practically no one. But that is the pathway. It is this thing called life for people who are not yet perfect, which means everyone other than Jesus.

Imagine a room full of every person that you respect and admire. Put every person that you look up to and want to be like in it. Do you know how many of those people have not made a major mistake in life? Not one. Out of all those people, I promise you every single one has made more than one huge mistake in life. I highly doubt that many of them have not made a major mistake in the past six months. I know I have already made two this year, and it's only February. That's an average of one per month, and February is not over yet so that number might go up.

What's the difference between you and the people you respect? It is not that they have made fewer mistakes than you. The difference is they have learned to process through mistakes, and when they fall short, they don't let it stop them. They learn from their mistakes. They grow. Then they go forward. There's your difference. If you and I are going to go from Simon to Peter, we must get back up from failure.

These concepts are important for all of us to grasp; they are true for every single person in the world. But there is another level. If you are the kind of person that takes big swings for the big things in life, then this is especially true for you. You have really got to change the way that you look at failure. If you are going to be content to bump along in an average life, you still need to get this. But if you are somebody who says, "Baby, I'm going for the brass ring. I'm going for all God has for me. I'm going to get out there. God, run me like a flag to the top of the flagpole. I don't care; I'll flap in the breeze, but I'm going forward." If you are that kind of person, it is supremely important that you understand how to deal with failure. If you are going to attempt great things in life, you better get this.

I'm a big baseball fan, so I can tell you that 1998 was one of the most amazing years in the history of baseball. What happened that year? All kinds of home run records were broken. Two guys were at the forefront of the record-breaking. It was such a big deal even people who were not sports fans knew what was going on. I know that because my wife knew, and she doesn't care anything about any sport. I asked her last week, "Do you remember the two guys who were battling it out for home run king in 1998?"

She said, "Yeah, Mark McGwire and Sammy Sosa."

Mark McGwire and Sammy Sosa. Who won? Mark McGuire, seventy home runs to Sammy Sosa's sixty-six. A lot of people know that those two led the league in home runs that year, but almost nobody knows who led major league baseball that year in strikeouts. Can you guess who? Mark McGwire at 171 strikeouts. Do you know who was number two? Sammy Sosa at 155.

When I was younger, I had a coach in little league baseball who once told the team this before a game: "My God, if we don't beat these guys... if we don't ten-run rule these guys, I'm going to be really ticked off." I thought that was a pretty strong way to say it at the time. I guess he read that reaction on my face because he looked at me and said, "Oh, listen to me, son. We got hitters on this team. That team over there? All they got is touchers." That stuck for me. I never want to be a toucher when I go up to the plate. A lot of people live life as touchers.

"I don't want to strike out. I just need to make contact."

Then they celebrate their slow roller back to the pitcher because at least they didn't strike out. If you are a toucher, don't worry about dealing with failure so much. But if you are a hitter, it is radically important that you learn how to deal with failure. To go from Simon to Peter, you must learn to fail intelligently.

In Philippians 3:12-14 the Apostle Paul says,

> *Not that I have already obtained all this, or have already arrived at my goal, but I press on to take hold of that for which Christ Jesus took hold of me. Brothers and sisters, I do not consider myself yet to have taken hold of it. But one thing I do: Forgetting what is behind and straining toward what is ahead, I press on toward the goal to win the prize for which God has called me heavenward in Christ Jesus.*

That is so important for us. Forget the past. Go for the future.

The Azusa Street Revival in the first decade of the twentieth century was one of the greatest revivals to ever happen here in America. I once studied this revival and dove deep into the notes, diaries, and journals of the people who were involved in it. One of the leaders, Frank

Bartleman, said he "begged the Lord to drop a curtain so close behind me on my past that it would hit my heels."[5] The leaders of that revival purposefully let go of what had happened the day before. Every day was fresh and new. They were moving past mistakes and even moving past good things that happened. They were not living on yesterday. I read about that revival decades ago, and I told Jesus I wanted to live that way.

A number of years ago I visited with an incredible Christian man who was a successful businessman, a powerful man of God, a generous giver, and a loving father. We were having lunch at a nice restaurant. As the conversation developed, I asked him if he would answer a few questions. He said it was all right, so I asked him my first question.

"What made you so successful?"

"Wow . . . I'll have to think about that for a minute."

I let him think. We sat there at the table for twenty to thirty seconds, then his eyes suddenly began to fill up with tears. Tears just started running down his face. That was not the reaction I expected. It took him a little while to regain his composure. Then he said this, and he had to kind of choke it out:

"If I had to pick one thing, Myles, it was when I was nine years old. My family was called to the hospital. My grandfather, an incredible and godly man we all greatly revered and respected, was facing his last moments. We raced to get to his bedside in time. When we got there, my grandpa wanted to greet each one of us individually. One by one we came to him. My turn came, and I went up to hug my grandpa. I hugged him, then I started to back away, but he pulled me back again. He whispered in my ear, 'You're going to be a great man.' Then he let go of me, and I walked out of the room. Within two or three minutes he died, but I could never shake that word. I knew it was truth. I knew that he'd spoken something out of God to me, and that's why I never ever wavered. Anytime I started to drift, I remembered that I was going to be a great man."

When I left the restaurant that day after hearing that story, all I could think was, "Oh, poor me. I didn't have a godly grandfather. I didn't even really have a grandfather; both of mine were already dead when I was a child." I was sitting in the car, whining and having my own private pity party behind the wheel. Then God spoke to me.

"How many times have I tried to tell you that? Won't you hear me? Won't you listen to me? I've been whispering that in your ear for years."

Paul said, "I press on to lay hold of that for which Christ Jesus laid hold of me," (Philippians 3:12). Jesus laid hold of you. Jesus came, sifted through the crap of this world, and found you. He sought you out because He wanted you.

Have you ever wondered why? I have. Why on earth did Jesus want me? Paul said he was pressing on to figure that out. Why did He want me of all people? Why did He want me? What did He see in me that I can't see myself?

What did He see in you? Why did He want you so bad? If you don't really know or if you are not sure, then you are in good company. You are in there with every other Christian ever, including the Apostle Paul himself. But I hope you are also in there saying, "I press on. I want to go from Simon to Peter. I want to go from who I believed I was to who I really am in Christ."

REACHING YOUR POTENTIAL

Philippians 1:3-6 says, "I thank my God every time I remember you. In all my prayers for all of you, I always pray with joy because of your partnership in the gospel from the first day until now, being confident of this, that he who began a good work in you will carry it on to completion until the day of Christ Jesus."

Do you know the name Michelangelo? He was a great painter, a great sculptor, and a great inventor. Did you know that Michelangelo started forty-four different sculptures, but he only finished thirteen? That means he walked away from thirty-one sculptures before they were finished. Everyone talks about the thirteen he finished. They are beautiful and on display in museums. What about the thirty-one? They look atrocious. Some of them have no head. Others are missing arms. I know a lot of Christians that are like those unfinished sculptures— deformed and incomplete.

The verse at the beginning of this chapter is clear. "He who began a good work in you will carry it on to completion," (1:6). God won't stop. He won't give up. He won't throw in the towel. God will not get to a place where He says, "I've had it with you. I've tried and tried and tried. This isn't working out. Forget it; I'm going to get a new piece of stone and start over." The great Michelangelo might have been that way, but God is not. Never will He say to you, "I give up. You're just not gonna make it." God finishes what He starts. He will bring to completion that which He has begun in you. It is wildly important that you believe that.

"Wait a minute, Myles. If God finishes what He starts, then why did you say there are Christians that look like unfinished statues?"

If a Christian is an unfinished work, the fault is never with God. Michelangelo's statues couldn't do anything; they just sat there. We are living beings. And, as living beings, sometimes we jump off the stand and run away before God can finish His work.

Let's stay in the world of art, but move over to Rembrandt. This man was one of the greatest painters that ever lived. Even his smaller, lesser-known paintings sell for tens of millions of dollars. Rembrandt's paintings are easy to spot because he chose to paint differently than everyone else. All the other painters of his time started with a white canvas and put colors onto it. Rembrandt started by painting the canvas completely black. Then he used color to bring the light forward. God often paints Christians like that.

"Oh God, make me a beautiful painting."

Then God starts blacking everything out.

"Wait, God. I don't like what You're doing. This doesn't look very good. This is not what I thought."

And in our ignorance, we jump off the easel and run out the door. We could have been worth tens of millions, but how do we end up? A canvas with a bunch of black paint slopped all over the front.

The problem is never with God. If there is a problem, it lies with us. God desires to finish what He starts in our lives. He has a plan for each one of us. Before you were born, God knew you. He knew the gifts and talents He was going to put in you because even then He had a destiny and a purpose in mind for your life. That's not just a nice thing to believe; that's what the Word of God says. Are you a believing believer or not?

God crafted you by hand to do certain things; He has a vision for you and your life. What is a vision? Vision is looking into the future and seeing yourself in it. But if it stops with just a picture of what you want in the future, then it is not a vision; it is a fantasy. A desire for the future becomes a vision when you add the steps that will turn the desire into reality. Real vision includes a strategy to make future things come to pass.

Destiny goes hand-in-hand with vision. When you are walking towards the vision God has for you—who he created you to be and what he created you to do—then you are walking in your destiny. And when you are walking in your destiny, you are reaching your potential in God. The goal is to realize all of the God-given potential in you to its fullest extent, but that happens only when you are in step with God's vision and destiny for your life.

The best part? With God's destiny for you comes a love for living. The only place where you are going to truly love living is in the place God created you to live in. As you live the life God crafted and designed for you, you will not be able to avoid happiness. You are going to wake up in the morning and say, "Woo hoo! Another day. I like it."

There is a sea of people around you who are experiencing just the opposite. They are simply making it through another day. Life is terrible, and they are just bummed out all the time. Nobody wants that. But what are you willing to do to make sure you don't end up there? To what lengths are you willing to go to walk in the potential God has for you?

There are five different principles that apply when it comes to reaching your potential. These principles are not complicated or deeply theological. As good as theology is—and it is good—I want to speak on a very, very practical level right now. I want you to see how these principles are immediately important in your life. They are very simple. They are easy to grasp. But if you do not grab onto them and begin to apply them to your life, you will never fully walk in God's destiny for you, you will never come into the vision He has set before you, and you will never reach your potential.

1. Be yourself. Then be all that you can be.

Do not try to reach someone else's potential. Reach your own potential.

I can look back at my own life now and see so many times where I was trying to live somebody else's life. Many times I have tried to be like somebody else because it looked like they had it together. It didn't matter whether it was in sports, academics, or church.

"He just has that geometry thing down. I wish I was like him in this math class."

"I just wish I could throw a baseball like he does."

"If only I could sing like she does."

I wanted to be like them instead of wanting to be like me. Our tendency is to always want someone else's gifts, but in the process we demean our own. When we focus on other people and how much we want to be like them, we devalue the things already within ourselves. Trust me, you do not want to do that.

You cannot be like somebody else and still fulfill your own potential. It's not going to happen that way. If you get caught in that path, you will live a frustrated, unhappy life. It is not a path to your blessing or to your destiny. In fact, it is a path to somebody else's blessing and somebody else's destiny. You cannot have those blessings. You cannot live that life, because God created that life for another person and not for you.

Be yourself. It took me many years to really learn this. This struggle does not just stop when you become a teenager or a legal adult or college graduate; it stays in your life until you deal with it. When I first became a pastor, the first thing I did was look around and say, "Who's good at this? Oh, look at him. He's doing a great job. I need to be like him." Thankfully I caught myself and chose to be like me instead.

I was on a mission trip when I first truly grasped this principle and it really broke for me. I was in India, one of three speakers scheduled to teach 1,400 pastors from all over Northern India at an eight-day conference. Then one of the speakers lost his passport, so it was down to me and one other speaker. This other pastor was known internationally as an incredible teacher. He was about seventy years old at the time, but he was the best teacher I have ever heard in my life. Every person I have ever talked with about this man had the exact same opinion of him.

We arrived on location the first day, and the conference leaders gave us the game plan. There were going to be four sessions every day, alternating between me and the other speaker. That meant we were each going to do two sessions a day, and almost every time I was going to have to get up and teach right after this amazing speaker.

Can I tell you something? That was more than a bit intimidating. Not only was this guy one of the best teachers in the world, he also spent years living in India planting upwards of two hundred churches. That meant he knew the culture backwards and forwards. If I have ever in my life been really, really intimidated, that was definitely the moment.

I sat down and listened to him speak the first session. The entire crowd was enthralled. He was connecting with them through all of his experience and bringing a great Bible teaching. I just sat to the side, thinking, "Oh my God. I don't teach like he does. I just kind of get up, start talking, and hope the words come."

Then it was my turn to teach. I found myself slowing down, looking at my notes, and trying to teaching very line-by-line like he did. It was a complete disaster.

During a break I went back to the home we were staying in and just sat there, rubbing my head. How did that turn into such a disaster? I wanted to blame it on territorial evil spirits, but I knew what it was. God spoke to me and told me, "You're trying to be him. Go back there tonight be you." So I stepped up to the podium that night, set my notes aside, and just kind of let it rip. That is who I am.

As that week went on, the Indian pastors got good ministry and I praise God for that. But no one there got more ministry than I did.

God began a process of breaking my desire to be like others and setting me free.

Now I can stand up and let it rip on any given Sunday morning to any given church. Almost always I can see some people nodding their heads; they get it. But you know what? Almost always I can also see other people thinking, "Can he stop walking around so much? Why is he talking so loud? Does he not know he has a microphone? I mean, he's gonna lose his voice." I know; I lose it all the time. But that is who I am!

John Mason said in a book years ago, "You were born an original, don't die a copy."[1] Be who you are. There is something in the fallen nature we inherited from Adam and Eve that causes all of us to want to morph into somebody else at times. We cannot let ourselves get pulled into trying to be somebody other than who we are. We have to catch ourselves and say, "No, I am not going to be somebody else. I will never reach my destiny that way. I will never walk in the fullness of God's potential for me until the only person I am trying to be is myself."

Be yourself. Then be the best *you* can be.

You have to be yourself in order to reach your potential. If God wanted Joey to be another Doug, then he would have made Joey exactly like Doug. He would have given Joey the exact same gifts, talents, and abilities as Doug. But he didn't. They are two completely different people. Joey's abilities are unique. They are different from Doug's. They are different from mine. They are different from everyone else's because God has a specific purpose and destiny for Joey. There is something that God wants him to accomplish with his life.

That brings us to this wonderful verse: "I can do all things through him who strengthens me," (Phil. 4:13, ESV) Translated literally, straight from the original Greek, this is what Philippians 4:13 says: "I am powerfully capable through Christ who powerfully capable-izes me." The first part of the sentence and the second use the exact same Greek word. I am powerfully capable! Do you actually agree with that? Do you believe that about yourself? You are powerfully capable through Christ because he powerfully capable-izes you. He made you that way. Be you. Be yourself. Then be all you can be through the strength of Christ.

2. Overcome what others think and say about you.

People are going say a lot of things about you. They are going to think a lot of things about you. But I am firmly convinced that when we get to Heaven, we are going to be shocked to find out how little other people actually thought about us.

You waste a lot of time trying to guess what other people are thinking about you. Want the truth? Nobody is even paying attention to you. Get over yourself. We let all kinds of concerns influence what we do and how we present ourselves. When you raise your hands in worship, are you wondering how many people are watching? Because most of the time that number is zero; nobody even noticed your hands go up. Get free from that stuff.

Proverbs 12:18 says, "The words of the reckless pierce like swords." Have you ever been pierced by some reckless words? Sticks and stones may break my bones, but words will never hurt me. It's a cute little rhyme with a nice thought, but it is flat not true. Words hurt. Words bring pain into our lives. They hurt us in the moment, but they can also continue to hurt us indefinitely. If we allow them to lodge inside this computer we call our brain, they will start running around in the hard drive. They get stuck in a loop going round and round and round inside our heads, and they just hurt and hurt and hurt. It is hard to get those words out sometimes. Yet people who reach their potential do just that. They get rid of those words. They don't allow the reckless words to hang onto them, and they move forward. If you want to reach your potential, you are going to have to do that.

Let me give you some examples. Beethoven composed some of the best musical pieces of all time. His childhood music teacher told him he was hopeless as a composer. Thomas Edison was undoubtedly one of the most successful inventors to ever live. His elementary school teacher recommended Edison's parents take him out of school because he was unable to learn a thing. These are true stories. Do you know the name Caruso? The great Italian tenor? Some say he was the greatest singer to ever sing. But when he was young, one of his instructors told him to take up an instrument because his voice was no good. How about Walt Disney? Disney was fired from his first job. The editor of the newspaper he worked at fired him because he had no creativity. And of course most know about Michael Jordan. Jordan was cut from his high school basketball team. The coach told him he couldn't play basketball.

It is easy to smile and shake your head at the words that were spoken to these people. When are you going to smile and shake your head at the words that have been said to you?

You'll never amount anything.

You'll never be able to do that.

You'll always be terrible at this.

When are you going to get to the place where you smile and shake that stuff off? Get up and go. If you are going to reach your potential, you have got to overcome what others think and say about you. That takes a determination: "Nothing that is said to me will ever keep me from my destiny."

Let me be clear about one thing because there needs to be a balance. I am not talking about godly council. I am not talking about someone who is spiritually mature and in a place of spiritual authority over your life speaking words of correction to you. The Bible says those words are life-giving rebukes and only a fool rejects that kind of correction. But most of the time godly correction won't include phrases like "You can't" and "You'll never." Rather, it will be things like "Stop believing this about yourself. Stop doing this because you are more than that."

Years ago I heard a story about an old golfer. This man was hanging out at the golf course one day when three young bucks, carrying the newest clubs and decked out in the latest golf apparel, stepped up to the tee box at the first hole. These young guys wanted a fourth player, and they noticed this old guy hanging around. One of them said, "You want to play with us, old timer?"

"Yeah," the golfer said, "I'll play with you on one condition."

"What's that?"

"I want three lookouts."

"Three lookouts?"

"Yeah. If you give me three lookouts, I'll play with you."

The young guys looked at each other and shrugged. None of them knew what a lookout was, but they agreed and started playing.

The first guy stepped up to swing. He drew back his club, but just as he was about to hit the ball, the old golfer screamed, "Look out!" The swing went terribly wrong, and the ball just barely got off the tee box. All three of the younger guys were confused, but they didn't say a word. The next guy got up, set his ball on the tee, and drew back. The whole time he kept glancing back at the old golfer, worried that the guy was going to yell again. It ended up being another terrible shot. They spent the whole eighteen holes worried about the next time he was going to yell, so all three of them shot an awful game. The old timer beat all of them, and he never even had to use his other two lookouts.

There is a moral to that story. So many of us go through life worrying about the next lookout. We worry about the next time someone is going to say, "Look out! You're going to mess up!" If you want to come into your potential, you have to get rid of that fear.

3. Choose your friends wisely.

"Whoa, wait a minute. I thought we were talking about reaching my potential."

Yes, exactly. This is big. Choose your friends wisely. A person seldom rises above the level of his or her closest friends. Proverbs 13:20 says, "He who walks with wise men will be wise, But the companion of fools will suffer harm," (NASB). Why does the companion of fools suffer harm? Because he starts taking on the foolishness of his friends. In other words, you are going to become like the people you hang with.

It is critical to understand this. The people that you are taking the trip of life with can either speed you up, slow you down, or stop you altogether. Your companions, the close friends in your life, have the ability to speed you down the road to your destiny. They also have the ability to slow you down or even stop you dead.

I do not hang around people who are not ambitious. Do you know why? Because I understand what the Bible says, and I believe it. I am going to become like the people I spend time with. If I take the trip with people who do not have ambition, then I am going to end up in the same place they are going—nowhere.

That does not mean I completely avoid people who lack ambition. I want to evangelize them. I want to impact their lives and bring them into the Kingdom, but I am not going to hang out with them regularly. They will not be my best buds. I want my best buds to be mountain climbers. I want to hang out with people who are going somewhere, especially if that somewhere is up.

Who are you hanging out with? Who are your best friends? Think about what they are like. In a short time, you are going to be like that.

"Oh, I'm not going to be like that."

Don't try to outsmart God here. You are not going to get around this. Pick your friends very, very carefully. Be careful who you spend time with. Hang out with people who are going places. Choose close friends who have high moral standards and vision for their lives. Spend time with people who do not compromise with the world around them. Hang out with people who take risks, dare to fail, and get up every time they fall. Those are the kind of people I hang around with because I want those qualities to rub off on me.

If your friends are growing, then you are going to grow. Iron sharpens iron. Deep calls to deep, and stupid calls to stupid. That principle works any way you slice it. Rebellious calls to rebellious. Offended calls to offended. Critical calls to critical. People with those qualities will drag you into the same hole they are headed into.

No one can get past this. There are a lot of people in the world. All you have to do is look at who they are hanging with, and it will tell you a lot about them. It will tell you a lot about where they are going to end up. Benjamin Franklin once said this: "He that lies down with dogs, shall rise up with fleas."[2] Don't lie down with dogs. Choose your friends wisely and carefully.

4. Face your fears.

Proverbs 24:16 says, "For though the righteous fall seven times, they rise again, but the wicked stumble when calamity strikes," (ESV). That doesn't mean righteous people stay down on the eighth time. God is saying that righteous people are always going to get back up. Micah 7:8 says something similar, "Do not gloat over me, my enemy! Though I have fallen, I will rise.

Who was the greatest boxer of all time? Muhammad Ali. He had quite a mouth—certainly not one of my favorite people—but he was a great, great boxer. Most people say the three boxing matches between Muhammad Ali and Joe Frazier were three of the greatest boxing matches ever. Muhammad Ali's style was very quick, and he threw lots of jabs. Frazier, on the other hand, was one of those guys that just came straight in and kept coming. Frazier would follow Ali around the ring, taking hits the entire time. Then he would get inside and land a couple good hits before Ali would dance away. Frazier just chased Ali all night long.

In their first match against each other, Ali pounded Frazier. It was a big deal, so they ended up having a rematch. At that point the whole world was watching. In round four or five of that second match, Ali knocked Frazier down. Frazier got back up. Close to round eight, Ali knocked him down again. Frazier got back up and got right back in Ali's face. By the time they got to round fifteen, Joe Frazier won and became the world champion.

I kept a picture of Joe Frazier on a bulletin board in my office for many years; it was one of my favorites. I pulled it out of a Sports Illustrated magazine the month after that famous second match. The picture was basically a mug shot of Frazier's face the day after the fight. Both of his eyes were swelled completely shut. His face was incredibly disfigured from being hit so much. He looked grotesque. People would walk into my room and say, "Oh God! What is that picture on your bulletin board?"

"Read the caption," I would say. "That is Joe Frazier the night he beat Muhammad Ali. Read the caption."

The caption said this: "The Battered Face of a Winner."[3] It was the face of a champion.

If you are still wondering whether or not you are going to get knocked down in life, let me answer that for you. You are going to get knocked down many times, and you are really asking the wrong question. Everyone gets knocked down. The question is this: Are you going to get back up? Will you get back up off the canvas and get back in the fight? Will you face your fears?

Falling is not the issue. Getting up is. Get back up, learn, and get better at whatever it is you just failed at it. Get back into the fight. Come at the problem with a different attitude that says, "I am going to keep growing until I whip this puppy." The problem that you face will not get any bigger, but you get bigger every time you try and fail. As long as you keep getting back up, it is just a matter of time. You are going to win this battle

If you want to reach your destiny, you are going to need some fight. You are going to have to look your problems in the face and stop whining about them. We like to come to church and sing about being overcomers, but as soon as a problem pops up in our lives, we want to be runner-around-ers. I like the mountains in my life because they give me something to overcome. They give me a reason to come in on Sundays and sing about being an overcomer with confidence. I live the life of an overcomer. To reach your potential, you have to approach the mountains in your life differently. You have to face your fears and get after it.

I have already given you a tried-and-true method for success from one of America's most successful businessmen. if you want to double your success rate and become successful faster than everybody else around you, do one simple thing. Double your failure rate.[4] That is the pathway to success. Look at failures as stepping stones to success, nothing more. Failures are not dead ends. They are opportunities to learn, to grow, to change, and to get better. They are stepping stones that you step on to get to success.

You have no need to fear failure. Look failure straight in the face and say, "Bring it on. I'm gonna learn from you. Everybody fails, but I'm not going to be one who stops. I'm going to be one who keeps going so that I can become who God created me to be." That is how to reach the potential God has for you.

5. Draw inspiration from others.

2 Timothy 2:15 says, "Study to show yourself approved," (KJV).

For many, many years now I have loved reading the biographies of great men and women of God. I have read hundreds of biographies about godly people who literally changed the world in major ways. One of the things that fascinates me is how incredibly different all of these people were. They came from different backgrounds. They had different levels of education. They lived in different places around the world. They had all kinds of different gifts and abilities. They were all so very different. But there is one thing I found in the life of every single one of these world-changers: they were all readers.

"That's not what I wanted to hear."

Well, that is the truth. Every single one of these people was committed to reading and learning and growing.

John Wesley, who started the Methodist Church, had a passion for reading. He did most of his reading on horseback. Every day he rode from village to village—anywhere from sixty to ninety miles—to preach the Gospel. Preach, then ride mile after mile to the next village. That is the way he lived almost every single day of his life. Do you know what he did while he was riding? He read books. He ended up learning six different languages. By the time he died, he had read thousands of books.

And Wesley was not just reading Scripture. He was reading all kinds of books. When Paul wrote his second letter to Timothy, he said, "When you come, bring . . . my scrolls, especially the parchments," (2 Timothy 4:13). Let me paraphrase, "Man, I'm missing you, Timothy. It's going to be good to see you, but I'm really missing my books. I want some good stuff to read. Can you bring me some?"

Paul was still studying. He was still reading. He was still pushing himself to grow. We need to take a hint from that. Oswald Sanders has a great quote about this. "If a man is known by the company he keeps, so also his character is reflected in the books he reads."[5] A Christian's reading is the outward expression of that Christian's inner hungers and aspirations. What are your inner hungers? What are your aspirations for the future? What are your dreams? Who do you want to become? What you are reading and taking in exposes the true answers to those questions.

Read books. Listen to tapes. Get sermon messages and listen to them over and over again. I cannot tell you how many times I have asked Christians of all ages who are outstanding and chasing after what God has for them about the last message they listened to over and over again. Every time I get a blank look. Every time I am disappointed.

I am who I am today in large part because of the messages I have listened to repeatedly. I am not deceiving myself; I am not delusional. I know I am not some great, amazing golden standard of a person. But God is using me today, and I attribute a large part of that to the things I have read and listened to. When I hear something that ministers to me, I get a recording of it and listen to it repeatedly until I really get it. I am so grateful for the invention of CDs because I listened to some messages on tape so many times the tapes wore out and stopped working. Even now I listen to messages that speak to me ten to twelve times before I set them aside.

How much do you want this? How serious are you about reaching your potential? I hope something is stirring inside of you, saying, "I've got to get out of this place I'm in." Even if you are in a good place, you could be in a better one. You could be in a phenomenal place in a matter of years. I want to challenge you right now. Rise up, lay hold of this message, and begin to press forward into what God has for you. How do you do that? Invest in yourself. Listen to messages. Buy books and read them.

"But Myles, books are expensive."

If you think education is expensive, try ignorance. It gets very expensive to go through life in ignorance. Invest in yourself. When you buy a book, it is not like buying candy that you eat up and it's gone. When you buy books, you are investing in who you are. Have enough confidence in yourself and enough vision for your life that you can say, "I am worth investing in." Set aside money to buy good books. If you don't know of any good books, ask your pastor for help. Most pastors will be able to recommend books that will impact you and your life.

"Well, I don't have any time to read books."

Turn off the stinkin' TV. Put away the phone. Power down the computer and the PlayStation along with it. Crack open a book. Open and read and learn and grow. Do you want to reach your potential? Are you serious about it? Or is it something you just want to get fired up about so you feel better for a little while without really doing anything? If you are serious about living out your destiny, then you need to study, learn, and grow.

People often come up to me after I speak to ask me how I come up with these messages and where I get my revelation from. I tell them the revelation comes to me because I have been reading, studying, and listening for almost my entire life. Many years ago the Holy Spirit came to me and gave me a picture of a big bookshelf that didn't have very many books in it. He asked me, "Do you know what that is?"

"What?" I said.

"That is your mind. There are all of these empty spots all over it. I want you to fill this bookshelf up by reading tons and tons of books. If you do that, it gives me all kinds of ability to use you. You are going to get in conversations, and in those conversations I can reach over, pull books off the shelf, turn to a page, and hand it to you."

That has happened to me many times. A passage or an idea from a book I read twelve years ago and forgot about will pop up in my mind in just the right moment. If we fill ourselves up with the good things of God, then God will draw those things out of us when we need them for ourselves and for others. Fill the bookshelf of your mind with good things. Draw inspiration from others. That means read, listen, study, learn, and grow.

In Philippians 3:12, Paul writes, "Not that I have already obtained all this, or have already arrived at my goal, but I press on to take hold of that for which Christ Jesus took hold of me."

Do you see the big question mark in the second half of that verse? There was something that Paul did not know about his life, and he was trying to figure it out. It was not something he just casually wished he knew; the question ate away at him on a daily basis. Why did Jesus take hold of me? What did He see in me that made Him want me and choose me?

In John 15:16, Jesus says these words: "You did not choose me . . . I chose you." You didn't choose Jesus. You simply responded to Him choosing you. The word translated as "choose" and "chose" in this verse is actually the Greek word *eklektos*. The meaning of *eklektos* paints a beautiful picture for us.

Imagine going to an outdoor marketplace, like one in the Middle East packed with stalls and people. Imagine walking the fruit stalls looking for a tomato. When you find a vendor selling tomatoes, you dig through his bin full of tomatoes, testing each one. None of them will do. You move over to the next bin and dig through it, piling up rejected tomatoes to the right and left. None of them will do either. You move on to another vendor and dig through his bins full of tomatoes. Nothing. You find another vendor, dig into his bin.

"Yes! I've got it! I found it!"

Eklektos. I choose this one. I carefully sorted through all of them, and I pick you. That is what Jesus says to each one of us. Other people looked at me and said, "Oh, he's a nice guy. He's a good guy. I don't know if he will make much of himself in life." Jesus said, "You are exactly what I'm looking for."

Why did He pick you? Why did He want you so bad? What did He see in you? Do you wonder? Does that question eat you up? That is why Paul pressed on. That is why Paul kept running. He was going with everything he had. To do what? To get to heaven? No. He was pressing on to find out why Jesus chose him.

Every single person has potential. Every single person has value. Yet Jesus sorted through everybody and pulled you out of the stack. Why did He want you? There needs to be something in you that wells up and wants to find out the answer to that question. Something that is determined to pursue Jesus and keep pursuing Him until you know what it is He saw in you.

Before you leave this message, ask the Holy Spirit what He is saying to you. Allow him to speak to you. Reflect on the principles and anything else that stood out to you about reaching your potential. Speak to the Lord. Tell Him you want to hear what He has to say to you. More than that, tell Him you want to lay hold of what He has for you. Begin something right now. This is not a time for finishing or finalizing anything. It is a time of beginning. Begin something more aggressive than anything that has come before. Begin something more passionate than anything that has come before. Step out from where you are in life and begin a quest, a journey towards your destiny.

THE DAY OF SMALL
BEGINNINGS

I n Zechariah 4:10, God speaks to His people and says, "Do not despise these small beginnings," (NLT).

At the time of this verse, the Israelites had been in exile for seventy years. The king of Babylon had sent his army into Israel, and that army absolutely crushed the Jewish army. Then the Babylonians laid siege to the city of Jerusalem and sacked it. When I say they sacked the city, I mean they destroyed it. They burned much of it and knocked down almost every single building, including the Temple of Solomon. The destruction of the Temple was a big deal to the Jews. The Temple was at the center of their lives. It was at the center of their spiritual existence and really the whole of their existence as a culture. They looked to the Temple; they looked to the city of Jerusalem. Now both had been completely destroyed.

Then the Babylonians did to Israel what they did to most of the countries they defeated—they exiled the people. The Israelites were not allowed to stay in their homeland because the Babylonians were smart enough to realize Israel might start rebuilding and reestablishing themselves as a nation, and then Babylon would have to fight the same battle over again. So the Babylonians took the Israelites and scattered them throughout the rest of the Babylonian kingdom.

At the time of Zechariah 4, the Israelites had been scattered for seventy years. Almost two full generations had lived and died in exile. Zechariah, a priest and a leader of the people, was one of the first to return to Jerusalem. God commissioned Zechariah to do something unbelievable, something that seemed totally impossible. He commissioned Zechariah to rebuild the Temple.

You might think that doesn't sound very impossible, but consider this. These people just spent seventy years in exile. They had no money, no financial backing. They had no political contacts. They had no way of working through any system to get things they needed. And, after two generations of exile, they had zero confidence in themselves. They saw themselves as some of the lowest people on Planet Earth. They were a conquered people with no vision for their future or their destiny. So you can imagine what was going through Zechariah's mind when God told him to do this unbelievable task. Imagine the thoughts that must have been bouncing around in his head.

"How is it possible for me to do this? How are we going to pull this thing off? God, are You sure? Is this really what You are calling me to do? Do You really expect us to do this? Come on! I don't mind being stretched to do something a little beyond my means, but You are asking me to do something completely impossible."

God replied to Zechariah, but not as you might expect. God didn't say, "Don't worry, Zechariah. I'll take care of all the resources that you need. I'm going to connect you with the right people. All of the funding is going to come in." Out of all the things God could have said to him to help him move forward, God said this:

"Zechariah."

"Yes, Lord?"

"Zechariah, are you listening?"

"Yes, Lord. I'm listening."

"Whatever you do, don't despise the day of small beginnings."

Zechariah was probably hoping for a little more than that. There were so many good things God could have said to him in that impossible situation. Why would God say what He did to Zechariah? Why might God say that same thing to us? The first reason is this: God knows that we have a tendency to do exactly that. Each and every single one of us has a tendency to despise small beginnings because they look like nothing.

"This looks impossible."

"I don't have the resources."

"I'm not the right person."

"I don't have enough education."

"You just don't understand my family history."

"You have no idea how many things I've messed up in the past."

We have a tendency to despise the day of small beginnings, but I believe there is another reason why God said what He did to Zechariah. It suggests something to us. It suggests that God knows something about small beginnings that you and I don't know. That is fascinating to me.

You might be facing a small beginning right where you are at this moment. In some area of your life, you might be stepping into something new, something different, or something uncomfortable. Maybe you were comfortable in a certain area, but now God is calling you to something bigger. If that is where you are, then I am glad you are reading this today. You are in the right place at the right time. God has a word for you.

Maybe you are building a new business. Maybe you are starting a new relationship. Maybe you are pursuing a new level of education. Maybe you are beginning the process of recovery from an addiction. Maybe your small beginning is simply a new, fresh word from God calling your life in a new direction. If you are in a small beginning like that, you are probably struggling a little bit right now. You might be struggling with discouragement. You might be struggling with a sense of isolation, feeling like you are all alone and without support. You might be struggling with some pain. You might be struggling with doubts—not doubting God or his Word, but doubting that His plans can come to pass in and through you. You might be struggling to establish new norms and habit patterns in your life. These kinds of struggles come often in those early, fragile small beginnings; that is why we despise them.

Did you catch the word *fragile*? Because the beginning of something new is almost always a very fragile stage. It is easy to mess up right at the start and miss what God had planned for the middle and the end. But God has a word for you. He wants to say the same thing to you today that He said to Zechariah hundreds and hundreds of years ago.

Do not despise the day of small beginnings.

The day of small beginnings is a painful, lonely time. It is easy to feel all alone. In fact, people around you—sometimes even people that love you—often line up against you when you are at the very start of something new.

"What on earth are you doing? Oh man, that's crazy. You've done some crazy things in the past, but this one takes the cake. You've been so successful for your entire life, but now you're going to lose it all."

When you are in the day of small beginnings, people around you will often misjudge your motivations. They will misjudge why you are doing what you are doing. These times can be difficult, and they can be demanding. So, so many people give up on the ideas they had in this part of the process.

Right now I am only talking about God-given ideas, not ideas we come up with on our own. I have seen people come up with a wild idea all on their own at church on a Sunday morning, then turn around and blame God when they go after it and it fails. I'm not talking about those kinds of ideas. That is a different message for a different day. But there are ideas God Himself gives to us, and we need to be careful to hold onto those ideas because it is easy to give up on them in the day of small beginnings. It is easy to abandon that dream or that business idea or that relationship, and then we will miss what God has for us. We will miss our destiny. That is why it is so incredibly important for each and every one of us to understand the truth in Zechariah 4:10. Do not despise the day of small beginnings.

This is a simple message, and—in case you haven't noticed—it is a repetitive one. I know I have used the phrase "small beginnings" a lot already, but you are going to see it even more. I am not apologizing for my repetition because this concept is so important to understand. If you stick with me and receive it, this word will take you to a completely different place in life. It will hold you steady during times of small beginnings so that you can graduate into everything God has for you. Do not despise the day of small beginnings. Do not reject the day of small beginnings. Do not get angry and frustrated in the day of small beginnings. If you do, you will never see the great days God has for you ahead.

Do not despise them. *Despise* is a strong word. We despise what we see no value in. If you don't see value in something, you will seek to remove it from your life rather than welcome it. If you don't see value in something, you will just try to get out of it as quickly as you can.

"Come on, God. Deliver me out of this. Get me where I want to go. I'm stuck here in this place of small beginnings."

God is saying, "Don't do that. I'm doing something very important in this day. Don't despise this day, this time, this season of small beginnings."

If I were to show you some pictures and videos of the very beginning of the very first Grace church, I can tell you what your response would probably be.

"Oh my God. That thing'll never make it."

In fact, I would probably only have to show you a picture of one thing: the infamous hole in the floor. We were meeting in an old building, just off the square. The subfloor of the building was about five feet below the wood floor everybody walked on. In one area the wood floor had collapsed, so we took metal folding chairs, put them in a circle around the whole, and wrapped them in yellow police tape. Every Sunday we had to warn the parents, "Please keep your children away from that area over there."

"It must have gotten better when worship started, right?"

It didn't. We had an overhead projector, so someone had to slide transparencies with the words to the worship songs on and off the projector. The good news is that the people handling the transparencies were real worshippers. That is also the bad news. They would start worshipping and forget to change the slide. We also didn't have a nice screen to project the words onto; they were just projected straight onto a rough, stucco wall. So even when we had the right slide up, about one word in every four was distorted and impossible to read.

If I could take you back to that time and stand you in that place, right next to the white butcher paper taped to the window with the bullet holes, you would look around and say, "There is no way this thing is going last a year. And if it lasts, it will just be a little thing that limps along." You would never believe that it could become the church it is today. You would never believe it could grow into GMI, Grace Ministries International, and plant an entire church network. You would never believe it could have a huge impact through missions to Kenya, Ukraine, Georgia, Austria, Poland, Bulgaria, and more. I could go on and on!

Don't despise the day of small beginnings. The church with the hole in the floor went on to host the first men's conference in the history of Poland, then the first one in the history of Ukraine, then in the history of Bulgaria, then in the history of Georgia. Thousands of pastors and leaders in churches of other countries have been trained because of the conferences led by GMI. On one of those trips overseas, I visited with one of those pastors. He came to me and said, "Oh, Pastor Myles. Thank you. You trained me to be a pastor all those years ago, and now I'm pastoring my own church."

I said, "Oh, that's super! How's it going?"

"Oh, it's going well. We're kind of small, but we're really starting to grow."

"Well, how big are you?" I said.

"Oh, we're like 1,700 people right now, but we're starting to grow a little bit."

That is a true story. But if you back up to the beginning of Grace Ministries International, it wasn't like that. We were a little church in a little building in a little town. Can anything good come out of Wharton, Texas?

Don't despise the day of small beginnings.

"Man, I would give anything to have a marriage like that. That is the best marriage I have ever seen."

Well, you should have seen it when they first walked into the doors of the church five years ago. Their marriage was a total mess. Then they got saved. They got baptized in the Holy Spirit. They began to walk in God's ways and live out marriage the way God intended. Things got better, but they were still a mess. But they didn't despise the day of small beginnings. What about you?

"Well, we're not fighting as much as we used to. The police don't come out to our house once a week anymore. But we've got all of this other mess. I just . . . I don't know if it will ever get fixed. Maybe I just married the wrong person. Let's just get a divorce and start this thing all over again. There is no way *this* marriage could be like *that* marriage, and I want *that* marriage."

Don't despise the day of small beginnings. Can I tell you something? God is committed to small beginnings. I love that about God. There are so many things that I love about Him, but I love this one thing especially. God is committed to small beginnings. And in those small beginnings, God is looking for something to happen on the inside of us. This something does not happen at any other time along the path. It does not happen in the middle. It does not happen at the end. It only happens in the very beginning, when we are in a hurry to get out of there. We just want to move beyond the beginning, but God says, "No, no, no. This is a precious, vitally important time where I am weaving things into the fabric of who you are that will enable you to be all I intend you to be and do all I have set aside for you to do." What happens in us during small beginnings is absolutely essential to us becoming the people God has destined us to be.

Everything begins small. Even Jesus, when he taught on faith, used the mustard seed as his example. Have you ever seen a mustard seed? They are tiny, one of the tiniest seeds in existence. Years ago somebody gave me a little vial with about four mustard seeds in it. I immediately opened the vial and poured a seed out into my hand. About three seconds later, I dropped it just trying to move it around in my hand. They are so small. There are seeds out there as big as footballs. Why didn't Jesus pick one of those seeds to use as an example? Man, what a big seed! A seed like that would be a pretty good beginning. But Jesus deliberately chose the mustard seed. He chose to use something tiny to make a huge point. From small beginnings, like mustard-seed size faith, come things like GMI. From small beginnings come things like model marriages and families.

God is committed to small beginnings, but He knows that we are not. Therefore He tells us to not despise the day of small beginnings because in that day He is transforming us and doing something amazing in our hearts.

For some of you, this message is ringing your bell. I am speaking your language. I am right where you live. That's because you are in a day of small beginnings in at least one area of your life right now. For others, you might not be in a day of small beginnings. But listen to me on this: even if you are not in a day of small beginnings right now, it is almost certain that you have a close friend or family member who is. I want to encourage you to do something today. Before you set this book down and move on from thinking about this message, take out your phone and send that close friend or family member a text. So many people lose it right there in the day of small beginnings, but a simple word of encouragement can do amazing things for people in that place. Encouragement is like a ray of sunshine piercing a dark sky. It is like a drink of water to a parched soul. Don't put off encouraging that person. Don't tell yourself you will do it later; you will probably forget. Before you leave the place you are right now, send that person a text.

"I was reading a message about small beginnings, and it made me think of you. I know that's where you are, and I know you're going through a difficult time right now. I want you to know something. I love you. I believe in you. I'm praying for you, and I want to encourage you to keep going in God."

Small beginnings take more people out than almost anything else out there. It is a critical time. I believe there are many, many people out there that you and I will never know about simply because they never made it out of a small beginning. They did not survive the day of small beginnings. Therefore, they never realized their dreams. If they had, we would know their names. They would be widely known for the amazing things that they accomplished. But they didn't make it through the beginning. So many people miss what God intends for them because they don't graduate out of the day of small beginnings.

Think about how many Bible characters faced small beginnings. How about Moses? What if he had despised the day of small beginnings? I imagine you know Moses. I imagine even if you are not a big Bible scholar, you probably know his story. You probably know what happened to him and what he did. But let's be honest. If you had never heard of Moses before and didn't know anything about him or his life, and if I showed you a picture of him as an abandoned baby in a basket made of reeds floating down the Nile River, what would be your first thought?

"Oh, good things are ahead!"

Not likely. It would probably be something closer to, "Uh oh. This isn't gonna end well."

What if we fast forward to Moses' life later on? He finds out his identity. He tries to free his people, the Israelites, in his own strength. He ends up killing a man, and he flees for his life. He crosses the desert and ends up in a foreign country, herding sheep and goats. If I gave you that background information and showed you a picture of him out there tending the animals, what would you think?

"Ah, I see it! Mighty deliverer. He is going to be used by God to deliver his people from four hundred years of bondage. I think some of the greatest miracles that will ever happen in history are going to be done through this guy. Yeah, that's him."

That's not what we would say at all.

"That's all that's left for him. Washed up. Washed out. Total failure. He's just marking off the days as they go by; he's got nothing to look forward to. He missed his chance. His life now is only good as a lesson of what not to do."

Let me tell you something very important. Never look at your life like a photo. Let the video run. Don't look at a snapshot of a moment in time. Let the video run.

What about Joseph? Again, we know his story. But if you didn't know anything about him and I showed you a picture of his brothers selling him into slavery, would you expect great things ahead? Fast forward and let's see how things are going. What's he doing now? He's in prison. When is he supposed to be released? Never. He's in there for life. Would you look at a snapshot of that and think, "That's exciting. I can't wait to see what God does next. That guy in prison is going to be somebody big. Prince of Egypt, right there."

Not one of us would see the great things ahead just looking at those snapshots. What's the lesson? Never look at a photo of life. Let the video run. We are so good at taking pictures of our lives. We take a picture, then we look at the picture and look at the picture and keep looking at the picture. We let those pictures define who we are. Never freeze yourself in time.

Here is one thing I see people do all the time when they are in the day of small beginnings: compare. People in chapter two of an area of life often look over at somebody else who is in chapter twenty and say, "I could never do that. I could never be that. There is no way I could get from here to there." Oh, if only you knew that person's story. If only you knew how they got from chapter two to chapter twenty. Don't compare yourself to people who are further along. If you do, you will end up despising the day of small beginnings.

Don't despise the day of small beginnings. Your best days are yet to come.

In Revelation 21:6, God says, "I am the Alpha and the Omega, the Beginning and the End." Alpha means beginning. Omega means end. God says that he is the Alpha, the beginning, and the Omega, the end.

Most people don't understand the meaning of that verse. We have heard it over and over. We have read it over and over. We all think we understand what God is saying, but we don't really get it. As human beings, we think in a linear fashion and in a finite way. God is infinite, and He lives outside of time and space. So when God says, "I am the Alpha and the Omega," He doesn't mean He was the Alpha over there at a specific beginning point in time and He will be the Omega way later at a specific ending point in time. He is not saying He was with you as the Alpha way back in the beginning of your life and He will be with you as the Omega at the end. That is not what He is saying at all. When God says, "I am the Alpha and the Omega," He is telling us that he is both at the exact same time.

In your alpha, God is already the Omega. In your small beginning, God is already at the end. What does that mean? It means this: whatever God intends for you to be in your omega—your end—He has already included that in your alpha. Whatever you are going to be at the end is already there in the beginning.

"Well, God, I need this. I need that. I'm not this. I'm not that."

God says you have what it takes. In Him you already have what it takes to be somebody. Will there be training and development? Oh yeah. Will there be growth in character? Absolutely. But everything you need is already there inside of you. Your small beginning is deliberately designed by God to get you to your omega. It is specifically designed to take you to the end of your destiny and your created purpose.

SON OR SLAVE

I'm taking a golden oldie out of the vault for this one. I have preached this message many times over the years in various places around the world. Even so, every time I teach this teaching, God speaks new things to me. Here's the message: son or slave. I want to encourage you read this one carefully. Even if you have heard me speak it before or if you are familiar with the concept, don't check out. There are some powerful truths from God's Word that we're going to mine out here.

Psalm 127:1-2 says, "Unless the Lord builds the house, the builders labor in vain. Unless the Lord watches over the city, the guards stand watch in vain. In vain you rise early and stay up late, toiling for food to eat, for he grants sleep to those he loves." There are two very powerful truths in just these two verses. These are important truths that have the potential to reshape your life, and that's not an exaggeration.

Here's the first one: God is a builder. God is in the designing and building business. He designed and built the universe and everything in it. He designed and built every star and planet, and Scripture says He calls them all by name. God designed and built Planet Earth, along with every tree, every plant, every animal, and every human being on it. God is the designer and builder of it all. Scripture says, in Hebrews 11, that Abraham went looking for a city whose architect and builder was God. God is a builder. Once you understand this truth, you can go through Scripture and see this truth just popping up again and again and again. God is a builder.

Here's the second truth, which ties perfectly in with the first: what God builds, He watches over. When God builds something, you don't have to worry about whether or not it will last. When God builds something, He watches over, protects, and preserves it. If God built it, it will not fall down. That's what Psalm 127:1-2 is saying. If God built it, then you don't have to watch over it. God will! If God built it, then you don't have to lose sleep because you're worried about whether or not it's going to be there when you wake up. If God is the one who built it, then you know what? You can be absolutely certain it will still be there. What God builds, he watches over. What God builds, He builds to last. He builds permanently. What God builds is unshakable.

That's an important truth because we live in a fallen, sin-soaked world. In Matthew 5:45, the Bible says that God "sends rain on the righteous and the unrighteous." That means good and bad things happen to both the righteous and the unrighteous. Bad things aren't just for bad people; bad things happen to good people as well. They are going to happen to each and every single one of us. There are going to be things that come into our lives that will shake us. You might think that's awful thing for me to say, but it's the truth. There are going to be troubles! Don't ask whether or not bad things will happen because the answer is always yes. Ask this instead: Will your life get all shaken up over them? Are you going to fall apart?

God is a builder, and what He builds is unshakable. When we get that truth, the light bulbs need to turn on for us. We should begin to say to ourselves, "Wow, I need to make sure my life is built by God." If you want to live an unshakable life, make God the builder of your life.

If you want your marriage to be unshakable, then you need to make sure God is the one building your marriage. If God is the builder, then your marriage will not be shaken by the circumstances of life. Trouble will still be trouble, but your marriage won't fall down. We want God to be the builder of every aspect of our lives.

God is a builder. What God builds is unshakable. He'll watch over it. He'll preserve and protect it. If you understand those things, then the natural response is to want that for your own life! Who wouldn't want that? I want a life where things happen, but I am still able to stand and walk through it in peace and joy. I want a life like that no matter what the circumstances are around me, even if those circumstances are unpleasant and not really what I want. I want to be able to stand in the storm instead of sinking. I want God to build every aspect of my life.

The next question is this: How? How does God do this? And how do I make sure my life is built by God? When you take this question to Scripture, you will find that God builds primarily in three ways. If you want your life to be unshakable, then you must embrace the fact that God builds in these three ways. God builds revelationally, God builds relationally, and God builds generationally.

This isn't theological mumbo-jumbo. I don't do theological mumbo-jumbo. We're going to look at each one of these, but I want to make this very practical because God is imminently practical in our lives. God speaks things that are not just stuff for theologians to argue about. God gives us things we can take and put into our lives because He loves us and He wants us to live abundant lives. He really does. I don't care what you've heard or where you've heard it from. If you've heard anything other than that, it's a lie. It's a flat-out lie. God loves you. He's a good dad. He wants you to walk in His blessings within His plan, so He gave you the Word to show you the way. If you will walk in His way, then you will receive His blessings, His peace, His joy, and His life. That is the way He will build your life.

1. God builds revelationally.

God build through revelation. We could look at many, many scriptures on this, but right now we're just going to look at Matthew 16:15-18. In these verses the disciples have just come back from Jesus sending them out in pairs of two. They've already reported back to Jesus. What was their report? Boy, people were healed. Demons were cast out of people. People received the gospel of the Kingdom. All of those wonderful things have happened, and they are celebrating. But then the conversation turns to the things people had been saying about Jesus. Some people were saying Jesus was John the Baptist, come back from the dead. Others were saying that He was Elijah. They are discussing all of that when Jesus interrupts their conversation with this question: "Who do you say I am?" (16:15). Suddenly it's very quiet around the campfire. Then Simon Peter speaks up.

"You are the Messiah, the Christ, the Son of the living God."

Jesus replied, "Blessed are you, Simon son of Jonah, for this was not revealed to you by flesh and blood, but by my Father in heaven. And I tell you that you are Peter, and on this rock I will build my church, and the gates of Hades will not overcome it," (16:16-18).

Now, if we give this a casual, quick reading in the English translation, it is easy to mistake what Jesus said here. A lot of people around the world have certainly misunderstood it. It sounds like Jesus was saying He planned to build the Church on Peter. But if you look at this passage in the original Greek language, you'll see very clearly that Jesus was using a play on words. He looked at Simon Peter and said to him, "You are *petros*." That's the Greek word there. *Petros* means a boulder or a large rock. So Jesus looked at him and said, "You are a large rock." Then Jesus said, "Upon this *petra* I will build my church."

"Different Greek word, but basically the same thing, right?"

No, no, no. *Petros* and *petra* are close in spelling, but they have two completely different meanings. *Petros* is a boulder or large rock; *Petra* is bedrock. If you've ever been to a quarry or seen pictures of a quarry, then you know what bedrock looks like. Layer after layer after layer after layer of rock, rock, rock, rock, rock, and rock. We're talking stories on stories of rock all the way down into the ground. That's *petra*.

So Jesus was not saying He would build His church on Peter. Peter was a big rock, a big part of what Jesus was going to do. Jesus was telling him that he was strong, stable, and immovable. That's who he was and who he was going to become. But Jesus was not talking about building the Church on Peter. He was talking about building the Church on the revelation that Peter had. That is the *petra*. He was saying that Peter's revelation is the beginning revelation for each and every single one of us. If God is going to build upon our lives through revelation, here's where it starts. You and I need a revelation of Jesus as the Son of the Living God.

"Well, what's the big deal? I mean, I know that. I got that in the Sunday school years ago."

Listen, you may have that knowledge. You may have that concept. But have you ever had a real revelation of that? That's a different thing altogether. When you get a real revelation of Jesus as the Son of the Living God, it changes the way you think, talk, act, and live. If you really, really believed that and had a clear revelation of it, you would live a very different life than you once did.

We need to get a revelation of Jesus as the Son of the Living God, the Christ, the Messiah. Let me put it in a kind of modern illustration. Jesus is not a five-star general. He's a million-star general, and you and I are just privates in the army! We're just privates, walking around on Planet Earth. Think you're better than a private? Think you're more of a captain? You still have a million-star general showing up on the scene.

Now I've got to carry this analogy forward. In the real army, let's imagine a one-star general shows up on the scene, walks up to a private, and says, "Private, drop and give me fifty." Can I tell you what doesn't happen in that situation? The private doesn't say, "Well, I'm just not really into push-ups." The private doesn't say, "Well, you know, I'll pray about that." He doesn't say, "You know, push-ups just aren't in my calling," or "General, you just don't understand what I've gone through in my life." That doesn't happen! The private is on the ground pumping them out before the words are out of the general's mouth! He doesn't know why he's doing them, but he's pumping them out. There aren't any questions. There's no argument. There's no debate.

Do you get it? When you get a revelation of Jesus as the Son of the Living God, you see Him as a million-star general. When He comes in and says, "Hey, do this," you do it immediately. If your response is like, "Well, let me think about that," then you haven't had a revelation of Him yet. You might have Sunday school knowledge, but you don't have a revelation. When you get that revelation, it changes everything.

I know the deal. I've been doing this for decades and decades in many different places and nations of the world. This is not just an American problem. It's worldwide. There are so many rebellious and unsubmitted Christians in the Church, and every one I've met says the same thing: "I just love Jesus." Really? Is that true? Because Jesus says if you love Him, you will obey him. If you really love Jesus, then you will obey Him. You will do everything He tells you to do, and you will obey those He puts in authority over you.

A revelation of Jesus as the Son of God is the beginning revelation, but it's not the end. God just came in with a bulldozer, cleared the ground out, and poured a slab on it. It's the biggest revelation that you and I can get, therefore it's the biggest piece of the puzzle we need in our lives. If God is going to build our lives, build our marriages, build our careers, build our ministries, or build anything in us, this is where it starts. This is the foundation stone of it all. Then, as we go on from there, walk in relationship with God, and press into Him and His work, He gives us more revelation. Each and every time His revelation comes, we are to say "Yes sir. Reporting for duty, sir. I got it." Then we walk those things out, and as we do, God builds our lives in an unshakable way.

2. God builds relationally.

In John 15:16, Jesus says, "You did not choose me, but I chose you and appointed you." You didn't choose Jesus. Jesus chose you! The word translated as *chose* is the Greek word *eklektos*. That's an interesting word because it does not mean what we expect it to mean from the English translation. We get this idea that it's kind of like picking sides in a sandlot baseball game.

"Uh, okay, I'll pick you. Hmm, and you."

That's not it! This word, *eklektos*, means to very, very carefully select something. The picture in this word is like someone going to a bazaar or a big market place. It's one of those that is just block after block of all kinds of shops and stalls, full of people. This someone is at this market, looking for a certain item. Maybe it's an exotic fruit or the perfect avocado. This person digs through bin after bin in stall after stall all the way down the street until finally finding the exact thing the search was for. That's the word *eklektos*.

Jesus very carefully selected you. He looked out into the future and said, "You know what? I need somebody in this time and in this place who can do these things. I'm going to take this person, put in the giftings, talents, and abilities to accomplish those things, and put that person right in that time and place to accomplish my purposes there." He chose you to do specific things. You were born with a created purpose, a God-given destiny.

God picked every single one of us. He could have left you where He found you, but He didn't. He picked you. He handpicked you for what He has for you in life.

John 15:16 says Jesus chose you *and* appointed you. Because He chose you, He now has the right to appoint you, to place you where He wants to. The Greek word translated here as *appoint* is the word *tithémi*. That word has two very clear, very strong connotations. The first = is geographic. The second is relational.

Because Jesus picked you, He has the right to place you geographically where He wants you to be. Why do you live where you live? Well, it better be because God placed you there.

Sallie and I live in Wharton, Texas. Never heard of it? Not surprising. Look it up; it's near Houston. If you think my wife and I live in Wharton because it's the most beautiful place we've seen on Planet Earth, you need help.

"Oh, you must have picked it because the weather there is so ideal."

Right. Yeah. Especially in July, when the temperatures skyrocket right along with the humidity. No. Why do we live in Wharton? Because God placed us there. I don't want to live anywhere other than where God has placed me.

After hearing me speak this message, several people have told me they can't hear God that well, especially about where to live. Listen, if your heart is right, God will meet you. He will make sure your foot ends up stepping in the right places. That's what the Bible says in Psalm 37:23, "The steps of a good man are ordered by the Lord: and he delighteth in his way," (King James Version). Just get your heart right. When your heart is at a point where you want to live where God wants you to live and do what God wants you to do, then God will say, "Okay, just walk. I'll make sure your foot lands in the right place." Trust God enough to know that He will make sure your foot lands in the right place. Because He chose you, He has the right to place you where He wants you geographically.

Because God chose you, He also has the right to place you where He wants you relationally. That is the second connotation in the Greek word *tithémi*. He puts you in the relationships He wants you in. That's really, really important. God places you relationally where He wants you. That's important to know because we all run into problems and difficulties in our relationships. Come on. All it takes to have conflict is more than one person. Actually, I've met some people who didn't even need another person. They could have conflict with just themselves, but that's a different teaching for a different day.

Some of us think that relationships are given to us by God for encouragement and support and all those other great things. Yes, yes, and yes! But don't miss this: another reason why God brings relationships into our lives is to cause friction.

"Why would He do that? I thought God loved me."

He does! He brings you into relationships to show you things that are in your heart. He wants to reveal to you things that are in there that you wouldn't otherwise notice.

Most of you reading this probably don't know me very well, at least on a personal level. If you did get to know me, you would learn very quickly that I am very much a work in progress. I'm happy with that. I know I haven't arrived. I have a long way to go, and that's okay. God made that clear to me years ago. He jumped in my life and told me, "Man, relax. You are in process. Just enjoy that process. I'm taking you from faith to faith and from glory to glory." We are in process, and we've got to get happy about that fact. *You* need to get happy about the fact you're in process. If you think you have already arrived, get in contact with me because you need some counseling. We are all in process.

One of the areas where I need the most work is this: I'm not the most patient person in the world. I think a lot of my family and friends would agree with that. I've grown a lot. Saying I'm in process doesn't give me an excuse to just stay the way I am. That's not it. I'm growing, I'm changing, and I'm not nearly as bad as I used to be. But I have a tendency to be impatient. I often care way too much about getting to the next thing.

I know of one way I could be instantly and totally delivered from all my impatience. It's simple. I just have to move up onto a mountaintop all by myself. I would no longer be impatient. What an amazing transformation! Delivered from impatience! Completely free!

Except I wouldn't actually be delivered. I would just be deceived. I would run out of provisions up there by myself, and they I would have to come down into town to buy some groceries. Then I would end up at a grocery store with twelve checkout lanes and only three of them working. All of that impatience would come flooding back as I stand there in line. In fact, it wouldn't be coming back because it never left. My impatience was just hidden while I was all by myself on the mountaintop.

Relationships bring that kind of stuff out in the open, and God's hope is that when we see it, we cry out to Him to help us grow and change. God uses relationships to build us. God builds relationally. Ephesians 4:16 says it this way: "From him the whole body, joined and held together by every supporting ligament, grows and builds itself up in love, as each part does its work." So we grow and build each other up.

"Whoa, whoa, whoa. That's not God building us up. That's us building each other up."

No, no. That's God in each one of us working to build each other up. God is the builder, and He works through us in the church. God wants to build us relationally.

I know there are lots of people today in lots of churches who think they're just not into this whole relationship thing. They think they just don't really like relationships, and they definitely don't want anything to do with that accountability junk. No speaking into each other's lives or transparency for them. You know what? That's fine. You can count yourself out of those things. You can have a seat to the side and watch God build the rest of us. But God builds through relationships, so if you want God to build your life in an unshakable way, then you have to embrace the way God builds through relationships.

In the beginning of the Church around the first century, there were two different concepts of maturity. People had two different ideas about what separated the mature from the immature. The Greeks and those influenced by them believed as a person accumulates information, knowledge, and data, that person becomes more mature. The Hebrew concept of maturity was quite different from that. The Hebrews believed as a person grows in relationship with God and others, that person becomes more mature.

I don't have to tell you which concept we buy into in America. It's all about the information. The more data you have and the more informed you are, the more maturity you have.

"I'm more mature because I know more."

No, not necessarily. Even in the Church you will meet a lot of different people who think they're mature because they have memorized so much Scripture, gone through so many Bible studies, and listened to so many tapes. Those things don't necessarily increase your maturity. The fact that you can spit out Scripture doesn't mean anything. You might be the next thing to the antichrist for all I know. Information does not make you mature.

Maturity comes when you have a great relationship with God, you have great relationships with others, and you have worked through some relational issues. That's maturity. God will build on that. If you're not in relationships, then God won't build on you. You might be saved, but you aren't unshakable. You might be going to heaven, but you're not going anywhere else between now and when you get there.

That's why, in Grace churches, we speak over and over about the importance of our life groups that meet on Wednesday night. It's so important that we build relationships with other people. It's important that we open our lives, share, and grow together, encouraging each other. It is necessary that we speak openly into each other's lives. God builds through that.

3. God builds generationally.

God builds revelationally. God builds relationally. And, lastly, God builds generationally. This truth stands out in Hebrews 3:1-6.

Therefore, holy brothers and sisters, who share in the heavenly calling, fix your thoughts on Jesus, whom we acknowledge as our apostle and high priest. He was faithful to the one who appointed him, just as Moses was faithful in all God's house. Jesus has been found worthy of greater honor than Moses, just as the builder of a house has greater honor than the house itself. For every house is built by someone, but God is the builder of everything. "Moses was faithful as a servant [or slave] in all God's house," bearing witness to what would be spoken by God in the future. But Christ is faithful as the Son over God's house. And we are his house, if indeed we hold firmly to our confidence and the hope in which we glory.

Scripture is making a comparison here between Moses and Jesus. First of all, what is the similarity? Both of them were faithful in God's house. Moses was faithful. Jesus was faithful. That's the similarity. What is the difference God gives to us in this passage? Moses was faithful as a slave. Jesus was faithful as a son. Big difference.

The New Testament book of Hebrews is a beautiful, powerful book. If you were to take the whole book of Hebrews and boil it down to one word, that word would be *better*. Time and time again, the book of Hebrews takes something from the Old Covenant and compares that thing to what is now in place in the New Covenant. And every time it shows us the Old Covenant and New Covenant side by side, it tells us that what is of the New Covenant is better. So it compares old to new over and over again, and every time it says the new is better. Better high priest, better blood, better sacrifice, better covenant, better, better, better.

Hebrews 3:1-6 compares two different ways of serving God. We used to serve God as slaves, but that's the Old Covenant model. Now we have a better, New Covenant model. Now we serve God in His house as sons.

I'm going to use the word "son" again and again in this chapter. Please do not take that as any sort of gender discrimination. I'm just using the word that Scripture uses, and I believe Scripture uses that word because it's setting Jesus as the example. So, because Jesus was male, the Bible uses the male term, *son*. It's not excluding women. If you are a woman, then every time you read the word *son*, you can take it to mean *daughter*. The important thing here is to not let the specific words used distract you from the message. The message is this: in the New Covenant, God is building on sons and daughters, not on slaves.

Here is the root of what Hebrews is saying. You can serve in God's house the old way, with a slave mentality, or you can serve in God's house the new way, with the mentality of a son or daughter. God is not building on the slave mentality anymore. If you want to serve God that way, that's fine and dandy. But if you want God to build your life, He is now building on sons and daughters. He has taken the Old Covenant model of serving with a slave mentality and replaced it with the better, New Covenant model of serving with a son mentality.

Think about this: slaves and sons both serve. Even if you serve from a slave mentality, serving in God's house is not a bad thing. That's not what I'm saying at all. Servanthood is a good thing. Jesus praised servanthood, saying that the greatest among us would be a servant (Matthew 23:11). I'm not down on servanthood. That's not what I'm saying. Please don't hear that. What I'm saying is this: slaves and sons both serve, but sons serve out of a different heart and a different mentality, and that is the kind of mentality God will build on.

Let me give you one simple example. Think back to Old Testament times and imagine a wheat harvest. There's a slave working out in the field, bringing the harvest in. Right next to him there is a son working, also bringing the harvest in. They are doing the exact same work. It's just as hot for one as it is for the other. They're both just as sunburned.

They're both just as tired. They're both dealing with aching muscles. Externally, everything is the same. The difference between them is internal. Inside the son, there's a completely different heartbeat and motivation. It's the same job, but the son has a different mentality.

God has replaced the slave model of serving and doing things for Him with the higher model of sonship. God tells us to fix our thoughts on Jesus and lock in on Him because Jesus is our example of the new model. God doesn't build on slaves anymore. God builds on sons.

Just think about things this way. If I want to build up and develop the members of my household, would I focus on somebody who comes and does work at our house sometimes? I'm obviously not going to do that. I'm going to focus on building and developing my children. That is what God is doing with us today.

Come with me to Galatians and let me show you this concept right in Scripture. This verse is Paul writing to the churches in the whole region of Galatia: "But when the set time had fully come, God sent his Son, born of a woman, born under the law, to redeem those under the law, that we might receive adoption to sonship," (Gal. 4:4-5). God isn't looking for slaves anymore. He's looking for sons. God isn't interested in people with a worker's attitude. He's not looking for somebody to clock-in and clock-out as an employee. He's looking for somebody with the mentality of a son or daughter. He's looking for a loving, honoring relationship.

I saw a bumper sticker a number of years ago. I passed the car, read what it said, and thought *wow*. It said, "Work for God. The pay isn't very good, but the retirement benefits are out of this world." You know, that's pretty cute. Pretty clever. But it misses the point. That's a slave mentality. I'm not just an employee for the Great I Am in the sky. I'm His son. I'm not just a worker in His house. I'm a son, and you're a son or a daughter in His house. We are not just building His house; we are building our house.

That's radical. I'm telling you, when this verse in Galatians was read to the Galatian churches, it was radical. I promise you, they were saying, "What? Back up. Read that again. What? You've got to be kidding me. We're sons? No, no, no, no. Read that again. That's incredible!" It was a radical truth. Sonship was a huge change from where they were in their mentality and their thinking. They were not just serving in God's house anymore. No longer were they just workers, just slaves. They were sons and daughters. Whoa.

I don't know how you're reacting to reading this right now. Odds are you are not reacting radically, but the truth is you should be. I've been doing this too long. There are so many people faithfully working and serving in the church, but doing it out of a slave mentality rather than out of a son or daughter mentality. I'm not just talking about people in American churches. I have seen this all over the world. And I'm not just talking about general church membership. I have seen this in pastors and leaders too. There are so many people serving God out of a slave mentality, and they are missing so much. They are preventing God from building on their lives generationally. God is not going to build on the old model anymore.

Galatians 4:6 says, "Because you are his sons, God sent the Spirit of his Son into our hearts, the Spirit who calls out, '*Abba*, Father.'" Daddy! Not just Almighty God, but Dad! Because you are a son. Because you are a daughter. You are not just a slave; you are not just a worker anymore. You are His kid! And just to make sure you knew it, He sent the Spirit of His Son to live inside of you so that, from the depths of your being, you can cry out to your Father.

I've been in so many different meetings in different places around the world where somebody gets up to pray, and their prayer makes my skin crawl. "Oh, Father God. Thou who hast spun the universe into existence . . ." I always want to ask them this: Do you really know who you're praying to?

While the church in Wharton was still young and my kids were still growing up, I owned a business for about ten to twelve years. A lot of times Sallie would come up to the office with the kids. She would pull up, and Susanna, my third child, would fly out of the door practically before my wife could put the car in park. That was predictable because with Susanna it's a hundred miles per hour or nothing. She would come running. I could always see her because I had a window to the parking lot right there in my office. I would look out and watch her jump out and run to the door. I always knew what was happening. She was racing to come see Dad.

So I would sit there, waiting for Susanna. Waiting. And waiting. And waiting. Where's Susanna? What's going on? Then all of a sudden I would hear this sound. I would get up a little bit from my desk and look out the doorway. And there she would be, crawling down the last few steps of the hallway. She would stop at the doorway of my office, saying, "Oh, Pastor Sweeney..."

Nah, not a chance. She would come around the corner at 150 miles an hour. She didn't care who was in my office, whether or not I was on the phone, or what I was doing. Didn't make a bit of difference to her. She's would run around that desk and leap into my lap from about four feet away.

"Why would she do that? The nerve of her, interrupting what you were doing."

Not at all! She did that because she knew she was my daughter. I'm her dad. I can build on that.

Did you know you can come to God like that? You're never interrupting Him. It's never a checklist, making sure you've done this and this and this before you can go to see Him. Even if you had done a checklist of bad things, He would still be excited to see you. He's always excited to see you. God can build our lives in an unshakable way when we get a hold of this truth.

John 1:12 says, "Yet to all who did receive him, to those who believed in his name, he gave the right to become children of God." Galatians 4:7 says, "So you are no longer a slave, but God's child; and since you are his child, God has made you also an heir." Romans 8:16-17 says, "The Spirit himself testifies with our spirit that we are God's children. Now if we are children, then we are heirs—heirs of God and co-heirs [joint heirs] with Christ."

Did you get that? We are joint heirs with Jesus. Do you know what a joint heir is? When something is passed down to you, then you are an heir. Now, imagine that something is passed down to three heirs. If they are just heirs, you know what they have to do? They have to value it up and split it out into three pieces. Each heir gets a third of the inheritance. That's an heir. A joint heir is different. Now, if those three heirs were joint heirs, that would mean that all three of them own 100 percent of the inheritance. It's owned jointly.

Now go back to the verse, Romans 8:16-17. We are joint heirs with Jesus Christ. Everything God has stored up to bless Jesus with, you and I have 100 percent ownership of. That's true. That's absolutely true. It's 100 percent yours.

I hear people teach on Psalm 2 all the time. They love to focus on the part where God, the Father, is telling his son, "Ask me, and I will make the nations your inheritance, the ends of the earth your possession." We think it's awesome that God is going to give Jesus the nations as an inheritance, and we miss the deeper truth. The nations are also mine! If you are a born-again believer, they are also yours. We are joint heirs. Here is the big question for you: Are you a son? Or are you a slave?

Before I leave this teaching, I want to give you nine different things that will help you see whether or not you have a son mentality or a slave mentality. These nine things aren't going to have a lot of additional points or stories to go with them, but I think most of them are easy to understand. This is a big issue. If you have a son mentality, then God will step in, bless you, and build on you in an unshakable way.

1. Sons build the house. Slaves just serve in the house.

Can you see the difference? One of them is there to build something. The other one is just there, just serving, just working, just looking for a paycheck. There is a big difference between the two.

When I worked in management at American Express, a lot of the other managers started asking me to help them with their interviews. They recognized I always picked good people, and their picks were hit-or-miss. I agreed to start helping some of them.

I'll never forget the first one I helped with. The manager I was helping was a great manager and a good guy. I really liked him a lot. He had an interview one day, and he asked me to come help. When I showed up, he told me to do the interview like I would normally do it, and then he sat off to the side. So I interviewed the potential employee. The interview lasted about an hour, then the candidate left. The first thing this manager said to me was, "What on earth just happened?"

"What do you mean?" I said.

"That's the weirdest interview I've ever been a part of in my life. You didn't go over his educational background or his work background," he said.

"Well, I can read his resume. That's all there," I said.

"Then what were you doing? I mean, you were just chatting. You just laughed and talked and visited for an hour. What was going on? What did that tell you?" he asked me.

"Oh, listen," I said. "All that I was trying to do is what I do every time I interview someone. I'm trying to figure out who's sitting across the desk from me. Do I have somebody with a slave mentality, or do I have somebody with a son mentality? You can always train someone with a son mentality. You can always teach them what they need to know. I need to know what I've got in front of me. If it's somebody with a son or daughter mentality, then that's who you want."

If you're working for somebody and you've had a slave mentality in that work, then I want to encourage you to repent. This truth isn't just for our actions inside the church. We are meant to have a son mentality in every area of our lives. That means wherever we work, we should not just serve in the house. Build the house. Consider it your own. You're not just there to serve and get a paycheck. You are there to build. That is what God calls us to. After you have come to repentance, talk your boss. Apologize for your slave mentality, and communicate your repentance. You might have to explain the different mentalities to your boss, but make it clear that from here on, you are going to have a son mentality. I believe that the employers out there in the world ought to be begging and looking actively for Christians, because Christians ought to be the best workers out there.

I go to a lot of different churches. In some places I'll see some kind of paper or trash on the floor. I like to watch for that kind of stuff. While I'm talking and visiting with people, I'll keep my eye on that piece of trash. In some places I'll watch dozens and dozens of people walk right by it without picking it up. Why? "I'm not the janitor. That's not my job." Hello, Mr. Slave. Hello, Mrs. Slave.

We're not here to serve, we're here to build. So are you a son? Or a slave? Are you there to serve? Or are you there to build?

2. Sons bond people to the Lord. Slaves bond people to themselves.

You can always pick out a slave, whether you are in the workplace or in church. It does not matter where you are or what organization you are in. Slaves are insecure, they have their own agenda, and they're always trying to capture people. They want to bond people to them so they can influence. Sons don't have an agenda of their own. They are just faithful sons in the house. The house is the agenda. Above all, sons seek to connect people with the Lord. Sons build relationship with people, connect those people to the Lord, and then try to connect those people with others.

Through all of the decades and decades I have spent building the GMI church network, no one has ever, ever been able to accuse me of bonding people to myself. I've never done that, and I never will. I'm not interested in bonding people to myself. That's a dangerous thing. It's also foolish to let yourself get bonded to someone else. I see people who come into the church and immediately bond with the worship leader, with a life group leader, with this pastor, or with that pastor. That's not smart.

When a big-name pastor goes down, I am rarely surprised by the fact that the pastor went down. But I am almost always surprised by the ripple effect it causes. It shocks me to see so many others fall right alongside the pastor. I remember when Jimmy Swaggart fell. Tens of thousands of people quit going to church! I was sad about Swaggart, but what happened to him didn't affect my relationship with God or my relationships with others in the body of Christ. I'm not bonded to Jimmy Swaggart. Bond yourself with the Lord. Spend outrageous amounts of time with Him. Bond yourself with Him and with people in the bigger body of Christ.

3. Sons see themselves as heirs and have a sense of ownership. Slaves see themselves as just a worker in somebody else's house.

You can tell the difference here when trouble comes. Trouble always magnifies this. Jesus himself pointed out that when the wolf comes to attack the sheep, the hireling hits the road (John 10:13). Why? Because he has no sense of ownership. Those aren't his sheep. What about David? When the lion came, what did he do? Well, he was a son. That lion wasn't having any of those sheep. They were his sheep because he had a son mentality. When troubles, difficulties, or attacks come, you will always find out who the true sons are.

If you read your Bible, then you know that Noah once got drunk. After the Flood he planted a vineyard, left the grapes out for a little while, got drunk, and fell asleep naked in his tent. One of his three sons found him like that, went out, and printed the first edition of the National Enquirer. Right? He told everybody. Then Noah's other two sons took a robe, put it on their backs, walked backwards into their father's tent, and covered Noah. Who do you think had a slave mentality? And who do you think had a son mentality?

4. Sons see the honor and reputation of the house as synonymous with their own. Slaves see themselves as separate from the house.

This is big. When Jesus visited the Temple, He saw all the money changers charging too much and ripping people off. What was His response? He drove them out because he was so passionate about the way they were dishonoring His father's house. If you have a son mentality, then you see the honor of the house as synonymous with your own. If you have a slave mentality, then the honor of the house really has nothing to do with you.

5. Sons think in terms of responsibility. Slaves think in terms of rights.

What do we have in America? Rights, rights, rights. It's all about rights, isn't it? I want my rights! Everybody is out there screaming about their rights. I don't see anybody out there screaming, "I want my responsibilities!" Why is that?

Sons think in terms of responsibility. Sons say, "I'm going to take this responsibility. I'm going to put the weight on my shoulder. It's mine. I'll do this. I'll take this." Are you a son? Or are you a slave?

6. Sons are family-oriented. Slaves are issue-oriented.

In other words, sons seek the greater good of the family. That could be a natural family, a church family, a business family, or any other type of family. The integrity, the happiness, the peace, and the growth of the family is more important than any issue the son could have. That's the way a son thinks. A slave just wants to be right. Slaves want to be right on all the issues, and they will argue no matter how much division and strife and damage it brings.

7. Sons embrace correction. Slaves reject correction.

That one doesn't need much explanation, does it?

8. Sons have puppy feet. Slaves come into the house full-grown.

Puppy feet. In other words, it's obvious that sons are going to grow. Sons grow and grow and grow because they are teachable. There's a lot they don't know, they are aware of that, and they are willing to learn. That's a great attitude. Keep that. Keep that for life. If there's one thing you could carve on my tombstone in truth, I want it to be this: "He was a constant learner." I want to continue to learn and grow. God will build on that. He'll build your life in an unshakable way if you embrace that way of thinking and living.

9. Sons embrace authority. Slaves don't.

Sons respond rightly to authority. They just get it. It's in them almost innately. They find authority, they accept it as delegated authority from God, and they line up underneath. That's the way they function. Sons accept authority even when it's not in church. They see their boss at work as a God-given authority in their lives. That's not what Myles Sweeney says, that's what Scripture says. Your boss is a God-given authority in your life. That does not mean you have to do absolutely everything your boss says, but it means you should be submissive. If the commands are not contrary to Scripture, obey them. If they are, then submissively decline. But your boss is a God given-authority. Speak well of that authority even when all the other employees around you are cutting the boss down. That's the kind of behavior that sets you apart as a son, not a slave, in the house.

Are you a son? Or are you a slave? I have one more question for you: Are you a learner? Learners do not just sit and read and say, "That's good." If you are a learner, then you are a doer. You will take something out of what you just read and apply it to your life. Are you about absorbing information? Or about learning?

If you want to take something out of what you read and actually see your life change, I encourage you to pick one thing. Maybe something in this chapter stood out to you. Maybe God has spoken to you through it. Maybe you recognized an area of your life where you have acted more like a slave than a son. All you need is one thing that takes you from hearer to doer. It may be something at school or in your workplace. It may be in church or in your marriage. It may be something to do with your relationship with your children or with your parents. Take just one thing, but choose how you are going to act on it. Choose how you are going to walk away from slavery and into sonship in your life.

Part 3

Overcome Obstacles

BEING RESPONSE-ABLE

God wants you to be successful.

Yes, I know I've said that before. This truth is worth revisiting.

God wants you to be successful in every area of your life. The Bible itself says He wants you to prosper (3 John 1:2), and it brings Him glory when you bear much fruit (John 15:8).

That doesn't mean you are supposed to wait for success to happen to you. It is not guaranteed without any effort on your part. You are responsible for participating in the process. God gave you the means to walk in success by giving you His Word. If you walk in the paths lined out by the Word, you will walk into success. If you build the characteristics described in the Word into your life, you will walk into success.

So how do we do that? What makes us successful in life? What are the biblical characteristics that we need to get? There are a lot of different answers to that question. The Bible gives us a lot of different characteristics that can help lead us to success in life, but I want to share one of the biggest keys with you today. If you are going to be successful in the various areas of your life, then you need to be responsible.

A lot of you probably checked out on me right there. Okay, be responsible. I understand what that means. Can I go now? No, not yet. The word "responsible" is actually two English words that were combined together years ago: "response" and "able." We need to be response-able—able to respond appropriately and properly to the different things that happen in our lives. We need to be responsible for the way we respond to circumstances, situations, events, good things, bad things, and everything in between. If we are going to be successful in life, we need to take responsibility for our responses.

If you study any psychology at all, one name that will pop up is Viktor Frankl, a very famous Jewish psychologist. Frankl is a big name in psychology circles. As a well-read, European psychologist, Frankl was well-versed in Sigmund Freud's teachings, Freud's view of life, and Freud's concepts of why people do what they do. Freudian Psychology has a primarily deterministic view of life.

In the field of psychology, there are stimuli and there are responses. As people walk through life, they experience different stimuli—external things that happen to them—and they respond. According to deterministic, Freudian thinking, who you are and what you do in life are determined by the stimuli you experience. You are shaped by all the things that happen to you in life.

That is true for animals, but it is not necessarily true for humans. Viktor Frankl discovered this during World War II. Frankl was taken and put into a concentration camp during the war because he was Jewish. He spent many years in that camp seeing brutal, horrific things happen to the people around him and experiencing those things himself. Frankl entered the camp with a deterministic mindset. Deterministic thinking says things like this:

"I'm a victim. It's not my fault."

"I am the way I am because of the things that happened to me. There is nothing I can do about that."

"I had a hangnail; that's why I turned into a T. rex the other day."

"The reason I am so difficult and cannot get along with people is because the wallpaper was too bright in the room I was born in."

Viktor Frankl went into the concentration camp with that kind of mindset, but he came out of it with a completely new way of thinking. In fact, he left with the belief that the deterministic, Freudian way of viewing life was a load of hogwash. From that day forward he began to lay out a new way of viewing life.

Is deterministic thinking true? For animals, yes. Freud and other psychologists came up with a lot of their ideas by testing animals. It is very possible to use stimuli to condition animals to do certain things. Maybe you remember Pavlov's dogs? That was a very famous experiment; it is taught in school all the time. Pavlov rang a bell, then fed his dog. He rang a bell, then fed his dog. He rang a bell, then fed his dog. He did this again and again and again. Before long, Pavlov's dog started salivating as soon as the bell rang, whether there was food or not. That is a deterministic deal. The circumstances determined the dog's response.

The problem with the views of Freud and other psychologists like him was they saw human beings as nothing more than just another species of animal. They believed humans were the same as other animals, just at a slightly higher level of evolution. They did not recognize that humans are totally, completely different. We are not animals. God created us very differently.

For animals, there is only stimulus and response. But here is what Viktor Frankl found from watching the people around him in the concentration camp: for humans, there is more than just stimulus and pre-determined response. Frankl watched the people around him experience the exact same horrible, terrible things in the exact same horrible, terrible environment. Then he watched some of those people come out of the camp bitter and angry, even evil and wicked as a result of the things that happened to them. But other people came out more loving, more gentle, more kind, and more compassionate than they had been before they went in.

After seeing that, Frankl started doing a series of experiments, and those experiments eventually proved that the deterministic view of psychology does not apply to human beings. This is because, for humans, there is a gap between the stimulus and the response. There is always a gap. That gap may be a just a millisecond or a matter of days, but there is always a gap. Stimulus, gap, response. In that gap you and I, as human beings, make a decision about how we are going to respond to the stimulus. We always have the ability to decide. We decide how we are going to respond.

This is critically, critically important, especially in American culture today. Successful people choose to not be victims. They say, "No, I will not be a victim. I will not let circumstances, people, and situations control or manipulate me. I am not going to live my life in a series of knee-jerk reactions. As a human being, I don't have to do that. I am not an animal. There is a gap. I can make the decision to respond differently, even from others around me."

Successful people don't allow themselves to fall into a victim mentality. Successful people respond properly to whatever comes into their lives. They are response-able. They take responsibility for their responses to the things that happen to them.

The victim mentality is a plague. Victimhood is everywhere. It's not my fault. I'm not responsible. Somebody asked me one time, "Myles, when did that start? When did the victim mentality really take off? Was it in the 60s, with rock and roll?"

I said, "No, it happened year one with Adam and Eve."

If you haven't read the story of Adam and Eve recently, I encourage you to go back and read it. The truth is right there for us. Adam and Eve were in the Garden of Eden, but they disobeyed God. What happened when they disobeyed? The infection of sin came rushing into the world for the first time. Now stop and think about this story for a minute. What was the first evidence that sin had entered the world? Was it murder? No. Was it idol worship? No. What was it? It was the transfer of responsibility. You know the story. Adam and Eve disobeyed God. God came. He found Adam and put a spotlight on him.

"What's going on here, Adam?"

"It's not my fault! The woman You gave me, she's defective."

Transfer of responsibility. Sin was in the world. Then the spotlight shifted to Eve. She looked around and said, "Whoa, wait a minute. I'm a victim! The serpent, see, he tricked me!"

Then the spotlight shifted to the serpent. "Oh man, I'm cooked goose. I've got nobody else here to blame."

Listen to me here. You don't have to be a victim. If you are living like a victim today, it is because you are choosing to be one. That is reality. You don't have to go through life as a victim. You don't have to go through life blaming everyone and everything for your lack of success. The culture that we live in is going to tell you that you are a victim over and over and over again. That message is constantly streaming around us. It is easy to take a bite out of that apple; it is low-hanging fruit. I'm a victim. It's not my fault. I am the way I am because of the things that happened to me. The problem is none of that is true.

"Well, I've had all these bad things happen to me."

Get in line. So have all the other people around you. Does that sound unloving? It's not. Let me tell you what would be unloving. It would be unloving to say, "Oh, you poor thing." Because then that person would stay in a victim mentality and never come to success in life. That sounds very unloving to me.

You may have gotten a raw deal in life, but if you want to be successful, you are going to have to become response-able. You are going to have to take responsibility for your responses to the things that happen to you, and you are going to have to respond the right way.

"I'm a victim. I got a bad deal."

No, you are not. You are not a victim of a bad deal, you are a victim of your response to the bad deal. That is where victimhood comes in. Maybe you did get a bad deal, but the real issue for you is your response to it. That is the problem. There are people all around you in this world that have gone through bigger, deeper, uglier things than you have, and they are doing incredibly well. Some of them are ministering out of the things they experienced and touching people's lives. How you live your life is not determined by what you went through. It is determined by how you respond to what you went through. If you are not successful in life, it is not because of what happened to you. It is because of how you responded to what happened to you.

This is not a popular message to preach today. We don't like to hear these things, but they are true. I am proud to be a part of a church where you do not have to look far to see how true this message really is. I know many, many people who overcame incredibly awful, ugly things. But they did not just overcome. Because of how they responded to those awful things, the bad things actually helped shape them into bigger, better, more godly people.

One man in particular comes to mind when I think of this. This man was brought up in a horribly dysfunctional family. Messy, messy upbringing. His dad was never there for him or for the rest of the family. So now you can look at this man's life and say, "Well, no wonder he is such a bad husband and a bad father." No, not the case. He is an incredible husband. He is an incredible father. How did that work? He did not allow himself to be a victim. He chose to take responsibility for how he responded to his upbringing and everything else in life.

Throughout the years that I have been married, about thirty or forty people at the very least have come up to talk to me about my wife, Sallie Sweeney.

"She is such an incredible woman and such an incredible wife."

"You are absolutely right," I say.

"How did that happen? How did she become such an incredible wife?" they ask. I give the same answer every time.

"There are a lot of different reasons, but one of the biggest is her parents divorced when she was nine years old."

Every single time I say that the person who asked stares at me like a calf staring at a new gate. It doesn't make sense to them, but that truly is one of the biggest reasons that Sallie is an incredible wife today. When she went through her parents' divorce as a young child, she made a decision. She said, "When I get married, we are going to do things differently." Now she is married. And boy, when there is a marriage conference, we are signed up for it. When she finds a good book on marriage, we read it together. We have always done all kinds of things to learn and improve our marriage because she decided at nine years old that she was going to pour into and develop her marriage.

"I'm a victim. I can't do that because—"

No, no. That is not the truth.

I remember one night years ago I was watching Larry King Live. It must have been one of those slow nights where nothing else was on, because I am not a big Larry King fan. But I was watching Larry King that night. He was interviewing a lady who was blind, and the interview captured my attention. She was talking about her life and all the things she was doing. She was an incredible mother and an incredible wife, and she was also making a major impact in the world by traveling around the United States to speak a very powerful life message to the youth of America.

Larry King was asking this woman about her background and about everything that had happened to her. She told him her story. When she was a young newlywed, a man had assaulted her. After the brutal assault, this man took a gun out, put it to her head, and pulled the trigger. He thought he had killed her, but she survived. Granted, she almost died. After that day, she spent almost two years in the hospital. She lost her sight and had to go through surgery after surgery in the very slow process of recovery.

After she finished telling most of her story, Larry King asked her, "How did you overcome all of that and become the incredible person that you are today?"

Her answer was so powerful. I made sure to write it down and save it. This is how she answered him: "I had to make a decision. I decided not to let this zero—this nobody on the scale of humanity—destroy my life. I decided not to let him control the rest of my life."[1]

Do you know how many people I meet who are controlled by things from their past? This woman decided that her life was not going to be controlled. She lived through an awful moment of assault. Then, because of what that man did to her, she lost her sight and had to go through an agonizing recovery process. But despite all that had happened to her, she decided that she was not going to let what that man did control or dictate how she lived the rest of her life. When we operate in a victim mentality, that is what you and I are doing. We are letting circumstances or people from the past control how we live today. They are dictating our lives.

If you are a prisoner of past tragedy, please hear me out here. I am not minimizing the tragedy that you went through. If you think that is what I am saying, then you are not hearing my heart. I am not saying that. I know there are awful, awful tragedies that many, many people have lived through. I know that absolutely horrific things may have happened to you in this sin-soaked world. No one is minimizing that. But what I am saying is this: those things don't have to control your life.

"Well, he hurt me! He ruined my life!"

Hurt you? Yes. I understand that, and I totally agree. Ruined your life? Mmm, no. Not unless you allow him to. That is a decision that you make. The hurt and the pain? Those are real. I am not asking you to live in denial. Jesus does not ask people to live in denial. Don't bury your head in the sand and act like all the bad things never happened. Don't just shove them to the back and try to forget all about them. No, they happened. They are real. They are painful. But you do not have to let them ruin your life and dictate how you live.

You very likely know people who are totally controlled by their circumstances and surroundings. Monday morning comes, and they are just determined to have a bad day. Why? Because it's Monday. Mondays are miserable. But then Friday rolls around, and they are happy. Why? Because it's Friday. Fridays are great. Really? You are telling me that a date on a calendar controls your life? It is just another twenty-four hours. It doesn't have to be miserable just because the calendar calls it "Monday." But if you decide that it is going to be miserable, that's all it takes.

I am not trying to deny that Mondays happen. Mondays happen to all of us, but they don't just happen on Mondays, do they? The important thing is not whether or not it's going to be a bad day; the important thing is how we respond to those days. Like Karen Carpenter said, "Rainy days and Mondays always get me down."[2] Well, if you let them, they will. Look at the rest of Karen Carpenter's life. What a tragedy. She died at thirty-two years old of a major eating disorder. It wasn't just rainy days and Mondays that got her down. There were lots of things that got her down, and what had been a promising life ended quickly and tragically.

The Apostle Paul says this in Philippians 4:13: "I can do all things through Christ who strengthens me." I know you know that verse. Let's apply it to what we are talking about here because that is a Kingdom principle. How does this verse speak to being response-able? By the grace of God and the power of the Holy Spirit, I can respond to all things with a good attitude. I can rejoice in all things.

"Well, you know, this thing happened. Then that thing happened. My day just didn't start off right."

Whoa, that's it? So you are going to go through the rest of your day miserable and make sure that everybody else is miserable just because of that? That's all it took? There has got to be more.

I know from my experience speaking this to large groups of people that there are two main responses to this message. Some of you reading this right now are getting it. You are seeing this in your life more clearly than you have ever seen it before. Light bulbs are turning on all over the place for you, and you want the freedom in your life that comes from being response-able. But there are at least a few of you reading this and responding very differently. You are angry right now. You are mad at me. Why are you mad at me? Because I am lousing up your life right now. I am taking away all of your excuses.

Galatians 5:1 says, "It is for freedom that Christ has set us free." What does that mean? When we were born again, what Jesus did on the cross became applicable to us. Now we have freedom. Why did Jesus give us that freedom? He set us free so we could have freedom. Freedom to what? Do whatever we want? No, that's stupid. That will take us right back into bondage. Freedom to what? To do the things we should do. Jesus set us free so that we would be free to walk in His ways. His ways bring life and blessing and success.

I say this with conviction: I, Myles Sweeney, am going to be successful in life. That is not just me being arrogant. I am going to be successful in life. I can say that. I cannot say that my bank account is going to be this or my career is going to be that, but I can say that I am going to be successful in life. I can say that because my success is not dependent on what happens around me. It is not based on what happens to me or what people do or don't do to me. My success is based on how I respond to all of those things. I know that I am going to be successful because I am not going to let anything knock me out of my destiny. How about you?

The story in John 5:1-7 shows us how Jesus responds to victim mentalities.

Some time later, Jesus went up to Jerusalem for one of the Jewish festivals. Now there is in Jerusalem near the Sheep Gate a pool, which in Aramaic is called Bethesda and which is surrounded by five covered colonnades. Here a great number of disabled people used to lie—the blind, the lame, the paralyzed. One who was there had been an invalid for thirty-eight years. When Jesus saw him lying there and learned that he had been in this condition for a long time, he asked him, "Do you want to get well?"

*"Sir," the invalid replied, "I have no one to help me into
the pool when the water is stirred. While I am trying to
get in, someone else goes down ahead of me."*

Now, what was the issue here? What was going on? This guy had
a victim mentality. How do we know? It is very simple. Look at his
interaction with Jesus. What did Jesus ask him? "Do you want to get
well?" Just on the surface, this seems like a dumb question. I know I am
not supposed to say that because it was Jesus who asked it, but really. If
anybody else had asked that question, we would all be wondering why
that person had asked such a dumb question. But Jesus was operating
in the fullness of the Spirit and saw more than just what was in the natural realm. Jesus was reading the sick man's mail. He knew everything
that was going on, and he knew the answer to his own question before
he even asked it.

Let me share a revelation that caused a big turning point in my life.
My life changed when I finally realized this: when the Lord asks me a
question, it is not because He needs to know the answer. He is never
looking for any insight or information I have. This was a shocking revelation to me as a young Christian. When God asks me a question, He
already knows the answer. Why is He asking the question, then? When
God asks a question, it is so that I, in the process of answering the question, discover what is really going on in my heart. If you have been there
before, then you know exactly what I am talking about.

So Jesus walked up to the sick man by the pool and knew exactly
what the real issue was. "Do you want to get well?" The King James
Version of 3 John 5:6 says it this way: "Will you be made whole?"
If I had been laying there for thirty-eight years, you know what my
answer would be?

"SURE! You betcha! There is nothing I want more!"

How did the sick man answer?

"I have no one to help me," (3 John 5:7).

He was basically saying, "These other people around me, they have a good deal going on. They have their families to help them out. My kids are just too busy. I'm not valuable enough to them. They aren't here to help me get in the water."

Can you hear the victim's whine now? Jesus knew what the deeper issue was. He saw that the man was lame; that was a real issue, and Jesus was not discounting that. But He saw that there was an even bigger issue at play. He asked, "Will you be made whole?"

Do you want to be a victim for the rest of your life? Or do you want to be made whole?

If you read on in the story, the sick man eventually says yes. Then Jesus tells him, "Get up! Pick up your mat and walk," (3 John 5:8). Most English translations add an exclamation point to that first sentence. Do you know why? It is because the words of the original Greek are in emphatic form. That means they were not said; they were shouted.

I know a lot of us have watched different movies about Jesus' life. In most of them, he is a namby-pamby weakling of a guy. That doesn't even come close to the kind of person he actually was, if you believe in Scripture. In the Jesus movies, this scene plays out with Jesus using this gentle, melodic voice to quietly tell the sick man to get up. That is not what happened. It is clear in the Greek. He shouted it. In fact, it is not even just his volume level that was different from the movie depictions. In the Greek, this short, two-word sentence is in a verb tense that implies repetition. That means he did not just shout these words once; he shouted them repeatedly.

"GET UP! GET UP! GET UP! GET UP! GET UP!"

"Well, I just don't believe that Jesus would talk to anyone like that."

Then you believe something that is different from what is in the Scripture. You bought into the softie Jesus. That is not real. Jesus was loving enough to deal with the real issue. Jesus understood that if he didn't deal with the victim mentality, the sick man would get healed physically, but he would still limp for the rest of his life.

What about you?

"I am a victim of the dysfunctional family that I was raised in."

"I'm a victim of my race."

"I'm a victim of my poor education."

"I'm a victim of this past relationship that damaged me."

Jesus would say the same thing to you that He said to that lame man at the pool of Bethesda. "Will you be made whole?"

The man at the pool of Bethesda gives us a great example of what living from a victim mentality looks like. What does it look like to be response-able?

Let me show you with a story. This is the story of a man named Richie Parker. Richie is an engineer who works for Hendricks Motorsports. If you know racing, you probably know that Hendricks Motorsports is the most winning organization in Nascar. They are the organization behind many big names including Jimmie Johnson, Dale Earnhardt Jr., and Jeff Gordon. Richie has worked there for eight years designing different car components. What makes Richie's story exceptional? Why is it a big deal that he works for Hendricks Motorsports? Because Richie Parker does the design work with his feet. He was born without arms.

What would life would be like if you never had arms? What challenges would come just with simple, everyday life? Even when Richie was very young, his parents made the decision that they were going to help him overcome every challenge and have as close to an independent, normal life as possible. If Richie was not able to do something on his own, they made it to where he was able to do it on his own. Trouble opening the refrigerator door? They kept a rope around the door handle that Richie could slip his shoulder into and pull. Trouble eating? They rigged a contraption that allowed him to use a spoon with his mouth, set the spoon down, and then turn the spoon around to eat from it.

People always said that he couldn't. He couldn't ride a bike. He couldn't drive a car. He couldn't live on his own. He couldn't take care of himself. Richie Parker did every single one of those things. Later in life, Richie looked back and said this: "I don't know that there's a whole lot of things in life period that I can say that I can't do. Just things that I haven't done yet."[3]

Richie Parker had every reason to think and act like a victim of his circumstances. He had a much better reason than you and I will probably ever have. But Richie made a decision. He made the decision to be response-able. What decision will you make today? Will you choose to be a victim and let other people and circumstances control your life? Or will you choose to be responsible for the way that you respond and walk down the path toward the success in life that God Himself has for you?

Becoming Offense-Proof

L et me start this chapter with one quick word from Jesus. In Luke 17, Jesus says, "Things that cause people to stumble are bound to come." Now, other translations condense the phrase, "things that cause people to stumble" down to one word: "offenses." So Jesus was saying this: it is inevitable that offenses must come. Did you get that double statement there? It is *inevitable*, and offenses *must come*. He made two statements of certainty, and He said them with great emphasis. You can't really tell in English, but if you look at this section in the original Greek, it has tremendous emphasis on it. It's a word you could put four or five exclamation points behind in mid-sentence. He was really trying to emphasize this; He was saying "Listen! Listen! Listen! Listen to me, saints! Listen to me, people of God! Listen to me, children of God! It's INEVITABLE that offenses MUST COME!"

They will come. No matter how you and I live our lives, no matter how righteous or pure we are, and no matter how perfectly we walk out our life, it's inevitable that offenses must come.

The Greek word there that's translated "offenses" is a fascinating word, like so many of the Greek words in the New Testament. This is the word *scandalon*. It's the word that we get "scandal" from, but if you go back and look at its origins, you'll find that scandalon means a bloody piece of meat.

You're probably wondering what on earth bloody meat has to do with offenses. Well, this is the picture. When people in those days wanted to trap a wild animal, they would first dig a deep pit in the ground. Then they would cover over the top of the pit with sticks and palm branches so that the animal wouldn't know that there was a pit there. Then they would make a tripod of three long poles, joining them together out over the center of the deep hole. From the apex, where the poles met, they would hang down a scandalon, a bloody piece of meat, for bait. When the animal came to take a bite of the scandalon, what would happen? It would fall through and find itself trapped in a pit. This is a perfect picture of what offenses do to our lives.

Listen, offenses will come. If we're not careful, we will reach out and take a bite of one of the offenses that's hanging out there for us daily, weekly, or at least monthly. They're hanging out there. If we're foolish enough to reach out there and take a bite of them, we're going to find ourselves in a pit. We're going to find ourselves in a place where we are stopped in our forward progress and limited in the things that God wants us to do in our lives.

It's inevitable that offenses must come. They will come through people. They will come through circumstances. They will come through situations. They will come again and again and again. This is a promise from Jesus. If you go down to the Christian book store and you buy one of those pocket promise books that has all the promises in the Bible, you won't find this one in there. There is no chance of seeing this one on a refrigerator magnet. Why? Because we don't want to think about it. But listen, it's a promise from Jesus to you and to me. And it's a *warning* to us.

Let me tell you something, if I had not learned how to become offense-proof—if God had not taught me this twenty-something years ago—there is no way I would be doing the tiniest portion of what I'm doing today. In the same way, you are not going to come into what God has for you—your destiny, your purpose, and your calling—if you don't understand this. You are going to miss so many wonderful things God has for you if you don't learn this truth, get this truth, and respond the right way to this truth. Keep yourself from biting into the scandalon, winding up in a pit, and missing what God has for you.

We need to learn this. This is critically important. In fact, here's a fascinating thing about offenses. Overcoming offense is so critical in our lives that Jesus Himself will engage in the offense process with us.

"What? Not Jesus!"

Oh yeah. See, some of us haven't read our Bibles really closely and carefully. God is so interested in making us offense-proof that He will engage in the process of dealing with our quickness to get offended. Time after time these things come, and we are so quick to get offended. He is telling us that He is going to help us become offense-proof.

In John 6:51, Jesus says, "I am the living bread that came down from heaven. Whoever eats this bread will live forever. This bread is my flesh, which I will give for the life of the world." Understand something: to the Jew, cannibalism—eating another person's flesh and drinking another person's blood—is the most abominable thing that one can think of. That's their mentality. And so here comes Jesus, who says to them, "I'm the bread of life, come eat me. Come drink my blood."

Then the Jews began to argue sharply among themselves, "How can this man give us his flesh to eat?"

Jesus said to them, "Very truly I tell you, unless you eat the flesh of the Son of Man and drink his blood, you have no life in you. Whoever eats my flesh and drinks my blood has eternal life, and I will raise them up at the last day," *(John 6:52-54)*

Jesus was not backing up one bit. The people that were listening didn't like what He was saying; they were taking offense. What did Jesus do? He upped the ante. He pressed forward.

On hearing it, many of his disciples said, "This is a hard teaching. Who can accept it?"

Aware that his disciples were grumbling about this, Jesus said to them, "Does this offend you?" (John 6:60-61).

Do you believe that Jesus was surprised here? No, I don't think so. Number one, Jesus had the Spirit of God without measure. You and I have it in measure, but Scripture tells us He had it without measure. He was flowing freely and completely in the gifts of the Spirit. He was reading everybody's mail all the time. So He was not surprised by his disciples; He understood what the deal was. He understood what their natural reaction was going to be.

So this is the situation. In John 6 we've got massive throngs of people who are coming to Jesus. Large numbers of people flocking, and they're all wanting to make Him king. They've got all these big plans, and things are on a roll. They're saying, "We are in *revival*, brother." So what does Jesus do? He says, "I've got a plan. Unless you eat my flesh and drink my blood . . . Does this offend you?" Then John 6:66 says, "From this time many of his disciples turned back and no longer followed him."

Jesus is going to speak the truth whether you like it or not. Jesus is going to speak truth to you and I, directly or indirectly, whether we like it or not. He is going to speak truth whether we accept it or not. He's going to do it, He's going to do it, and He's going to do it. And in the process, hopefully, you and I will become offense-proof.

Next we are going to look at a passage in Mark 3. Let me give you a little bit of background on this one. Jesus is teaching in Capernaum. He goes to a house and starts teaching in it, and so many people come that the crowd fills the house, the outer courtyard of the house, and the street outside. Big crowd. We pick up the story in Mark 3:31-33.

*Then Jesus' mother and brothers arrived. Standing out-
side, they sent someone in to call him. A crowd was sitting around him, and they told him, "Your mother and
brothers are outside looking for you."*

"Who are my mother and my brothers?" he asked.

Now, let's think about this for a minute. Here is Jesus' mother and
brothers. They come up on the scene. There are all these people there.
They can't get in, so they pass the word in to Jesus.

"Tell Jesus His mother and brothers are here."

"Ok . . . hey, tell Jesus His mother and brothers are here."

"Oh, all right . . . tell Jesus His mother and brothers are here."

Word passes through the crowd, finally getting to Jesus. Someone
says, "Hey, Jesus! Your mother and brothers are here." What does Jesus
say? "Who are my mother and my brothers?" (3:33).

"Hey, Jesus said, 'Who are my mother and my brothers?' Pass it on."

"Ok . . . Jesus said, 'Who are my mother and brothers?'"

The message gets all the way to the guy standing by Jesus' mother
and brothers. He turns around, looks at Jesus' family, and pauses. Then
he turns to the guy next to him and says, "Uh, you tell them. Jesus said,
'Who are my mother and my brothers?'" I bet nobody actually wanted
to tell them what He said.

What's going on in this story? To find out you have to back up to
earlier in the chapter. Mark 3:21 says, "When his family heard about
this, they went to take charge of him, for they said, 'He is out of his
mind.'" Jesus' mom and his brothers didn't come there to sit in on the
teaching or to be ministered to by Him. They came there with a purpose: to give Him a new jacket. It was a nice white one with long sleeves,
and it zipped up in the back.

Jesus knew what was going on. His family was offended by what
He was saying and doing. All the rumors were coming in. I mean, it

was okay for a while; He was just a little out there. But, after more and more stuff came in, they finally said, "Man, the guy has lost His mind. He's giving us a bad name and ruining our rep. We need to go take charge of Him."

Before you pick up stones to throw at Jesus' mother and brothers, stop and ask yourself this: have you ever been offended with Jesus? I know you're not supposed to say that, but come on. If you have walked with Him for any length of time, chances are good that you have been offended with Him at some point. I can tell you story after story of times that I have been really offended with the Lord because He didn't do things *right*. Which really means He didn't do things my way.

Here's one. My parents were Methodists, and my family grew up just nominally attending the Methodist church. Their son, you know, was just this crazy, fanatical Christian who actually read his Bible at home. They had a real problem with that. "It's bad enough that you read your Bible at church, but if you read it at home, you've become a fanatic." That's what they said to me. My whole family was that way.

Then I left my job at American Express to move back to Wharton. They were saying, "What on earth are you doing? You're throwing away this career! You're making so much money! What on earth are you doing? Why are you coming back here? This is crazy!" Within a number of years, the church started in Wharton, and I was asked to lead it. I resisted for a while, but I finally said, "You know what, this is God."

So I was leading the church, and this thing was growing. But it was practically a Charismatic church. Oh my goodness. My family was freaking out. They weren't even tolerant of the church in conversation, so Sallie and I were both sure they would never walk through the door.

We were in church one Sunday morning, and the service is just about to start. This is an absolutely true story. One of the church members walked up to me and said, "Hey Myles, your mom and dad just walked in."

"Yeah, right. Funny," I said.

"No, they're really here," he said.

"Stop. Quit. That's not even funny to me."

"No! Turn around and look!"

I finally turned around, and I was completely floored.

"Sallie, my mom and dad are here."

"No way."

"Turn around and look!"

We couldn't believe it. They didn't tell us a thing, just showed up. I started talking to God. *Yes. Thank you, God.*

Then worship started. *Oh, now wait. Now, Jesus. You know where my parents are. Can we have a nice calm Sunday today? Will You speak to the worship leader very quickly and make him change the songs to where they're nice and mellow?*

Huh uh. That isn't what happened. First song, boom! Loud and exciting. Everybody was jumping around and raising their hands, and I was off to the side, thinking, *No, no, no. Lord! Don't you understand? My parents! They're already freaked out! They just walked in the door and they're only going to be here two minutes! They're gone! Tame this thing down.* At the same time I was also thinking, *Well, hopefully no one gives a word. They really won't understand that.*

Two songs into worship, the Lord gave me a word. *No, Lord. Not gonna do it.* But the word was just as clear as a bell, and it kept coming. I decided that I couldn't live in disobedience to God, so I went up to the stage and took the mic.

Not only was this a word, it was a weird word. I spoke it to the congregation, "I don't understand this, but this is what God said to me. This is a word for somebody here this morning. Your name is not Juliet. That's not even a part of your first name, middle name, or last name, but you know I'm talking about you, and you know that the Lord knows specifically who you are by me calling you Juliet this morning. It means something to you, but it won't mean anything to anybody else. You are

Juliet, and you know that you are Juliet. Will you please come forward? God has a word for you."

We waited. Nothing happened. I said, "I really have a sense that it's a visitor here this morning. If you're nervous about this, don't be nervous. Just come forward. God wants to bless you; He's got something for you." Nobody came, and finally I realized nobody was going to come. I sat down thinking, *Now that's even worse.* I couldn't imagine what my parents were thinking in the back.

Worship ended, I preached, and we had a ministry time at the end. At the end of the service, I was at the front talking to people. My parents made their way up, but they were also visiting with some people. They were standing not six feet away from me when a girl walked up to me.

"I'm Juliet," she said.

"Well, how do you know that?" I said.

"Yesterday somebody asked me if I had seen the movie 'Shakespeare in Love.' I told them no, but they said that my hair looks just like Juliet's in the movie. Only God would know that. What do you have for me?"

With that the Lord gave me what He had for her, and I shared the word with her. She began to cry. I asked her if she'd given her life to the Lord. She said no; she hadn't grown up in church, but a friend of hers had been reaching out to her and had shared the gospel with her that week. She said, "I know this morning that God is real, and I'm ready to give my life to Christ."

I prayed with her. While she was weeping, I was thinking, *I'm excited about this, but I know what's going on over there. My parents are flipping out.* I finished praying for her, I gave her a hug, and I congratulated her on her decision that morning. Then the Spirit of God just nudged me. You know those little nudges? He said, "Pray for her."

I asked her, "Hey, can I just pray with you before you leave? I'd just like to pray a blessing over you." She said yes. I reached out, and as soon as I touched her forehead it happened. The Spirit of God rushed in. In one second she took off praying in tongues. I was just standing there thinking, *Oh my God.* She prayed in tongues for about thirty seconds, and then boom. No catchers, she just fell over. I thought, *I'm not even looking. I'm not—Jesus, how could You do that to my poor parents? Do You have any idea how long I've been trying to evangelize them? With one Sunday You've messed it all up.*

Have you ever been there before? Ever been offended with God?

Do you remember Michal, David's wife? She got offended because David was celebrating the goodness of the Lord. David danced before the Lord, worshipping Him for His presence among the Israelites. Then Michal caught him and told him how very much he embarrassed himself out there. She was offended. After that encounter, the Bible says she was barren for the rest of her life (2 Sam. 6:20). Did God strike her barren? Maybe. But I think it is more likely the bridegroom never had intimacy with her again. He withdrew his presence from her. Be careful; we can become barren if we get offended with what God is saying and doing in our lives.

There is another example in Matthew 15:10-13.

Jesus called the crowd to him and said, "Listen and understand. What goes into someone's mouth does not defile them, but what comes out of their mouth, that is what defiles them."

Then the disciples came to him and asked, "Do you know that the Pharisees were offended when they heard this?"

Then Jesus said, "No! You're kidding! I had no clue they might get offended over what I said. Oh! Let me run over there and solve the situation. We can't have them offended, now. I'll work that out. I'll modify things and water them down a little bit so they are palatable to them." Is that what He said? No. Here is how He actually responded:

"He replied, 'Every plant that my heavenly Father has not planted will be pulled up by the roots,'" (Matt. 15:13).

There are two powerful truths here, and we need to make sure we get both of them. Here is truth number one: there is a kind of offense in the very will and purpose of God.

There are times when people start coming to a church that God never called them to be a part of. Sometimes those people will hear His voice and move on. But there are other times when God uses an offense to move them on. That's what Jesus said. Do you see that? He was talking about offenses when he said, "Every plant that my Heavenly Father has not planted will be pulled up by the roots," (Matt. 15:13). In other words, God will move them on and plant them in another place where they can grow because they were never intended to be there.

We need to understand that because sometimes there may be somebody that you've been trying to get to church forever who finally comes and seems to really like it. Then the pastor says something they disagree with, or the worship leader plays a song that they don't really like, and all of a sudden they're gone. If you're not careful, you will get offended at the pastor, the leaders of the church, the worship team, or whoever caused the exit. You may even get offended at God! God was just moving them on because they were not meant to be planted in your church.

There's another thing that can happen. Sometimes it's somebody who *is* intended to be planted here. They may be here for a while, but the next thing you know they get sour about something. They get offended, and they won't deal with that offense. Maybe they just don't like something or have a different opinion. "Well, I don't like this. I don't like that." Someone like that will begin to cause problems. They become a sour apple, and God will move that sour apple before it ruins the whole bunch. Sometimes God will use an offense to make that happen.

We need to understand that God sometimes uses offenses to serve his own purposes. If we don't, then the same thing I've seen happen so many times in so, so many churches around the world will happen again. Somebody gets offended and hurt over something. That person decides to leave the church. Then a whole bunch of other church members line up like little ducklings behind the offended church members, and they all walk out of the church together. "Well, I'm offended because they're offended. I'm offended that—"

Offenses are one of the ways God keeps His house clean. That is absolutely true, and we need to understand it.

Here is the second powerful truth that we need to get from Matthew 15: Jesus never let up on the Pharisees. And—listen to me, saints—He's never going to let up on the Pharisee in you. Some of us need to be delivered from the idolatry of our personal opinion.

People amaze me. They have for years. I've been leading people for decades, and I'm still constantly amazed. I have watched different people do the same thing time and time again, and I am still amazed it happens another time.

It is amazing when a person with a tiny bit of experience in ministry and maybe half the information at best comes to me thinking they have all the answers. What's wrong with that picture?

"Well, I don't understand. Why are you doing this? Why are they doing that? Why did you pick them? Why did they do this? I just don't understand why we don't do more of this."

It is great to have questions. But if you have questions, you know what? Ask questions. Don't make statements. Go to your pastor ask questions. Go to an elder and politely request a meeting. Don't go to others and make statements.

I cannot tell you how many times someone has come up to me and said something like, "Well I've got my notebook on eschatology." Really, do you now?

The last person I sat down with told me he had a problem with my view on end times. He said he believed in dispensationalism. I simply started asking him if he knew about several different aspects of dispensational teaching. I went through eighteen points from the very core of dispensational teaching, and he didn't know about a single one of those eighteen points. True story.

"Oh, I didn't know dispensationalism taught that."

I knew more about what he believed than he did. It seemed like he hadn't studied one bit, yet he came to me because I was the one who was ignorant and didn't understand. That was not the first time I faced a situation like that, and it will not be the last.

There is a kind of offense that comes from God. God will sometimes take people who are going to be a problem and move them on. God uses offenses to clear out people who are not going to be teachable, be plugged in, or be healthy members of the church.

"Well I've got my notebook about why women shouldn't teach in the church."

Really?

"Well I've got my notebooks on why the gifts of the Spirit died in the first cent—"

You know what? Take your notebooks and shove them. Back on the shelf! What did you think I meant? Hey! Get your mind out of the gutter.

There's a kind of offense that is in the will and purpose of God. Jesus confirms this again in John 11:1-6.

> *Now a man named Lazarus was sick. He was from Bethany, the village of Mary and her sister Martha. . . . So the sisters sent word to Jesus, "Lord, the one you love is sick."*

When he heard this, Jesus said, "This sickness will not end in death. No, it is for God's glory so that God's Son may be glorified through it."

This is sounding really good, isn't it? I mean, I like this Jesus. I dig this guy; I am right there with Him.

"Now Jesus loved Martha and her sister and Lazarus. So when he heard that Lazarus was sick, he stayed where he was two more days," (John 11:5-6).

Do what? Jesus was basically saying, "I tell you the truth, I love you so much that I'm not coming until you're dead. I love you so much, Mary and Martha. I love this whole family so much that I'm not coming until Lazarus dies." That is exactly what He said and did.

And get this: when Jesus finally came, Mary stayed at home. Martha ran out to greet Him, but Mary stayed at home. She was offended; she wasn't coming.

Listen, I've heard so many teachings about Mary and Martha for years and years. Do you know the story from Luke 10? Mary is sitting there on the front row taking notes while Jesus is teaching. Mary is that charismatic girl, glitter in hair and on fire for Jesus. Martha, that old house tramp, is in there cooking and cleaning; she's got her priorities all whacked up. What's wrong with her? Can't she get her act together? Doesn't she understand what's important?

The story is a little different here at Lazarus's tomb. Mary is offended and at home. Martha, the one who was so busy cooking and cleaning and serving and working in the background, was the one who came out to meet Jesus. She's the one whose faith Jesus was going to respond to by bringing Lazarus forth from the grave.

But even though that's true about Martha, listen to what she says. Listen to this "greeting" that she gives Jesus when she comes to meet

Him in John 11:21, "'Lord,' Martha said to Jesus, "if you had been here, my brother would not have died."

No "Hello." No "How are you?" No "Nice suntan you got there, Jesus." Nothing like that. She just walks up to Him and says, "Man, if you had just come when you should have, my brother wouldn't be dead right now. He'd still be alive."

Later on Mary finally did come out of the house to see the Lord. Here are her first words to Jesus: "When Mary reached the place where Jesus was and saw him, she fell at his feet and said, 'Lord, if you had been here, my brother would not have died,'" (John 11:32). Does that sound familiar? The exact same words Martha said. Exact. Verbatim. Same words. Do you get the idea maybe the two of them had been talking?

What was the problem there? They were offended.

"Where were you, Jesus, in my time of need? I've served You. I've been faithful to You. I've told others about You. And then, when I had a crisis moment, You weren't there. You said You loved me, but You didn't show up when I needed you, and I'm offended."

Jesus loved Mary enough to deal with her offense. Offense is simply ego, pride, and uncrucified self. That's all it is. I have to have things on my timetable, the way I think they should be done, and if you don't do it that way, then you must be wrong. That's uncrucified self—fleshy, nasty stuff. And Jesus says, "You know what? I am not budging one inch away from you. I'm going to deal with this thing, and I'm going to get it out of you."

Do you know what Jesus does? Sometimes He comes to us to just mess with us, mess our hair up, and poke us in the chest. Don't you hate it when He does that?

"Why is He doing this? I thought He loved me."

He does! He's trying to get you to come to a place where you're offense-proof. He's trying to set you free and deal with your ego and your offense. He loved Mary enough to deal with her offense, and He loves you and I enough to deal with ours. He loves us enough to set us free from that stuff.

Hebrews 12:6 says, "The Lord disciplines the one he loves, and he chastens everyone he accepts as his son." I once had the privilege of hearing Jamie Buckingham, an incredible writer and man of God, speak at a conference, and I like the way he paraphrased that verse: "For whom the Lord loves, he beats the hell out of." I don't mean that in a crude sense; I mean that in a strict, literal sense. If Jesus loves you, He will work to drive that hellishness—anything from hell and not from heaven—out of our hearts and our lives.

Christians are like tea bags. You don't know what's inside of them until you drop them in hot water. Then everything in them comes streaming out.

"Oh hallelujah, bless God. If it got any better, there'd be two of me. Oh, praise God, brother. Hallelujah."

"Are you blessed?"

"Oh, I'm blessed."

"Are you blessed?"

"Oh, I'm blessed beyond belief. I'm double-blessed. I'm triple blessed. Oh, I'm quadruple-blessed—"

Put a Christian like that in a hot situation with people, circumstances, or situations that aren't going their way. It's painful, it's unpleasant, and all this stuff comes out. God deals with us in order to get that stuff out of us. He's not dealing with us because He's trying to punish us. He wants what is inside of us to come streaming out. His hope and prayer is that, when we see it, we say, "Gah! That's gross! Is that stuff still in me? I thought I had dealt with that. Lord, help me get this out of my life." If we repent and turn, He'll set us free from it. That is His hope; that is His prayer.

I just hope you're not getting offended by this message on offenses. There is another story about offense in Matthew 11:2-6.

When John, who was in prison, heard about the deeds of the Messiah, he sent his disciples to ask him, "Are you the one who is to come, or should we expect someone else?"

Jesus replied, "Go back and report to John what you hear and see: The blind receive sight, the lame walk, those who have leprosy are cleansed, the deaf hear, the dead are raised, and the good news is proclaimed to the poor. Blessed is anyone who does not stumble [take offense] on account of me."

"Are you saying, Myles, that John the Baptist was offended?"

Yes, that's exactly what I'm saying. Why would John the Baptist be offended? I'm not sure; Scripture doesn't really tell us. But you can guess at it. I think it might be that things did not turn out exactly the way John the Baptist thought they were going to. I mean, who better to be Jesus' number two man? His wasn't an immaculate conception, but it was a pretty special birth. He is the one who prepared the way for Jesus. Even though it's a bit of speculation, there might have been something there.

"Well, I just can't believe that John the Baptist would be offended."

Well, then don't believe it. But think about what Jesus said to him. Why did He say, "Blessed is anyone who does not stumble on account of me," (Matt. 11:6). Do you think the Lord knew something? And think about John's question. "Are you the one who is to come, or should we expect someone else?" (Matt. 11:3). Now, excuse me. Wasn't John the Baptist the one who baptized Jesus in the River Jordan? Wasn't he the one who saw the Holy Spirit land on Jesus in the form of a dove? Wasn't he the one who stood in the river with Jesus and heard the Father's voice speak from heaven? Wasn't that the same John the Baptist? Yes, it was. Do you think, just over a quarter and a cup of coffee, maybe he knew who Jesus was? Absolutely. Then why was he asking the question?

Jesus' answer to him was essentially this: the only thing that's important is God's will being done. It is important that the Kingdom of God advances; the part you play in is not.

Oh, this is so big. This is such a big problem in churches all over the world.

"Well I've been in church here for years. I thought by now I'd be a Life Group leader. I thought by now I'd be on the worship team. Why'd they pick him? I could have done that! I've got more background. I know more Scripture. Why'd they pick her? I've got more gifting than her."

Jesus says the only thing that's important is that the Kingdom of God is advancing. Our particular place in it is not important. How many kingdoms are we building here? There is only one worth building.

There is another example of offense in 1 Samuel 30:1-6.

David and his men reached Ziklag on the third day. Now the Amalekites had raided the Negev and Ziklag. They had attacked Ziklag and burned it, and had taken captive the women and everyone else in it, both young and old. They killed none of them, but carried them off as they went on their way.

When David and his men reached Ziklag, they found it destroyed by fire and their wives and sons and daughters taken captive. So David and his men wept aloud until they had no strength left to weep. David's two wives had been captured—Ahinoam of Jezreel and Abigail, the widow of Nabal of Carmel. David was greatly distressed because the men were talking of stoning him; each one was bitter in spirit because of his sons and daughters. But David found strength in the Lord his God.

These people were grieved, and they were unhappy. Things hadn't turned out very well for them, so their first thought was to find the leader and stone the guy. As long as I have spent in leadership, that sounds awfully familiar. Leaders, this one is especially for you. One of the things you have to understand as a leader is this: the greater the scope and impact of your ministry, the greater the offenses coming your way will be.

I remember one morning, years ago, I was spending time in my office, praying and complaining. Have you ever complained to God? I know I'm in good company because about a quarter of the whole book of Psalms is just David complaining. On this particular morning I was just being open with God. It's not like He is surprised when I share something that's on my heart with Him. He already knows it's there. So I was just being honest with Him, saying, "God, I'm unhappy."

"What are you unhappy about today, Myles?"

"I'm unhappy because I'm catching all of this flak. I'm taking arrows in my back for stuff I didn't even do—conversations I never had, meetings I didn't make it to, and barbecues I supposedly went to with people I've never met before."

I told Him about all the stuff that was happening to me. I was really unhappy because the things I was facing weren't fair or right. I cried out to the Lord; I put it all out there before Him and waited for an answer, but I didn't get one. Nothing. So I went on with my day. About four or five days later I was working, and all of a sudden I got a little prompt from the Holy Spirit. He said, "Google some of the well-known ministers."

"Lord, was that You?"

"Google some of the well-known ministers. Men that you know and respect."

I've travelled with some well-known ministers. Been with a lot of them. I started googling, and what I found blew me away. Almost every single person I searched had multiple websites—not web pages, whole websites—that were all about twisting their words and tearing them down. Whole websites! The Lord said to me, "The more influence you have and the greater your sphere of ministry, the more opportunity you're going to have to be offended."

Listen, God has to deliver us from our offenses so that He can use us. If we are easily offended, He will not be able to use us fully. Here's the good news: God doesn't flunk you out. If you are offended, He is not going to expel you. But He will not promote you to the next class until you pass the test.

We're going to look at one last example of offense in Genesis 4:2-1.

> "Now Abel kept flocks, and Cain worked the soil. In the course of time Cain brought some of the fruits of the soil as an offering to the Lord. And Abel also brought an offering—fat portions from some of the firstborn of his flock. The Lord looked with favor on Abel and his offering, but on Cain and his offering he did not look with favor. So Cain was very angry, and his face was downcast."

Why didn't the Lord look with favor on Cain's offering? Because he brought it in the course of time. It wasn't animals vs. grains because God tells us clearly later in His Word that grain offerings are just as acceptable as animal offerings. What happened, then? Abel brought the first of his produce. Cain brought his offering in the course of time, when he got around to it.

Cain's anger is a classic case of offense. Have you ever knocked yourself out doing something, but nobody recognized or appreciated any of the time, effort, and energy that you gave? And maybe the situation was even worse than that because somebody else took credit for all your hard work. Ever been there?

Cain was offended because his best efforts, in his own mind, were not appreciated, valued, or recognized. One thing that's very clear from the rest of the story is this: Abel didn't coddle his offended brother. Abel didn't say, "Oh, poor you. Man, you have a right to be offended. I understand; I'm with you, bro." If he had said those things, I don't think Cain would have risen up to kill him. Abel didn't coddle his brother; he went out there and spoke truth to Cain. And because Abel spoke truth, Cain rose up and struck him.

This is happening in churches all over the world. A brother or sister in the Lord tries to come and speak truth to someone, and the receiver of truth rises up against the person who spoke the truth. God shows us the consequence of this in Genesis 4:12, "When you work the ground, it will no longer yield its crops for you." Let me help you understand what that means. When you are offended, God says your work will no longer be fruitful. You're going to spend just as much time and energy doing it, but there's not going to be any fruit because God will not bless it.

In the rest of Genesis 4:12, God says Cain will be "a restless wanderer on the earth." Offended people cannot have lasting relationships because of the offenses in their hearts. They go from relationship to relationship, sometimes even from church to church. Why? Because they have an offense in their heart. Every time something reminds them of their past, they're gone.

"You know what? I'm getting my stuff, and, by God, I'm moving on. I don't have to take this. I'm gonna go somewhere else."

Usually everything is wonderful in the new place for six months to a year. Then something else happens.

"Well, I'm getting my stuff and I'm going over to *this* church. And then I'm going to *this* church. By God, I'm not taking this. Jesus, rapture me out of here because I can't get along with anybody!"

They become a Christian vagabond with no real home and no impact in the world.

In Revelation 3:18, Jesus says to His church, "Buy from me gold refined in the fire." Refined gold doesn't have any impurities in it. It is very soft, very pliable, and not at all corrosive. It is pure gold. The other impure elements added into gold make it hard, not pliable, and more corrosive.

Here Jesus is saying, "Buy from me gold refined in the fire." Can you see the parallel there? Our hearts are like pure gold; they are soft, they are pliable, and they are tender. God can mold them and shape them. But when we allow impurities to come in, they mess everything up. Hebrews 3:13 says our hearts are hardened by the deceitfulness of sin. Perhaps no other sin issue is as deceitful as offenses because when we are offended, we always feel that we are justified. We are deceived into believing we have a right to be offended, to be upset, or to be angry. If we don't deal with offenses, they are going to harden our hearts and open the door for other things to come into our lives. We're going to bite into that scandalon and find ourselves in a pit.

1 Peter 1:6-7 says, "In all this you greatly rejoice, though now for a little while you may have had to suffer grief in all kinds of trials. These have come so that the proven genuineness of your faith—of greater worth than gold, which perishes even though refined by fire—may result in praise, glory and honor when Jesus Christ is revealed."

God allows—sometimes even causes—offenses in our life, and those offenses act like a refiner's fire. In Malachi we get a picture of God as a refiner, a smelter of silver, and it's a picture of Him over our lives. Do you know how silver was refined in Bible times? They would put impure silver in a big, tall bowl, and then they would heat that bowl up so all the impurities would bubble up to the surface. The refiner would sit over it and use a long, skinny spoon to skim the impurities off the top. Then he would heat it up some more, more impurities would come, and he would skim them off and throw them away. And then he would do it again. And again. His job was not finished until he could lean over the bowl, look into the pure silver, and see his reflection *perfectly*.

That's God. That's the way He works in our lives. He heats things up, impurities come to the surface, and He skims them off. He heats our lives up, issues come bubbling up that we didn't know were in there, and He takes them away. His work is not finished until He can lean over, look into our lives, and see His reflection clearly.

There's an interesting story in 2 Samuel 2. If you read it, which I encourage you to do, you will find the house of David competing against the house of Saul. There is a major battle between the two. In the story David and his mighty warriors find Abner in their midst. Abner is the head warrior of the competing tribe, the house of Saul. David's warriors take off after Abner, thinking this is their chance to kill him. One of David's mighty men, Azahel, was said to be as fleet as a gazelle. Azahel outran all of David's warriors, and he closed in on Abner. He closed the distance while the other warriors got further and further behind. Azahel finally caught Abner, but Abner turned around and killed him on the spot. The other warriors pursued Abner until they came upon the body of Azahel on the ground. When they saw his corpse, they stopped, turned, and went back home.

I read that story years ago and felt that God was trying to say something to me through it. I read it again and again, six to eight times. I just kept reading it, and the Lord would still prompt me to read it again. No matter how many times I read it, I still wasn't getting what God was trying to speak.

I read the story and asked God what He was trying to tell me two or three times almost every single day for several weeks. Then one morning it just clicked within me. The Spirit of God said to me so clearly, "Myles, what's going to make you stop? What's going to make you stop pursuing that which I have called you to pursue? What's going to make you stop?"

Many years ago Sallie and I were sitting in the hospital of Wharton, Texas. Our fourth child had just been born, a little baby boy. We were celebrating, and I had just come back to the recovery room to be with

Sallie. Then the OB-GYN and the pediatrician came in together with long faces. *Uh oh, this doesn't look good.*

They told us that our son had Down syndrome, holes in his heart, and breathing problems. They said in order for him to survive, he would burn more calories than he could possibly take in, so he would continue to lose weight until he died. And that was only if nothing else killed him first. This was their advice to us that day: "I know this is horrible, but you should just take him home. Try not to get too attached to him because he won't be here in thirty days, max."

Let me tell you, when you hit moments like that in your life, the devil is not quiet. He sidles up next to you and says, "Ohhh. All those sacrifices for all those years. All the things you walked away from in business. All the money you turned down. All of the crap you've had to put up with for all the things you've done. All the times that you've been away from your wife, been away from your children. And this is what you get."

I grabbed Sallie's hand and said, "You know what? Here's what the devil is telling me right now. He's speaking loud and clear. And I want to tell you something, and I'm gonna say it to him right now." I just stood there, with nobody else in the room, and I said, "Devil, let me tell you something. If you think this is gonna slow me down, you better guess again. You have seriously misjudged me. You think that you're gonna knock me out of the saddle? It's going to take more than this. If you think this is gonna slow me down, guess what. I'm riding even faster than I've ever ridden before. I am going after this thing with even greater passion."

Through the years, when different people have shot all kinds of arrows in my back, accused me of things that I never said, and imputed motives to me that I've never even dreamed of in my life, I just stop and say, "Devil, is that all you got?" I do! I like speaking to him. "Is that all you got? Is that it? You got nothing! You think that's gonna slow me down? You think *that* is gonna keep me from what God is calling me to do? You think that is gonna knock me out of my destiny? Oh, you are *CLUELESS*! Ha! You are clueless! It's gonna take a whole lot more than that to knock me out of my saddle."

When unpleasant situations and circumstances come into my life and tempt me into offense—when that scandalon, that bloody piece of bait, is hanging there calling me—I just stop and say no. It's going to take more than that to keep me out of my destiny.

How about you? What's it going to take to knock you out of the saddle? What's it going to take to cause you to slow down? To back up? I can tell you one thing that will do that to you: offenses. Don't take the bait. Don't allow offenses in your life. Drive a stake in the ground today and say, "Never again." This could be a life-changing moment for you. That's not an exaggeration. If you become offense-proof in your life, you will find so much freedom, and one of the devil's main ploys to keep you from becoming who God has called you to be will now be gone.

A POVERTY SPIRIT

The spirit of poverty is a key issue in the Church. Part of the reason it is so key is that when most people hear or see the term *poverty spirit*, they think it doesn't apply to them. Why? Because their minds immediately jump to money. You know what? You can be doing well financially and be absolutely broke in so many other ways. You can be broke emotionally. You can be broke relationally. You can be broke spiritually. The poverty spirit touches all aspects of our lives, not just our finances.

If you have been influenced by a poverty spirit, I want to help you identify that spirit in your life and break its power over you. I want you to be completely set free from the spirit of poverty so that you can walk into the fullness of what God has for you—not just in your finances, but in every single area of your life.

Let's start with a truth. Sometimes we don't know why we think the things we think, say the things we say, and do the things we do. Sometimes we have no clue where our thoughts, words, and actions come from. They can be caused by things others taught us in the past. They can come from the way we were raised. They can rise up from situations and life experiences we faced that influenced us. The problem is many times a spirit of poverty will come in behind those things and look for opportunities to influence the way we think and talk and live.

It is important for us all to identify the reasons behind our actions. We need to be aware of our habit patterns and behaviors because they are not always just normal. They don't always come from, "That's just the way I am." The things we do automatically, whether we see the reason for them or not, are most often influenced by external things—events, people, and sometimes spirits.

Let me give you a simple example. I remember going over to my grandmother's house on Breezy Lane many times as a child. When we would visit in the dead of summer, it would be hotter inside her house than it was outside. We always asked her, "Nani, why don't you turn the AC on? You've just barely cracked a couple of windows. It's a furnace in here!"

"Well, honey, you just never know. You just don't know what's going to happen out there in the world."

"But you got money in the bank."

"Yeah, but you just never know."

My grandmother lived through the Great Depression. That event influenced her in ways she was not even really aware of. She would not do some things as simple as turning on the air conditioner because she subconsciously feared an experience in her past. Silent motivations often get behind the things we do. They manipulate us and pull us and push us in ways we are not even aware of.

In Luke 9:51-55, the Bible tells the story of Jesus going into a town. He sends a couple of His disciples ahead to let the people of the town know He is coming. When the town hears that Jesus is coming, they tell His disciples to keep Him away. They had heard of Jesus and did not want Him in their city. The disciples return and tell Jesus the news. Then they say, "We've got the perfect plan, Jesus. Let's call down fire from heaven and consume this whole village." Sounds pretty biblical to me. But Jesus tells them, "You don't know what spirit you are of," (9:55, NASB).

He didn't tell them they had bad thinking. He didn't scold them for screwed-up theology. He didn't encourage them to have a bit more mercy in their lives. He told them they were being influenced by a spirit, and they did not even know it.

The spirit of poverty can affect communities, cultures, and whole nations. It can affect entire churches, and it can certainly affect individual Christians. So let's define it. If you look up *poverty* in the dictionary, you'll probably find a definition like this: "A lack of money, a lack of resources, inferiority, or poorness." It is not just a lack of money or resources; poverty includes inferiority and poorness. *Impoverish* is another word that goes right along with poverty. It means, "To cause to become poor, or to exhaust the natural strength or fertility of soil." In other words, impoverished soil is no longer as productive as it was designed by God to be. It is no longer able to produce the fruit God designed it to produce. When you and I are impoverished—affected by a poverty spirit—we no longer produce the fruit God Himself designed us to produce.

In the beginning, God spoke to Adam and Eve and told them this: "Be fruitful," (Gen. 1:22). That was not just a good suggestion. It was a command from God. God commands us to do the same. In John 15:8, Jesus says, "This is to my Father's glory, that you bear much fruit." He is not glorified when you and I are doing okay. He is not glorified when we are surviving, just getting by. We glorify Jesus when we produce much fruit. The more fruit you produce, the more He is glorified. So many of us need to understand this and declare it over our lives. I am going to lay hold of that truth. I am going to grab it. I am going to appropriate it for my life. I am not just surviving. I am not just getting by, bumping along, or making a living. God has more for me and my life than that.

God commands us to produce much fruit. Whatever He has called you to be and do, you can certainly be and do. God will never command you to do something you cannot do. So if God tells us to be fruitful, then you know what? You can be fruitful.

"Well, I just don't understand how to be fruitful right now."

I think God understands better than you do. Have you asked Him about it?

"Well, you don't know my situation."

I think God knows your situation better than you know it. God says no matter where you are, no matter what circumstances you have been through, and no matter what you are going through today, be fruitful in the midst of it. Be productive.

There are seven different characteristics of a poverty spirit. These seven characteristics are meant to help you recognize a poverty spirit influencing your life or a certain area of your life. Use these characteristics to examine your life and identify areas where you are living under the spirit of poverty. Recognizing it is the first step to experiencing freedom.

1. Inferiority

You are not good enough.

That is not true, but if you believe it is, then it will become true. That statement can easily become a self-fulfilling prophecy in your life.

I know many different people who are very successful. I know many different people who are doing very well financially. I know many different people who are incredibly smart, even brilliant. All of these people seem incredibly successful to everyone around them, but I have had the opportunity to counsel a lot of people like this and get behind the scenes with them. Do you know what I have found? Most of them are absolutely controlled by a sense of inferiority. They are ruled by it. For many, the inferiority complex is what drove them to put on a façade of success in the first place.

What about people who are just full of themselves? Very few people are actually just purely arrogant. Most arrogant people are just putting up a false façade to cover a tremendous lack of self-confidence and a festering wound of inferiority.

Proverbs 23:7 says, "For as he thinks within himself, so he is," (NASB). The way we see ourselves is the way we will tend to walk out life. I believe I am this way; therefore, I act and think and talk and walk this way. It will become reality whether it is true or not. I believe I am inferior, therefore I act and think and talk and walk like I am lesser.

Many of us pick this inferiority thing up early on in our lives because of a lack of affirmation from our parents. That is such a problem. If you are a parent, let me say this to you today: make sure that you give your children plenty of affirmation.

"Well, my children are gone out of my household."

And that changes what? Give your children plenty of affirmation.

"Well, I'll just pick it up with my grandchildren."

That is good. But make sure you give your children plenty of affirmation. They might be young; they might be teenagers. They might be still in your household; they might be gone. They might be fifty years old! It does not matter; you can still give them affirmation. They still need it.

Become encouragement merchants. Be like a barge going down the river, packed full of those big metal shipping containers filled to overflowing with encouragement. Stop regularly and drop off encouragement. Dock often at the lives of your children and unload some encouragement.

2. Perceived Inadequacies

The second characteristic of a poverty spirit is perceived inadequacies. Sound like the same thing as number one? They may be similar, but they are not the same thing. Perceived inadequacies specifically result in the inability to see yourself as a resource to meet needs outside of your own.

When we do not see anything of real value in ourselves, we will not give anything to other people. This is one of the biggest things that keeps people from working or serving in the church. They simply believe they do not have anything to give.

"Well, you just don't understand, Pastor. I'm on the receiving end."

Well, I understand the difference between the Sea of Galilee and the Dead Sea. The Sea of Galilee receives water in and gives water out, and it is fresh and full of life. The Dead Sea receives water in from the exact same source, but it has no outlet. That's what makes it dead.

If you want to be full of the life of God, you not only need to be a receiver, you need to be a giver. And being a giver starts with seeing yourself as having something of value that God Himself has put inside of you. If you do not believe that, you will not develop yourself. I have seen this with so many people. They just do not invest in themselves. They never develop the different areas of their lives because they don't see the point. If you see nothing of value in yourself, then you see nothing to develop.

I have seen people who do not work at all towards developing interpersonal relationship skills. They don't know how to communicate with other people. They have not learned how to build friendships. They have no conversation or communication skills. When asked about it, one of the reasons they give most often is, "That's just not the way God made me." Nonsense. The truth is they do not believe they have anything in them worth giving out. If they saw and understood the beautiful, powerful, wonderful things God put in them, they would see themselves as worth developing. They would make sure those amazing things got communicated out to others.

3. Limited Vision

Some people always seem to be a day late and a dollar short, and not one of them ever knows why. People like this always point to a lot of superficial reasons why they come up short, but the root issue goes way beyond any of those surface-level problems. After decades of experience counseling people like this, I can tell you this mindset always comes from something much, much deeper. Most of the time it is simply this: they have no vision for more.

People like this are just trying to get by. They are just trying to make it. They would never try to have a lot so that they could give and be a conduit of blessing to others. Through that limited vision, they have invited a poverty spirit to work in their life. They are not moving into all God has planned for them; they are not receiving and walking in all of the blessings God has given them.

4. Hoarding Mentality

A hoarding mentality drives people to accumulate more than they need in the present. They hoard and accumulate things because they fear lack in the future.

Let me be clear; I am not talking anti-savings. It is wise to save. It is good to plan for retirement. The hoarding mentality takes the idea of saving and goes to the extreme. Have you ever met someone who just has all kinds of different stuff? They don't need it. They don't use it. They will never wear it again. But they can't get rid of it.

"But I might need it someday."

You have not needed it for years. Besides, you ain't never gonna to be able to wear that pair of pants again. Give the stuff away. People who understand the truth do not need to hoard things. God will bless you. He has taken care of you, and He always will. Be a generous person and give the stuff away.

"Oh, well, I'm just a hoarder. That's the way I've always been."

Then give the stuff away! That is how you get free; you force yourself to do the exact opposite. Give stuff away. And I am not just talking about stuff that you don't need anymore. Give stuff that is important to you away.

I can still remember the very first time that God told my family to give one of our cars away.

"Oh, that's nice. You got a new car and passed your old one on to someone else."

No, no, no. We gave it away and became a one-car family. Sallie would drop me off at work, and I would borrow my secretary's car if I had to run errands or go see a client because I did not have a car. I got questions all the time.

"Why don't you have a car?"

"Because we gave ours away."

"Why on earth would you do that?"

"Because God told us to."

There was no other reason why we would do it, that's for doggone sure. At that point in my life, it was the nicest car I had ever owned by far. The one we gave away was much nicer than the one we kept.

You have to learn how to get this truth in your life. It is so easy to look around at generous people who are well off and think it is just so easy for them to give. It is so easy to think they are just not where you are and that is why they give. Listen, I *was* where you are when I got these things in my life, and that is why I am here today. Most people who are successful today understood these principles when they were not successful, and that brought them to where they are now.

Proverbs 11:25 says, "A generous person will prosper; whoever refreshes others will be refreshed." A hoarding mentality is evidence of a poverty spirit.

5. Insecurity About the Future

Are you always anxious in the present because you fear the future? That is evidence of a poverty spirit. Even when things are going really well, some people cannot seem to really enjoy life. Why not? Because they are certain the good things will not last. They are just waiting for the other shoe to drop.

"I mean, I'm blessed right now. But I know I'm probably going to fail. Just a matter of time. I'm probably going to lose all of this. I know I'm not a perfect person. I did this and this in my past, and I know I'm not doing everything correctly now. So sooner or later it will all catch up to me, and God is going to punish me."

Whoa. Read your Bible, child of God. God does say there is something back there behind you that you cannot outrun. No matter how fast you run or which direction you take, it will catch you. It will overtake you. It will overwhelm you. Do you know what Scripture says that thing is? It is not your past; it is the blessing of God. The blessing of God is the only thing back there behind you, and it is going to overtake you.

"I think God told me to do this, but I haven't done it yet. That's why all these bad things are going to happen to me."

That is absolute nonsense. That is a poverty spirit making you fearful about your mistakes and all of the bad things that are going to come because of them. Insecurity about the future is evidence of a poverty spirit.

6. Hopelessness

The word *hopelessness* is not even in the Bible. We serve the God of all hope. Hope gives you something to anticipate. Something to look forward to. As the old saying says, "Hope is the music of the future, and faith is dancing to it now."

We should, as children of God, have things that we are excited about. Things may be going poorly. Things may be going okay. Things may be going great. It matters not; there are always better days ahead. I believe that. Do you?

The more a poverty spirit influences your thinking, the more difficult it will be for you to look to the future optimistically. The more a poverty spirit influences your thinking, the less excited you will be for what is ahead in your life. That goes for the short-term and the long-term. But there is always reason for hope.

"Well, Pastor Myles, you don't know my situation."

I may not, but I do know the situation of Lazarus. He was dead, and he had been dead for four days. The Bible says that he was already starting to stink. Jesus told them to roll the stone away from the tomb, and the disciples said, "Uh, Jesus . . . he's been dead for four days. He stinketh." Your situation might be bad, but is it worse than that? All Jesus did was speak three words, and everything changed.

It doesn't matter what your situation is. When God enters it, everything can change in a moment. It doesn't always happen in the blink of an eye; it could take a long haul of walking with God faithfully through situations that He wants you to learn from. Regardless of how God works, there is no reason for any child of God to ever come into hopelessness.

There is no such thing as a hopeless situation. It may be an incredibly difficult situation. It may be an incredibly painful situation. But hopelessness shouldn't ever be on the table. If you are a born-again believer, your Father specializes in impossible situations. That is when He does His best work. He loves it. When everyone else is saying something could never happen, that is when He loves to step in and change things dramatically.

As Christians, we need to get this. There are people who are going through difficult things. There are people who are deep into hopelessness, but we have good news. And the good news is not simply that there is a ticket out of hell and into heaven. The good news is that God is for us. God has a wonderful future for us. Jeremiah 29:11 says, "'For I know the plans I have for you,' declares the LORD, 'plans to prosper you and not to harm you, plans to give you hope and a future.'"

7. Victim Mentality

I can tell you honestly, I have never watched an entire episode of Dr. Phil, not a single one. But someone told me about one episode because they had heard me speak about the victim mentality, and I went and watched the clip on YouTube. It was phenomenal. In the clip, Dr. Phil was talking about spousal abuse, and he started taking call-in questions from people. One woman called in and started talking about how she was a victim of spousal abuse. Then Dr. Phil asked her how long it had been going on. She told him fifteen years. Dr. Phil paused for a moment, then he said this: "Ma'am, let me tell you something. You're not a victim. You're a volunteer."[1]

You were a victim the first time it happened, maybe even the second or third. After that, you were no longer a victim. You're a volunteer.

There are a lot of volunteers in the world today. They may have gone through difficult things in life that were out of their control, but now they are volunteering to let the devil continue to beat them up in the same way over and over and over. They choose to walk in a defeated mentality.

A victim mentality keeps people from seeking solutions to the problems that they face. This mentality says, "I'm a victim. I am not responsible for my reactions. Somebody else did things to put me in this spot, and somebody else is going to have to pull me out because I am not responsible for this."

Have bad things happened to you? Have bad things been done to you? Get in line.

"That's not very merciful, Pastor Myles."

I disagree; that is one of the most merciful things I can say to victims right now. Get in line. You are not unique. Heads up: this is a messed-up, jacked-up world we live in. It is not the world God designed. It is a sin-soaked world where—newsflash—bad things happen to good people. In fact, bad things happen to all people. Bad things will happen to us and even worse things will be done to us, but we always choose how we respond. You do not have to be a victim.

How do you stop? Refuse to be a victim anymore. Rise up in the strength of Christ and declare, "I am tired of this. I am done with this. I am not living this way anymore. I will overcome." Make a decision in God to say, "I am not a victim."

When you believe that you are a victim of something or someone, you let that event or that person dictate and control the way you live. And if you let it continue, you let the control continue. Stop living in reaction to the things that happen to you; live in the moment with God. There is always an excuse for why people do what they do.

"Well, my daddy—"

Whoa, whoa, whoa. Don't give me your daddy story. You are going to have to sell that somewhere else because I'm not buying. Are you a child of God? Then you are filled with the Holy Spirit. You are filled with the very life of God. You can be anything God destined you to be and do anything He destined you to do. You are not trapped by your past. You can take one giant step out, never turn back, and go on to be everything God called you to be.

"Well, I screwed up. I missed my chance."

That is a lie from the pit of hell. You may have messed up. You may have missed something, but you can start fresh because God has new things for you. He does not take those things, throw them away, and say, "Now you can't have them because you were so bad back then." That is nonsense. God is not the God of second chances. I have heard that so many times, but it is just not true. God is the God of 10 millionth chances. He always has a fresh start for you.

"Well, my parents just didn't show me any affection."

Then why don't you make a commitment to show affection to your kids?

"Well, my parents didn't encourage me."

Then learn from that. Realize the importance of encouragement and make sure that you give it to your kids.

"Well, my parents didn't teach me all the things they should have." The answer is the same every time. Make a commitment to not do the same thing to others; choose to do something different in your life.

If you break the victim mentality, sometimes hard things from the past can even be beneficial to you. I have an incredible marriage. I have an incredible wife; that is why I have an incredible marriage. One of the reasons she is so incredible is because her parents divorced when she was nine years old. Every time I share that, I always get the same response. People respond with pity, and speak of her like she is a victim of what happened. She is absolutely not. She learned how hurtful, painful, and damaging divorce is. I know one thing: my wife is going to do everything she can to make sure we have an incredible marriage, and I am with her on that. Every time there is a marriage conference available, we go. We find the money somewhere. It doesn't matter if we have to eat beans and tortillas until the end of the month; we are going to go to that thing. That was from day one in our marriage. Bad things can turn into good in your life if you let them.

You were not born to be a loser. I do not care what you have heard or what has been said to you. I do not care what you believe in your own mind. It is absolutely not true. If you have it tattooed on your arm, get it removed. You were not born to be a loser. When you were born again, everything changed. God took the old away. He made things new and predestined you for success. You did not just get a ticket to heaven; you got a gigantic storehouse of all kinds of other things that come with salvation. At your new birth, God predestined you to be a winner in every single area of your life.

There is a powerful story in 1 Kings 17:1-18.

Now Elijah the Tishbite, from Tishbe in Gilead, said to Ahab, "As the Lord, the God of Israel, lives, whom I serve, there will be neither dew nor rain in the next few years except at my word."

Then the word of the Lord came to Elijah: "Leave here, turn eastward and hide in the Kerith Ravine, east of the Jordan. You will drink from the brook, and I have directed the ravens to supply you with food there."

So he did what the Lord had told him. He went to the Kerith Ravine, east of the Jordan, and stayed there. The ravens brought him bread and meat in the morning and bread and meat in the evening, and he drank from the brook.

Some time later the brook dried up because there had been no rain in the land. Then the word of the Lord came to him: "Go at once to Zarephath in the region of Sidon and stay there. I have directed a widow there to supply you with food." So he went to Zarephath. When he came to the town gate, a widow was there gathering sticks. He called to her and asked, "Would you bring me a little water in a jar so I may have a drink?" As she was going to get it, he called, "And bring me, please, a piece of bread."

"As surely as the Lord your God lives," she replied, "I don't have any bread—only a handful of flour in a jar and a little olive oil in a jug. I am gathering a few sticks to take home and make a meal for myself and my son, that we may eat it—and die."

Elijah said to her, "Don't be afraid. Go home and do as you have said. But first make a small loaf of bread for me from what you have and bring it to me, and then make something for yourself and your son. For this is what the Lord, the God of Israel, says: 'The jar of flour will not be used up and the jug of oil will not run dry until the day the Lord sends rain on the land.'"

She went away and did as Elijah had told her. So there was food every day for Elijah and for the woman and her family. For the jar of flour was not used up and the jug of oil did not run dry, in keeping with the word of the Lord spoken by Elijah.

Some time later the son of the woman who owned the house became ill. He grew worse and worse, and finally stopped breathing. She said to Elijah, "What do you have against me, man of God? Did you come to remind me of my sin and kill my son?"

The two main characters in this story paint a very powerful picture. It is a contrast between someone with a poverty spirit and someone without a poverty spirit. The widow very clearly represents what it is like to have a poverty spirit, whereas Elijah represents a Christian who believes God will always provide for every need. In other words, Elijah very clearly represents what it is like to not have a poverty spirit. Understanding that picture and contrast, it is worth it to look closely at these two and their words and actions.

The word of God tells us in the New Testament that Elijah was a man just like you and me (James 5:17). He was not a superhuman being or anything special; he was flesh and blood. There were no telephone booths or colorful tights involved. He struggled with doubt. He struggled with fear. He struggled with disappointment and rejection. But he did not struggle with a poverty spirit.

Elijah demonstrated two specific character traits in this story that we can learn from. These two traits are critically important to breaking free from a poverty spirit.

Number one: he was not picky. He was not picky about the way God provided for him. He did not care what the immediate source of his supply was because he knew ultimately everything came to him from God. Elijah was confident that God was providing for him, and he had an attitude that said, "God can provide for me any way He wants to."

I know a lot of Christians who are not like that. They are always looking for a "Red Sea" experience. They want God to part the waters or maybe turn the sky purple. They are looking for some huge sign from God, and until they see it they will not believe God is at work in their lives.

God definitely works in big ways sometimes. You know the stories—somebody in financial need receives a $100,000 check in the mail from a distant relative. Praise God. That check was from God, but He does not always work that way. In fact, He often works in very practical, simple ways. What about the other people in financial need who learned principles from the Word of God, applied them faithfully, and slowly walked out of debt and into financial prosperity? We all identify that as good, but we don't identify that as God. That story is just as much the work of God as the other.

Take God's provision the way He gives it to you. Stop looking for somebody else's experience. Walk in your own experience with God. Thank Him for the process whether it is a short process of receiving or a long process of teaching and developing. It may be hard to see it, but those who walk out the long process often end up in better places. Those who run through the short process just get a check in the mail; those who faithfully walk the long process get character and wisdom that help them replicate success over and over again in their lives.

There is one other point in this story that it is important not to miss. Ravens were unclean animals. We are talking about Old Testament times here. Jews did not eat ravens. They did not touch ravens. They had nothing to do with ravens because ravens were unclean animals. Yet God himself provided for Elijah through those unclean animals. That may not seem like a big deal to us, but to a Jew that would have been shocking.

Here is the takeaway: God does not always send an angelic messenger. Religious people often get hung up on this. Many years ago, Oral Roberts made a big announcement to the people in his ministry. By mentioning him I am not endorsing him or all of his teaching, but the story is valuable. Roberts announced that he had just received an enormous check, to the tune of millions, from a very wealthy gentleman. But the gentlemen who gave the check owned a big horse racing track, so it was gambling money. Christians around the world began to condemn Roberts mercilessly for accepting the check because it was dirty gambling money. When that happened, at least five or six people in the church I was pastoring came to me and said, "You wouldn't take that money, would you?"

I said, "Oh, you bet I would."

"You're joking. You're not serious."

I said, "Oh no. I'm dead serious."

So many Christians have an Old Testament mentality rather than a New Testament mentality. In the Old Testament, if unclean things touched you, they would make you unclean. In the New Testament, Jesus is the model. Jesus touched unclean things and made them clean. Jesus touched lepers. He didn't become unclean or get leprosy; the lepers became clean. Jesus touched dead people. They came to life. That is the model for you and me.

"You wouldn't take that money."

Sure I would.

"That's dirty money!"

Not when it hits my hand. When it hits my hand, it turns righteous. Then I take it and put it into the Kingdom of God.

If you are reading this and having a hard time with it, let me just ask you to do one thing. When someone gives you a check for a million dollars of "dirty money" and you don't want to take it, just give them my name. Tell them where they can find me.

Throughout the Bible, God used unholy people to accomplish his purposes. King Artaxerxes of Persia gave Nehemiah all the money and resources he needed to rebuild Jerusalem. Artaxerxes was an idol-worshiping cat. He was an evil person, a heathen, but he funded the rebuilding of Jerusalem. Later on King Cyrus, another evil outsider, gave the money and resources needed to rebuild the Temple.

Things like this happened again and again in Scripture. Rahab was a prostitute in Jericho who helped the Israelites take down the city. She gave the Israelite spies inside information, hid them from the authorities, and let them out of the city. If she hadn't helped, they probably would have been captured, and the whole thing might have taken an ugly turn from there.

God uses all kinds of means to bring us blessing in our lives. Don't miss the provision of God simply because it comes in a way you are not comfortable with.

Here is the second character trait of Elijah that we can learn from: he was open to change. If you are walking in God's ways and your brook dries up, do not panic. It may simply be God Himself moving you to something new and better. If you are not obeying God and your brook dries up, that is a different ballgame. In that case, repent, learn from your mistakes, and trust God to meet you in that place and take you forward. But if you are obeying God and your brook dries up, don't panic.

People with a poverty mindset respond with panic. Why? Because they see a disaster. People without a poverty spirit respond with peace. They do not see a disaster; they just see a change. It doesn't matter how bleak everything looks; they know when they walk with God, they can trust Him to provide. People with that trust don't see disaster in change; they see opportunity.

What about the widow? The widow was full of hopelessness. She had it in spades. When Elijah stepped onto the scene, her plan was to eat the last bit of food with her son and then die together. That was her vision for the future. Even after God provided for her miraculously, her trust vanished at the first sign of trouble. When her son stopped breathing, she immediately accused Elijah of staying with them simply to remind her of her sins and kill her son. Elijah prayed for the boy, and the boy was healed, but the widow's response had already revealed her heart.

The widow's hopelessness and response to trouble are evidence of a poverty spirit, but the most important evidence is this: she didn't see herself as a resource. This is such a problem. In 1 Kings 17:12, she tells Elijah, "I don't have any bread." Is that true? Technically yes. But a poverty spirit will always lead you to focus on what you do not have rather than what you do have. A poverty spirit leads you to hone in or lock in on anything and everything that you lack. I don't have this. I'm missing this. I don't have that.

Well, what *do* you have? Everybody has something. At the very least, everybody has experiences. It does not matter if your past is full of horrible mistakes; you can learn from all of them. Sometimes mistakes are better teachers than success. I know that is true in my life. Learning from mistakes is painful for a time, but you do not tend to repeat them, do you? At the very least, you also have gifts. Every one of us has gifts that God placed inside of us.

So here is the question. How do you see yourself?

"Well, I'm not good enough."

Really?

"I don't have an education."

Really? Is that what this is about? That's what is limiting you in your life? Is that what you believe?

"Well, I just don't have gifts."

You do. Don't buy into that.

If you believe you are in lack anywhere in your life, in many cases there is a poverty spirit working through those beliefs to push you, pull you, limit you, and restrict you. A poverty spirit wants to keep you from becoming who God destined you to be, doing the things that He created you to do, and experiencing the fullness of His blessings in your life. Ask the Lord to identify that spirit in your life and break its power. Don't keep carrying it with you. Leave it right where you are. Make a decision to believe in the abundance and provision of God, and walk in the fullness of what God has for you from this day forward.

EMBRACING CHANGE

How do you respond to change in your life? Change happens to everyone, but dealing with it can be a challenge. Some people are willing to change, and by that I mean they are willing to be dragged, kicking and screaming, into change. Others learn to actually embrace change. It is even possible to become a person who loves change.

In Isaiah 43:18-19, God says to His people, "Forget the former things; do not dwell on the past. See, I am doing a new thing! Now it springs up; do you not perceive it?" Saints, this verse implies a question. It's practically right there in the verse. Why on earth would anyone miss the new thing that God is doing? Why would a person not perceive, or see, the new thing that God Himself is doing in middle of his or her life? The answer is simple. People will miss the new things God wants to do in their lives if they do not heed the command in Isaiah 43:18—don't dwell on the past.

"Forget the former things," (43:18). If you don't do that, you will miss the new things God wants to do in your life. We tend to fixate on the past, and that causes us to miss the things God is saying and doing, present tense.

Are you tracking with me? Do you get that? If you are focused on the past, then you are going to miss the new thing God is doing in your life. This is so simple, but it's so profoundly true, and it happens to so, so many us all the time. I catch myself there all the time. I get hung up on and focused on the wrong things, and I miss the new things God wants to say to me. Even today, if I focus on the past, I will miss the thing that God is wanting to do in my life right now.

Years and years ago, Sallie and I spent some time in Moscow, Russia, ministering to a group of church leaders. We had one afternoon off, so we decided to go sightseeing. Our meetings were not very far from Red Square, so we walked down to see it. It was pretty incredible to think about all the tanks that used to roll through there every year, trying to intimidate the rest of the world.

We walked all around that very beautiful square, but over on one side of it was an ugly, little, brown, cube-like building. We weren't sure what it was, so we asked somebody. That person told us it was Lenin's tomb. We learned that you could actually go in there, so we got into a long line of people to go inside Lenin's tomb.

I remember I was laughing and talking as Sallie and I walked in, but one of the soldiers stepped in front of us and said, "*Quiet!*" We didn't know it was such a big deal. I mean, the guy was dead. I didn't think I was bothering him. But it was a big deal. It was *Lenin's tomb*.

We walked in there and filed past his body. Let me tell you, the guy had been dead for decades, but he looked like he had just died that morning. Why? Because every week they took him out and put more embalming fluid in him to keep him fresh-looking.

That strikes me as very similar to what a lot of us do with our pasts. We pump embalming fluid into them and revisit them all the time. In truth, we need to be cremating our pasts. I'm not just talking about the times we have failed, although we do need to burn and forget those. We need to burn even the places of past joy and success. Rejoice over those times and be encouraged by them, but then burn them and move on. If you are dwelling on any part of your past and not forgetting the former things—good or bad—then you will end up camping in one place, and you will miss the new thing God wants to do in your life today.

Have you ever been driving down the road a little over the speed limit, only to look over to the side and see you're passing a highway patrolman?

Now, of course this has never happened to me. I can't believe you would think I would do such a thing. I've just heard of people this has happened to; they've told me stories.

Do you know what I'm talking about? You're driving along and— oh dear. You see the patrolman. Your heart sinks. What do you typically do in that moment? You start looking intently in your rearview mirror. You're staring back, wondering if he is going to pull you over. But when you do that, you almost assure that he's going to turn his lights on and pull you over. Why? Not for speeding anymore, but for DWI. You were so focused on what was going on behind you that you started swerving all over the road.

We get so focused on what is behind us that we can't drive a straight line into our future. I have spent years and years and years in ministry, and I can tell you this: I have met so many, many people who, sadly, spend most of their lives looking in the rearview mirror. They spend their lives focused on what's behind them, worrying about what has already passed. Not a single one of them is driving a straight line into the future. In fact, most of them are standing dead still, and the emphasis is on dead. Their lives, their destinies, and their futures are all on hold.

In Deuteronomy 1:6, God says this to His people: "You have stayed long enough." Don't you love that? God didn't beat around the bush. He didn't give them a bunch of nice words. He just told them straight. "You have stayed long enough."

I wonder how many people God would love to say those exact same words to today. How long do you plan to stay here? How long are you going to camp? How long are you going to stay in this area of your marriage? How long are you going to stay in this area of parenting? How long are you going to stay at this level of training or education at work? How long are you going to stay at this level of spiritual growth? How long are you going to stay in this place of ministry? How long are you going to stay here? "You have stayed long enough," (Deut. 1:6). It's time to change. It's time to get up. It's time to advance.

Embracing change is a value of mine, and it is a value I have tried to instill in every organization I have ever been a part of. I want to be an individual who moves on. I want to be a part of a church that corporately moves on. And right now I want to share with you three simple keys to embracing change in your life. If you will take these keys and apply them to your life, they will change the direction and momentum of your life.

1. Don't stay in a rut.

Do you know what a rut is? A rut is a repeated, boring, and unrewarding activity. A rut is nothing more than a grave with both ends kicked out of it. That's all it is. I once saw a sign at the beginning of a dirt road out in the country. The sign said, "Pick your rut carefully. You're going to be in it for a long time." This is what happens in our lives. We get into ruts; we get into habit patterns in our thoughts and actions. Sometimes those habit patterns—those ruts—enslave us.

Many of us know the old saying, "Practice makes perfect." That's not actually true. I tell people this over and over because it is so important for us to understand. Practice does not make perfect. Practice makes permanent.

I played baseball from a young age all the way through college at the University of Texas. After just three or four days of practice at UT, I went out and bought a handball glove because I needed the extra padding inside the glove. My glove hand was turning black and blue from catching hundreds and hundreds of ground balls. It was brutal! I never knew somebody could hit you that many ground balls in a day. It was just over and over and over. The coaches hit ground ball after ground ball to you, and if you ever once did anything wrong, they would stop, call you over, and show you how to do it right. Then they would hit you more ground balls until you had done it over and over again the right way.

Practice doesn't make perfect. Practice makes permanent. If you do something the wrong way over and over, it just becomes permanently wrong. Golfers understand what I mean. If you practice a bad swing over and over, what do you get? You don't get perfect. You get a bad swing. Then you consistently hit big banana balls like I hit—the ones that go off into the woods. When I play golf, it's a lot less golf and a lot more nature walk.

Practice doesn't make perfect. I wish it did! It just makes permanent. That can be good, or that can be bad. Sometimes we do things over and over and over and end up in ruts—habit patterns that aren't good for us or for our lives. We need to diligently find the areas in our lives where we are in ruts, and we need to break out of them. Break free of those ruts. Begin to set new habit patterns in your life.

There is another way to stay out of ruts. It's very simple: do something new. Hello. That's some rocket science right there. Do something new. When was the last time you did something for the first time? Think about that for a minute. Don't hurry and read to the next point, think about it. If you can't think of anything, then you're in a rut.

If you are not embracing change and growing, then you are living in Boredomville. Boring people live in Boredomville. They have boring jobs, they have boring lives, and they go to boring churches. A lot of people in this world think Boredomville is the only place to live. They think it's the only place on Planet Earth, and that's just the way of life. Not so! I've got good news for you. There are lots of other places that you can live other than Boredomville, but there's a condition. To make it out of Boredomville, you have to be willing to do things you have never done before. You have to be willing to embrace change and get out of your rut.

If everything in this world is boring to you—your marriage, your job, your school, your life—then go home, look in the mirror, and say, "Hello, Mr. Boring." That is what makes boring jobs, boring marriages, and boring lives: boring people.

Oh, it's in the Church, too. We're not immune. God is the same yesterday, today, and forever, but I've got news for you. You are not God. He doesn't need to change, but you and I do. Let's be honest about it; the Church is terrible with this. When the doors open on Sunday morning, it's like the California Gold Rush. Got to go get my seat. I staked my claim to it. It's got my markers on it. And if there's ever somebody else sitting there, the question is this: what are you doing in *my* seat?

That's not the only way we resist change.

"Well, bless God, I only read the King James Version. If it was good enough for Paul, then it's good enough for me."

Really? I didn't know Paul was alive in 1611.

"Well, I only read the New American Standard Bible."

That's great. That happens to be my favorite, but I read them all. I like reading some of the different nuances that come out of the Greek and Hebrew words. If you only read one translation of the Bible, you miss out on that. Come on, don't get in a rut.

I went to a church a few years ago where everything seemed fine and normal until worship started.

The steps of a righteous man are ordered by the Lord.
[ting, ting, ting]
Ordered by the Lord
[ting, ting, ting]
Ordered by the Lord
[ting, ting, ting]

I was waiting for a dinosaur to come through the door because I must have parachuted into Jurassic Park.

I'm not trying to be unkind. But so many of us on the road of life get stuck in places that God intended for us to go *through*. They are not necessarily bad places. Some of them are good places that were meant to be a part of life and growth and development. But when we camp in places we were meant to go through, it becomes a problem.

Ladies usually like this message. Know why? Because most of them are married to big boys with bigger toys. Men who don't want to take responsibility or leadership are stuck in a place they were meant to go through. They want to stay in adolescence; they don't want to grow up and become real men.

The same thing happens with churches. I know a lot of churches and a lot of Christians in churches who get stuck in places God was trying to take them through. It was a great season. It was a wonderful thing. God was trying to put something amazing in the life of that church or in the lives of those Christians, but the tendency is to just camp there. God often has to tell us, "This isn't the destination point. I'm taking you through here because you need what's here for the future. I want you to get this, but this isn't the destination. I'm bringing you through here to another place."

This happens everywhere. Through the years I've had lots of different people tell me, "Myles, you've changed." Do you know what I say every single time? "Thank you!" Some of them didn't mean it as a compliment, and I knew it. I say thank you because I'm not going to let my life, my destiny, my future, and my growth get hijacked by somebody with an unbiblical, stale, moldy view of how I need to stay the same and be the same. I don't want to do that!

I want to give you some good counsel. This one's free, on the house: don't listen. Don't listen to every yo-yo that walks into your life with a word for you. Come on, be smarter than that. Before somebody speaks into your life, they need to meet three conditions. Number one, their lives must prove that they have a love for the Lord Jesus and His Church. Number two, their lives must prove that they love you. Number three, their lives must prove that they are going forward in building the Kingdom of God. This is how I have done things for many, many years. Once somebody meets those three criteria, my life is an open book, and my ears are open to them; tell me what you see. If they don't meet those criteria, then they might as well keep their words and advice to themselves.

I have listened to many people over the course of my life, and my life has been greatly enriched and challenged because of them. But I only listen to people who know me well. I don't listen to people looking into my life from the outside with a judgmental attitude, saying what they think without any information. The only people who have really spoken into my life already had their noses in my business; they knew what was going on, they knew my heart, they knew what I needed to do, and they were speaking boldly as a friend. I will always welcome that; I need that. Listening to people like that is the way to grow. Do you have that in your life?

Corporately, every Grace church has a strong desire and passion to grow and change. I have been very open about that for decades now, but there are still people who complain when there is change in the church. You think things are changing in Grace churches all the time? You're doggone right they are.

The gospel message is sacred. It cannot be tinkered with, messed with, changed, adulterated, or watered down. The message is sacred and unchanging, but nothing is sacred about the packaging that message comes in. If you feel like anything in the packaging is sacred, then you are religious. Get delivered from that. The packaging is not sacred. The Grace churches are going to embrace change. We don't change for change's sake, but we are constantly asking questions like these: What we can do to affect more people? What can we do to get more people in the doors? We don't just want to get bigger. We want more people here so that their lives can be touched and transformed by God! That's what we're all about. Nothing else.

Before we leave this issue of ruts, let me be clear on something. Don't confuse activity with accomplishment. Don't do that. Just because your wheels are spinning doesn't mean that you're going anywhere. If the scenery isn't changing, you aren't making progress. This is a key point because if your wheels are spinning without moving you forward, what's happening? You're just digging a deeper rut. Don't stay in a rut. Break out of your ruts.

2. Don't ask the dumb question.

Ecclesiastes 7:10, God says, "Do not say, why were the old days better than these? It is not wise to ask such questions." God just called that a dumb question. Don't ask it. That is a dumb way to think.

"Well, I remember the good old days when—"

Whoa! Stop. Don't go there. It's not wise to think that way.

Now, why would God say it's foolish for you and I to ask that kind of question and think that kind of way? Because He knows just a little bit about you and I. He knows the way we think. He knows our tendencies as human beings, and he understands what is going to happen when we go down that road. When we look at the past, we have a tendency to enlarge it and glorify it past what it was really like.

Have you ever gone back to your elementary school building as an adult? Did anything strike you about it? Man, I thought that playground was huge. It's a little, dinky thing. I got scared every time I went up the ladder on that slide. I could have fallen off of that thing and not broken anything. And the classrooms are so small. They seemed so big back then.

Why is that the case? Because when we look at things in the past, they tend to look bigger and better than they really were. When we go through something at a younger stage in our lives, things look bigger than they really are. And when we reminisce about the past, many times we add an unrealistic glow to the picture. Right? The truth is if you and I could get into a time machine and go back in time, we'd find that the places that were so big and so wonderful either shrank or never really existed in the first place.

It's not wise to ask such questions. It's not wise to think that way.

"Well, I remember, back in the beginning of GCF Wharton, how wonderful it was back there on Milam Street."

Really? Is that the way you remember it? With the floor caved in, the metal folding chairs around it in a circle, and the police tape woven through them so nobody would fall in the hole? With the white butcher tape and scotch tape covering the windows? Come on, we romanticize things. We really do.

"Oh, but the worship was so wonderful."

No it wasn't! I praise God for it, but it wasn't. With the tin roof and wood floor, it was like worshiping in a tin can! The sound was bouncing everywhere.

"Yeah, but I remember the incredible sense of community and unity that we had back then."

Well, I'm glad you were living in la-la land. We never had so much conflict over so many issues. There were all these hardheaded people, and we just had one thing after another after another every week. It wasn't a glorious place of unity. That's crazy.

This happens everywhere and in every stage of life.

"High school. Those were the greatest years of my life."

No they weren't! Have you forgotten about the acne? The nerdy way you talked and acted and dressed? Oh my goodness. You would never put those clothes on today. The only reason you put them on then was because you were paralyzed by fear. Why don't you get a life? You don't want to go back there!

It's the same way with marriage. Exactly the same.

"I just wish we could go back to those wonderful feelings we had back in the honeymoon period of our marriage."

That's the whole problem. You want to go back to shallow infatuation rather than move forward into a life of *agape* love, laying down your lives for each other.

Listen, I've been doing marriage counseling for many years. I have yet to meet a guy who really loved his wife when they first got married. I'm not saying a guy like that doesn't exist out there somewhere, but I am saying I have yet to meet one. Infatuated with her? You better believe it. Every guy loves how he feels when he is around her. He says, "I love you," but he really means, "I love the way you make me feel." If you want to go back to that, then you are living in la-la land. That was not real love.

Go forward. Grow forward into a more rich, fulfilling life. If you do that, stuff is going to start falling off and it's going to blow you away. You've just got to press in deeper. You've got to learn to be a real man of God, or a real woman of God. Learn how to lay your life down in *agape* love.

I have heard people in the churches I have led say things like, "Well, I remember back when it was just one hundred of us. I knew everybody and all their children's names. I wish we were back like that again." Really? If that's where you are, can I be honest with you? If that's in your heart, even if it doesn't come out of your mouth, then you are selfish and self-centered. I wrote that with a smile on my face because I don't mean to hurt your feelings, but it's important that I tell you the truth. That attitude says, "Everything is all about me."

New people are coming into the church regularly, and their lives are being touched by God in powerful ways. Whether you realize it or not, that is happening all the time. Think about those people. When you wish for things to be the way they were when your church was small, what are you really saying? "To heck with those new people."

I am thrilled to be part of a church that doesn't want to stay small. If my church ever decides to play things that way, then I am out of there, baby. Honestly, that's the truth. Don't care how much I love all the people in it; I'm gone. I am not going to be part of a church that is just all about a small congregation. One hundred is a great number, unless you're number 102 and number 105 coming through the door.

As for any church I lead, we are not stopping at one hundred. In fact, we are not stopping at two hundred or five hundred or even one thousand. God wants to touch more lives, so we are going to do whatever it takes to partner with him in doing that. We are going to grow. We are going to change.

3. Don't get full.

A great friend of mine and a tremendous man of God I was very close with years ago told me a story one time. I traveled a lot with this man; we spoke in several different places together. He's telling me this story, just crying his way through it. It had just happened with him earlier that day.

> *This morning I was praying and spending time with God. Man, I was just having this wonderful time with the Lord. His presence was there. Then the Lord spoke very clearly to my heart, Myles. God said, 'You are so full.'*

> *I said, 'Oh, thank you God. What a wonderful word.'*

As tears welled up in his eyes and began to run down his face, he continued.

> *Myles, it took me ten or fifteen minutes of sitting there before I finally got it. It wasn't a compliment from God.*

*God was saying I am so full that he can't put anything
else in me. I got it, and I just said, 'God, I see myself as
full. Lord, empty me out. Let me see how much more you
want to do in my life.'*

Can I tell you something? You must have a desire for more and
a capacity for more in order to grow and change. If you're going to
embrace change, don't get full.

In Genesis 17:1, God says, "I am God Almighty." That is how most
English versions of the Bible translate the Hebrew name of God, *el
shaddai*. But if you really study that word and look at what Hebrew
scholars have to say about it, *el shaddai* means something so much
more than just "God Almighty." By using those words, God was literally saying, "I am the God of more than enough."

That is what God was saying to Abraham, and that is what he wants
to say to many of us. "I am the God of more than enough. I have plenty
of whatever it is you need." Since there is no lack of supply in God, that
really leaves us with only two real issues on this point.

The first issue is this: How much do you want? You will never
change what you can tolerate. That is great truth. You can go to counseling week after week after week after week and not experience any
freedom. If you can tolerate the problem, you won't change it. If you
can tolerate an extra fifty pounds, you know what? You won't change.
If you can tolerate a getting-by marriage—limping along through life,
held together with scotch tape and Band-Aids—then you won't do
what it takes to change. You might go to counseling, lamenting about
how your marriage is a wreck and begging for help. Then you'll start to
get help and get better, but your marriage will only get about halfway
to where God wants it to go at most before you call it quits. That's good.
That's enough. Whoa, whoa, whoa, you were just getting started! How
much do you want? If you can tolerate a getting-by life, then you won't
do what it takes to change.

Here's the second issue: How much can you contain? Or, said another way, how big is your container? You know, as Christians, a lot of times we pray silly prayers. We pray like this: "God, can you please fill my cup?" What? What are you talking about? Fill your cup? That's a silly prayer. If a challenge in that at all for God, it's squeezing His blessings down to such a small amount that he can fit them in that dinky little cup of yours. We need to stop praying, "God, can you fill my little cup?" Instead, let's start praying according to the Word of God, "Lord, increase my cup. Expand my capacity so that I can receive more of you."

Then we need to begin to do what it takes to expand ourselves so that we can receive more from God. Have a daily time in the Word of God, not because it's the religious thing to do or what they taught you in Sunday school, but because it's life and death! His Word is life to me. I get in there and it speaks to me and it challenges me and it enriches me and it encourages me and it convicts me and it expands me. I love His Word! Love it. Can't wait to get in his Word again. What about your prayer life? Come on, expand.

"I'm not going to expand, Myles. I'm just gonna jump up and down on Sunday mornings. Oh, hallelujah."

Well, that's the Charismatic version. I don't really understand that one.

Listen, you have to get into the Word. You've got to pray. You're going to have to develop a devotional life. Have those times with God where it's just you and him. Get lost in His presence. Fall in love with Him afresh. Start now. Expand.

Both personal and corporate times of worship expand us. What else? We need to get together with other Christians frequently. Get together with Christians who are growing and have a similar vision, heart, and destination to you. Fellowship with them frequently because God builds through relationships from one Christian to another. Don't separate or isolate yourself. Don't fall into that nutty, foolish teaching of Christian isolation that's out there in the world so much today.

Scripture says God builds us up through the corporate body of Christ. Embrace all of these things because they enrich our lives, they challenge us, and they expand us.

Let me share one last verse with you. Psalm 84:5 is perhaps my favorite verse in the Bible. It says, "Blessed are those . . . whose hearts are set on pilgrimage." Where are you today? Is your heart set on pilgrimage? Are you moving forward? Blessed are those who are moving forward. Blessed are those who are embracing change. Blessed are those who are growing.

My house is a pilgrim house, and my church family is a pilgrim family. God has called us to go from faith to faith and from glory to glory. God has called and commanded you and I to embrace change— to get up, to advance, and to go forward. That's exactly what I'm going to do, that's exactly what my household is going to do, and that's exactly what my church family is going to do. I want that to be part of our DNA, our MO.

How about you? Are you a pilgrim? Or are you a settler? Is there an area of your life where you have camped, settled down, and gotten comfortable? It could be your marriage, your workplace, your professional growth and development, your walk with God, your personal devotional life, or any other realm in life. Is there any area where you have decided that you're comfortable? Is there anywhere you have stopped growing?

"You have stayed long enough," (Deut. 1:6).

God wants to call you out of that place today. He wants you to step out and embrace change in every area of your life. Don't wait until you're comfortable before you move. Receive the life and freedom God has for you, and embrace change.

Part 4

✟

Learn
God's Ways

GRATITUDE: CHANGING YOUR DESTINATION

This message is critically important. Gratitude is huge. Gratitude has the power to change your destination. Where you end up in life is largely determined by how much gratitude you have or don't have. Most of us don't think about it in that way, even in church, but it's the truth. Gratitude can change your destination, and it can also change how much joy you have on the journey to that destination.

This is one of the big keys of life. If I had asked you, before you started reading this, to give me the top five character qualities you think have a major impact on destination and quality of life, would gratitude honestly be on that list? Probably not. And if I had asked you to expand that list to ten, fifteen, or even twenty things, would gratitude have made the cut? Probably not, and that goes for all of us. Most of us would forget about gratitude, but gratitude is huge. It has the power to change your life. Gratitude is absolutely necessary.

Now I understand, just as you understand, that we should choose to be grateful. We should choose to have gratitude, first and foremost, because of what God has done for us. We should give thanks because we have a good and gracious Father in heaven. And we should definitely be grateful for what He has delivered us from and what He has brought us into. That should be more than enough to make you and I grateful people. But right now I don't want to focus on all the reasons why we should be grateful. I want to focus on gratitude as a wise decision. It is wise for us to choose gratitude. And let me add to that—choosing gratitude is vital. If you want to live the abundant life that Jesus died on the cross to give you, then gratitude is not optional.

God sent His son on the cross not only to take us out of something, but to bring us into something.

"Well, that's heaven. You know, our someday pie in the sky."

No, that's not what Scripture says. Yes, heaven is in there, and praise God we can look forward to that for eternity. We can't even imagine how wonderful that's going to be. But Jesus said that He came to give us life right now. The eternal, abundant life He came to give us does not start when we die. It starts right now!

The question, then, is this: how do we walk in it? Gratitude is a big key to walking in the life Jesus gave us, but we have to choose it. You may have noticed that I said that a few times already, and I'm going to say it again and again because I want you to get that truth. You have to choose gratitude. It's a choice. It's a decision that we all face.

Gratitude is not a talent. People who live their lives with a lot of gratitude don't live like that because they were just wired that way. They are not like that because of their personality. They had to choose to be grateful. All of us have the same ability and opportunity for gratitude. Whether or not we live gratefully is a decision that we make.

It's not going to just happen in your life, either. You are not going to wake up one day and say, "I don't know what happened, but all of a sudden I'm grateful! Must have been the second song the worship team did yesterday." It doesn't work that way. You and I have to choose to be grateful. It's a decision that we have to make and that we should make because it's wise. It's vital. It's not optional.

Here's a good question for each and every one to ask ourselves: Where does gratitude rank on your list of virtues? If you had to categorize all of the virtues and character qualities you could think of, would you put gratitude in with the essentials? Is that the way you think about gratitude? Or are you like most people, who put gratitude under the "nice to have" category? And when I say most people, I'm talking about inside and outside the church. We don't think of gratitude as a critical part of living a good life. It's just a nice add-on. It's down there with things like being cheerful and praying for your pastor. Nice, but not really necessary. That's how most of us approach it, but the truth is gratitude is absolutely essential for us if we are going to live something even remotely close to an abundant life. Gratitude has the power to change your destination. Nothing less.

Even though gratitude is essential to the Christian life, we put our focus on all of these other things and other virtues. What about faith? Oh, we need faith. We've got to have faith for Christian life. Faith, faith, faith. I've got to get faith. I need faith. I've got to get more faith. Faith, faith, faith. Well, while you're getting faith, you might want to get gratitude. Have you ever tried to sustain persevering faith without gratitude? Try it and see what happens. If you don't have gratitude mixed up in there with your faith, you know what's going to happen? Before long, you will lose the whole reason why you are being faithful. Then you will be just another one in a long, long line of religious people doing religious things in a very disciplined way without any life. Come on, you can't do this without gratitude. Try to be somebody who loves other people unconditionally without gratitude. It won't happen! When the disappointments and the betrayals come—trust me, they will—you're going to get bitter, you're going to withdraw, and you might even become cynical.

What about ministry? Try to engage in ministry without gratitude. And I'm not just talking about the pastors and the worship team because every single follower of Christ has been called into ministry by God. We are called to engage in the work of building His Kingdom with the gifts He gave us. How are you going to do that without gratitude? If you don't have gratitude, then you're not going to last. I've seen it over and over and over in some of the best, the brightest, the most committed, and the most passionate Christians ever. Without gratitude, it is simply a matter of time before you end up with a martyr complex. Poor me; I do all the work around here and don't get the acknowledgement I deserve. That's what happens every time there is ministry without gratitude.

Listen, every single Christian virtue, if divorced from gratitude, will be stunted in its growth. If you don't have gratitude mixed in, all of the other virtues and character qualities will never grow into anything close to fullness, and they probably won't last long either. Whatever stunted growth you have will be there for a season, and then it will be gone.

This is why the Apostle Paul told the Colossians to be "overflowing with thankfulness," (2:7). A lot of us come to the Bible and make the same mistake over and over again. We get to a verse like that and think, "Oh man, here's another thing I have to do. Okay, got to be overflowing. Add that to my good Christian to-do list." No! God is not putting something on you. God, as a loving father, is wanting you to walk in peace and enjoy an abundant life. God wants you to walk in that, so He tells you to be "overflowing with thankfulness." Is that a command? Yes. But it's a command for *your* benefit, not His. You couldn't even get to real gratitude if it was just about checking a box on a to-do list. Real gratitude is not just doing grateful things. Real gratitude is doing grateful things from a grateful heart. It's not just actions on the surface that give an appearance of gratefulness, it is a heart that is full of gratitude pouring itself out through grateful things. That's real gratitude. Is that kind of gratitude in your heart? Does it just live on your to-do list? Or is gratitude off your map completely?

Where you end up in life is largely dependent on how much gratitude you have or don't have. If you end up in a wonderful place—the place God destined you to be in—it will be largely because you chose gratitude in your life. There are many factors involved here, but gratitude is one of the key factors.

If you're in a good place at work right now, it's largely because you have been grateful for the jobs you've had. That's a sure thing because you are never going to get to a wonderful place without first being grateful for where you are. That's the way life works. If your marriage is really good right now, it's largely because you have been grateful for your spouse. God wants us to be grateful because it produces good results in our lives.

We're going to look at the story of Jesus and the ten lepers in Luke 17. If you know the Scripture well, you probably saw this one coming from a long way off.

> *Now on his way to Jerusalem, Jesus traveled along the border between Samaria and Galilee. As he was going into a village, ten men who had leprosy met him. They stood at a distance and called out in a loud voice, "Jesus, Master, have pity on us!"*

> *When he saw them, he said, "Go, show yourselves to the priests," (Luke 17:11-14).*

Why would he say that? It's a simple answer. Under the Mosaic Law, if someone was healed from leprosy, then they were required to go immediately to the Temple and have the priests inspect them to confirm that they were legitimately healed because leprosy was a very contagious disease.

> *When he saw them, he said, "Go, show yourselves to the priests." And as they went, they were cleansed.*

> *One of them, when he saw he was healed, came back, praising God in a loud voice. He threw himself at Jesus' feet and thanked him—and he was a Samaritan.*

Jesus asked, "Were not all ten cleansed? Where are the other nine? Has no one returned to give praise to God except this foreigner?" Then he said to him, "Rise and go; your faith has made you well," (Luke 17:14-19).

There were ten lepers. All ten of them were healed, but nine of them just went on their way. They didn't come back. They never came and expressed gratitude.

Now, before we get out our stones and throw them at the nine, let's pause and think for a minute. At least in some way you can kind of understand it. I mean, they were overcome with shock, surprise, amazement, and excitement. They had been living a nightmare with no good future ahead of them. All of a sudden it came to an abrupt end; they were healed. Those guys were in a hurry to get home. They were in a hurry to go tell their families and show them the amazing thing that had happened. Maybe some of them were thinking they would go and thank Jesus at some point in the future. Apparently that window of opportunity never came around.

Here's the point. More often than not, we don't reject gratitude. We simply neglect it. We don't intend to not be grateful. It's just that we just never get around to it. It's about the fourth or fifth thing on that to-do list of stuff we just never get around to or follow up on.

Nine of the lepers neglected gratitude, but one of them came back. He came back because his heart was filled with gratitude. He didn't neglect gratitude. As he headed back, he didn't care how dusty the road was. He didn't care that he was making the journey alone. He didn't care that he might look foolish. He didn't care who heard him praising God with a loud voice. He didn't care about the dirt at Jesus' feet getting in his face and his eyes and his nose. He didn't care about any of that. He couldn't care less. He was filled with gratitude, and he just had to express it.

There is a good chance that you are familiar with this story. Even if you haven't read it before, it is likely you have heard a message preached about it in the past. It's a familiar story, but I want to share some insight that the Lord gave me about this story that made it even bigger and even more powerful, especially for those who want to develop a lifestyle of gratitude.

Luke 17:14 says this, "And as they went, they were cleansed." The Greek word translated here as "cleansed" is the word *katharizó*. *Katharizó* means cleansed, cured, or healed. It's a unique word in the Greek language used when lepers are healed because their leprosy is said to be cleansed away from their body. Luke 17:15 says, "One of them, when he saw he was healed, came back." The word translated there as "healed" is the Greek word *iaomai*, which is a less specific word for healing used often in the New Testament. Then, in Luke 17:17, Jesus says, "Were not all ten cleansed?" Here Jesus uses the word *katharizó* again. Finally, in Luke 17:19, Jesus ends the story by saying, "Your faith has made you well."

In the original Greek, the word in Luke 17:19 is not *katharizó* or *iaomai*. In fact, it's not any word that is commonly associated with healing at all. Jesus was not saying that his faith brought healing to his body. Here he uses the word *sózó*, which means salvation. All ten lepers received healing, but only one of them received healing and salvation. All ten received a great gift from the Lord, but only one of them received even more. What was the difference between that one and the others? Gratitude. Gratitude is the reason that he was blessed with more.

Now what about the other nine? They missed out. Why? Ingratitude. Ingratitude is a killer. There is something extremely distasteful and repulsive about ingratitude, especially when you're the one whose generosity or sacrifice went unnoticed. It is just distasteful. But how often are we the offending party when it comes to ingratitude? So, so many times we neglect to say thank you for benefits, blessings, and kindnesses. And the words part is we are oblivious to the ingratitude present in our lives.

"Oh, it's not ingratitude."

Yes, it is. Neglecting gratitude is ingratitude. Because of our fallen nature, the default position in a human being's life is ingratitude. You don't have to choose ingratitude. It will choose you. Ingratitude is automatic. It's there. If you don't want it there, then you have to actively choose gratitude. You have to develop it.

If you don't develop gratitude in your life, then you give Satan a vacant field where he can come and set up his little shop of horrors. If you don't develop gratitude in your life, you are leaving an empty space where the enemy knows just what to build. Think that's a little strong? Think that's an overstatement? It's not. Take a look at the message of Romans 1.

If you are familiar with Romans 1, it is likely because of the second half of the chapter. That part is all about progressing into depravity by choosing one thing that leads to another that leads to another, culminating in not only homosexuality, but a society that accepts homosexuality. It's a warning against going deeper and deeper into depravity and further away from God.

I do not think that homosexuality and the other sins it mentions are meant to be the main focus of the chapter, although I am not backing off of them one bit. I think there is a bigger message that Romans 1 is trying to get across. The spiral of depravity is really the created telling the Creator, "You don't know what You're doing. You don't have a clue. I know better than You. You made me wrong." It's showing the ultimate act of rebellion against God.

But here's the question: What was the beginning point? What started the whole slide downwards? The answer is in Romans 1:21, "For although they knew God, they did not honor him as God or give thanks to him." They did not give thanks to God. Ingratitude was the starting point of the slippery slope into complete godlessness.

Ingratitude opens the door in your life for all kinds of evil things to come in. It is like opening Pandora's box. If you open the door to ingratitude in your life, lots of other stuff will come with it—ugly stuff you don't want in your life. Ingratitude is a killer.

Consider the area of marriage as an example of this truth. If you, as a husband, are ungrateful for your wife, that opens the door and allows all kinds of stuff to come into you, into your marriage, and into your family. In 2014, a study reported that almost 60 percent of men who identify themselves as born-again Christians view pornography at least once a month.[1] You think maybe there's some ingratitude involved? Makes perfect sense.

What about you, ladies? As a wife, are you grateful for your husband? I'm telling you, ingratitude starts a vicious, ugly cycle. It opens the door to all kinds of awful, destructive things.

What about you, children? What about you, young people? Is there any ingratitude for parents and what they have done? No, that never happens. Ingratitude for parents is not ever really a problem, right? No, not right! Ingratitude for parents is huge. It's everywhere. It's so pervasive in our world and in our nation that it's considered normal and natural!

"Well, you know, parents aren't perfect."

Guess what. You're not going to be perfect when you're a parent either, and I don't think you want to start that sowing-and-reaping deal in your life. But more than that, I don't think you want to open the door of ingratitude and bring even worse things into your life.

Dr. James Kennedy—a powerful man of God, a great speaker, and a great writer—once said this: "An ungrateful person is only one step away from getting their needs met in illegitimate ways."[2] That is so true. Listen, when we give in to the whining, complaining, and murmuring of an ungrateful heart, we embark on a downward slide that will leave us in a place we never could have imagined or wanted for ourselves.

So, how do we avoid ingratitude? If we don't want its negative effects in our lives, what do we do? The obvious thing would be to choose gratitude. Even when we are choosing gratitude, though, ingratitude will try to creep back into our lives. We need to beware of its deceptions. I am going to give you six things that cause ingratitude in our lives. The more that you are aware of these causes, the easier it will be for you to combat ingratitude itself.

Unrealistic expectations

You know, we can expect a lot in life. In fact, if we are not careful, we can get to a place where, no matter how much we are given, it is never enough. But there is a deeper problem with the expectations so many people have. This one pops its ugly, little head up over and over again: we are expecting and trying to get from others what we can only get from God.

For instance, we tend to expect others to love us continuously, without stopping. No matter where we are, what we have done, or how we have been, we want everybody to love us nonstop. Can I tell you something? That expectation is not realistic. I don't care how wonderful the people around you are, no person is going to love you like that. Nobody. If you put them on that pedestal, they're coming down. God is the only one who can love you truly without stopping.

Here's another one: we tend to expect everybody else to forgive us immediately. That's a common expectation, but it's not realistic. No matter what I've done, forgive me now, right now. Wow, I can't believe you haven't already forgiven me. What's up? It looks like you're holding onto that.

When people don't meet expectations like these, it is not because there's anything wrong with them. They're human! They haven't arrived yet, and neither have you. You are expecting things from them that you can only expect from God, and having those expectations will produce ingratitude. You are setting yourself up for frustration and failure, which will open the door for ingratitude in your life.

Forgetfulness

God warned the Israelites over and over again to not forget the One who delivered them out of bondage and slavery once they got into the Promised Land. That's one of the key words of the whole book of Deuteronomy: remember. Deuteronomy 5:15 says, "Remember that you were slaves in Egypt and that the Lord your God brought you out of there with a mighty hand and an outstretched arm." Deuteronomy 8:2 says, "Remember how the Lord your God led you all the way in the wilderness these forty years." Deuteronomy 8:17-18 says, "You may say to yourself, 'My power and the strength of my hands have produced this wealth for me.' But remember the Lord your God, for it is he who gives you the ability to produce wealth." Remember, remember, remember, remember. But the Israelites didn't remember. On the contrary, they forgot.

Later on in the book of Deuteronomy you can still find the word "remember," but it is tied with the word "forgot." Deuteronomy 32:18 says, "You deserted the Rock, who fathered you; you forgot the God who gave you birth." You forgot. Forgetfulness and ingratitude go hand in hand. If you are regularly thanking God for the good things He has done, is doing, and will do, then you are not going to forget them. If you are not thanking Him for those things, it's probably not that you have rejected gratitude. You've just neglected it, right? But those things are not in your mouth. They're not on your mind. They're not in your heart. You will forget them, and your forgetfulness will lead you into ingratitude.

Entitlement

When I use this word in the pulpit, it usually gets a lot of agreement from the audience. At least in our churches here in Texas, very few people will argue with you if you say that we live in a society with a lot of entitlement. There are a great number of people in this nation that need help and assistance from the government, and praise God that help is available for them. But there are also lots of people who don't have needs and are taking advantage of the system. They do that because they have an entitlement mentality, and that's a problem.

But this issue of entitlement goes way, way beyond government and civics. It touches just about everything in our lives. If we're not careful, we can start thinking that God owes us the simple blessings He chooses to grant us. That's just a very small step away from pure ingratitude. When we start to think that our house, our car, our clothes, our marriage, our family, and all of the other blessings in our lives are owed to us and beneath what we deserve, do you know what happens? Ingratitude has all the oxygen it needs to live and thrive within us.

Some people truly believe that God owes them. They usually won't say that in so many words, but it's in there. And you usually don't have to read between too may lines to pick it up, either. Listen. Let me be clear on this. God is not the debtor. You are. He doesn't owe you anything. You owe Him everything, but, first and foremost, you owe Him gratitude for all that He's done for you.

Comparison

Now, when I say that word, I think the first thing that most people think of is keeping up with the Joneses, right? You know what that is; it's all about keeping track of what money and material things other people around you have and comparing it with what you have. They have more? I've got to catch up. It is constant comparison with others, which is always dangerous ground to walk on.

But let me tell you, there's more to comparison than just keeping up with the Joneses. Comparing your sacrifices, hard work, and commitment to that of others is just as dangerous and destructive as comparing material things. Whether it is in church, at home, at work, or anywhere else, that is not a place you want to be in.

No matter what you compare, the focus of comparison is always on the self. When you are focusing on yourself, it is impossible to have gratitude for others and what they have done. Get the focus off of yourself. Stop comparing yourself to other people. Stop competing with other people. Comparison is just your flesh trying to take other people and put them in your shadow. Comparison wants to belittle people next to your own life, which is so much bigger and more important. And when our focus is there, ingratitude is inevitable.

Blindness to God's Goodness

Lamentations 3:22-23 says, "Because of the Lord's great love we are not consumed, for his compassions never fail. They are new every morning; great is your faithfulness." The writer of Lamentations was keenly aware of God's goodness. He was not blind to it. He said God's love and compassions were new every morning. That means this guy woke up every morning aware of God's goodness; he saw it and it was a big deal to him. Every morning God's mercy, His grace, His blessing, and His goodness were new in this man's life. He was grateful every morning.

Well, that's the writer of Lamentations. What about you? And what about me? Are we keenly aware of God's goodness to us? Are we mindful of His blessings? Or are we blind to them?

There's an old story about a guy who comes to the pastor and says, "Pastor, I am at the end of my rope."

The pastor says, "What's the problem? What are you going through?"

"I just can't take it anymore," he says. "There are nine of us living in our tiny, one-room house, and it is just about push me over the edge. I can't take it anymore."

"I've got good advice for you," the pastor says. "I know how to fix this. Go home, take your goat, and bring him into the house with you."

The man looks at the pastor like he's not sure what to think. "Are you kidding me? That's crazy."

"No, no, no. Trust me. It will work," says the pastor.

So the guy goes home. Seven days later he comes back to the pastor. He looks haggard and even more beat down than he had been the week before.

"Well, how's it going?" asks the pastor.

"You wouldn't believe how awful it is in this house. We cannot stand it. That goat is nasty, filthy, and he stinks to high heaven. It's unbearable."

"Good," the pastor says. "Now go home and let the goat out of the house. Come back and see me in a week."

The guy leaves, then comes back a week later. As he walks into the church there is a smile on his face and a bounce in his step.

"How's everything going?" the pastor asks.

"Oh, pastor. Life is beautiful. Life is wonderful. We enjoy every minute of the day now that the goat is gone and there are only nine of us in the house."

Life is all a matter of perspective. It's about how you and I look at it. Don't be blind to God's goodness in your life.

Circumstances

Matthew Henry was an incredibly gifted, phenomenal Puritan preacher who wrote one of the most well-known and well-respected

Bible commentaries ever written. This man lived a big life that impacted many, many people.

One day Henry was mugged and robbed in the city of London. This is an excerpt of what he wrote in his personal diary shortly after that:

> *I thank Thee first because I was never robbed before; second, because although they took my purse they did not take my life; third, because although they took my all, it was not much; and fourth because it was I who was robbed, and not I who robbed.*[3]

This is a true example of choosing gratitude and intentionally building a lifestyle that's centered around gratitude. A person who has chosen gratitude like this can see anything—and I mean anything—through the eyes of gratitude. People who do not live like this will always accuse grateful people of being in denial or pretending reality doesn't exist, but that's not what they are doing at all. They see the exact same things in the exact same amount of detail as everyone else around them. But they also see more. Much, much more.

Some of you may be familiar with the name Richard Wurmbrand. He had a bit of an odd name, but he was an incredible man of God. Wurmbrand was a pastor in Romania during the era of the Soviet Union. The Romanian authorities imprisoned him for preaching the gospel because Christianity was illegal in Romania during that time. He spent fourteen years in prison, tortured almost every day. I won't go into every gruesome detail of what they did to him, but, just to give you an idea, he came out of prison with eighteen holes burned into his body. And yet, in his memoirs about that time, he wrote, "Alone in my cell, cold, hungry, and in rags, I danced for joy every night."[4]

Gratitude is not about circumstances. It's really not. Gratitude has much more to do with what is happening inside of you than what is happening outside. That is the difference between grateful people and people who only show gratitude occasionally.

Martin Rinkart was a Lutheran pastor and another incredible man of God. He was the pastor of a church in the city of Eilenburg, Germany during the Thirty Years' War. Because it was a fortified city, it became a refuge for people throughout the region and beyond; people flocked to it by the tens of thousands. Eilenburg didn't have enough resources to support all of the refugees, so conditions deteriorated rapidly. Rinkart refused to move. He ministered to every person he could as deadly waves of pestilence and disease swept through the city on a regular basis, wiping people out by the thousands. In one year alone, he performed over 4,500 funerals.

In the midst of all this tragedy, pain, and suffering, Rinkart wrote what he called a family grace, which was a short song he and his children sang before each and every meal. His family grace has become almost an unofficial anthem for the country of Germany. They use it for different state events and special occasions. It has also become a well-known hymn around the world. You might even recognize the title: "Now Thank We All Our God." I know that hymn. That means it didn't just stay in the Lutheran hymnal; it made its way over to the Methodist hymnal as well. In fact, it has become a very popular song.

If you just read the song without knowing its background, the tone of joy and gratitude might lead you to picture the songwriter scribbling it on a napkin at a Thanksgiving feast—table full of food, family laughing and rejoicing, pumpkin in the middle perfectly round and orange. That was not the setting for this song at all. Rinkart wrote this song of gratitude in the midst of abject loss. He was in the middle of hopelessly depressing circumstances full of pain and suffering.

There are many, many stories and examples just like these. I love to read the biographies of great men and women of God. I've been reading them for decades, so I can tell you lots of stories. Instead of doing that, though, I'm going to summarize a key point for you. I've found that many of these great men and women of God knew something that a lot of us in the Church today don't know: the only thing worse than going through awful circumstances is going through them with ingratitude.

Ingratitude is a killer. Understanding the causes of it can help us to avoid ingratitude, but that's not going to last long if we don't replace it with something else. What is the best thing to replace it with? The opposite: gratitude. If we want to enjoy the full, abundant life God desires to give you, then you need to cultivate a lifestyle of gratitude.

Gratitude is a lifestyle, and it is not an easy one. You have to fight for it. You have to be intentional about it. You have to swim against the current because our human nature is not grateful by default. It is not an easy lifestyle, but it is a grace-infused one. In other words, you and I cannot do it in our own strength, but God gives us His strength and power to live it out.

Don't take what you have read so far and try to pump yourself up into gratitude.

"I'm going to do this. I'm going to be that."

You will fail. Trust me. That is not weakness on your part; we all need to draw on the grace of God—His strength, His power, and His ability. Without God's grace, what's coming next will be fruitless.

Are you ready to be a person that is filled with gratitude? Do you want to change your destination and change how you live? Grateful people brighten the environments they're in. It doesn't matter if you are at work, school, church, home, or anywhere else; you will have an impact simply because of your gratitude. You will affect those around you with the joy and peace and fullness that comes with living the grateful life God created you to live. Do you want that? More importantly, are you willing to do what it takes to build, cultivate, and develop a lifestyle of gratitude?

If we are going to be grateful people, then gratitude cannot just be something that we pull off of the shelf just when we want it or need it.

It needs to be a natural response to our daily lives. That just upped the ante a little bit, didn't it? Gratitude takes more than just a surface-level changing of our minds.

You could read this and say, "Oh, that was great, Myles. I am going to think of gratitude as more important, and I am going to avoid ingratitude. I want to be more grateful. Good talk." That may get you somewhere, but it's not going to get you very far. To truly live a life of gratitude, you need to do things repetitively to change your habit patterns until gratitude becomes a natural response. We come preprogrammed toward ingratitude, and we have to engage with the process of reprogramming our minds and turning our hearts toward gratitude.

There are four simple and practical ways that you can cultivate a lifestyle of gratitude. These habit patterns will help you build a gratitude response and begin to default to gratitude. If you need to build a lifestyle of gratitude, this is how to do it.

Speak Up

If you want to develop a lifestyle of gratitude, then you have to speak up. God's Word tells us to speak out the things on our hearts. Here is what that means in the realm of gratitude.

There are times during our days and weeks and months that grateful thoughts pop into our heads automatically. It doesn't matter if you have a lifestyle of gratitude or not, grateful thoughts happen sometimes. Maybe you found some money on the ground. Maybe you were dreading a call to customer service, but ended up talking to a bright, happy employee who works everything out for you. There are so many situations where it is possible to have a spontaneously grateful thought.

Grateful thoughts are good things. There is definitely nothing wrong with having thoughts like that, but if we let thoughts in our minds suffice for gratitude, then we have a problem. That's not what the Bible tells us to do. Hebrews 13:15 says, "Through Jesus, therefore, let us continually offer to God a sacrifice of praise—the fruit of lips that openly profess his name." According to this verse, what is praise to God? The fruit of our lips. In other words, praise to God does not just live in our minds; it must be spoken.

In the same way, gratitude is not The Quiet Game. It has to be spoken. Gratitude begs to be expressed to both God and others. One great saint of the past once said, "Silent gratitude is not much use to anyone." Make your praise ring out. Don't keep it in your head.

"I don't think this is a big deal, Myles. As long as it's in my heart, I don't think it really matters whether or not I verbalize it."

That's great. You can think that, but that is not what Scripture says. The speaking out of praise and thanksgiving is a topic addressed many times throughout the Word. Let's just hit one highlight right now—Psalm 145:1-6.

> *I will exalt you, my God the King;*
> *I will praise your name for ever and ever.*
> *Every day I will praise you*
> *and extol your name for ever and ever.*
> *Great is the Lord and most worthy of praise;*
> *his greatness no one can fathom.*
> *One generation commends your works to another;*
> *they tell of your mighty acts.*
> *They speak of the glorious splendor of your majesty—*
> *and I will meditate on your wonderful works.*

Here we see the word "extol," which is another term that is used to describe the act of speaking out, especially in talking about the good qualities of someone or something. We also see the generations teaching, informing, and telling others of the Lord's great works. Then, at the end, both types of gratitude work together. There is speaking out—external—and there is meditating—internal. That is just one passage of Scripture out of many that give the same idea and the same command over and over again. Don't just think it. Say it. Say it. Say it!

I'm in a different place today because the Lord taught me this years ago, and I put it into practice in my life. There are so many times that a spirit of heaviness broke off of me because I began to speak words of gratitude and words of thanks. Anxiety, depression, despair, worries, and fears can all be broken off of our lives if we take God's prescription: speak it out. If you have a really bad sore throat and the doctor gives you a prescription, what are you going to do? You take the prescription so that you don't end up in the destination of having a sore throat. This is the same concept. God has given us a prescription to get out from underneath the heaviness of life. Speak it out. Praise him. Speak out your gratitude to him and to others. Don't just think it. Say it.

Sing out

Singing out is another teaching from the Bible and another prescription from God. If we want to cultivate a lifestyle of gratitude and end up walking in the abundant life God has provided for us, we need to sing out.

Psalm 28:7 says this: "The Lord is my strength and my shield; my heart trusts in him, and he helps me. My heart leaps for joy, and with my song I praise him." Psalm 147:7 has a similar message, "Sing to the Lord with grateful praise; make music to our God on the harp." Gratitude is a tune that you and I can dance to. There is a melody line running through it; it's something we can sing out and should sing out.

This is something the modern Church has fumbled away. The people of God in the Old Testament understood this; they got it. They read the same verses we read from Psalms, but they understood their purpose and practiced singing them regularly. In the Old Testament, time and time again, the people of God spontaneously lifted up a song of gratitude to the Lord. Their gratitude wasn't limited by western culture. Today we are intensely concerned about our images and reputation. Back then, people just experienced life.

"You don't understand something, Myles. I'm not much of a singer. You haven't heard my voice."

Well, have you heard mine? My friend, here is the truth: it doesn't have to sound good to be good. That's not the issue. It's not about how it sounds to you or to everybody else; it's about how it sounds to God. That should be liberating! It doesn't matter whether you're in a church service, mowing your yard, driving in the car, or walking to your mailbox. Whatever you are doing, start to worship God and sing out a song to Him.

There is something about singing out our thankfulness that has an incredible power to it. Combining songs with gratitude has the power to embed gratitude into our hearts and lives even faster than speaking it out. I think it has something to do with the power of worship. Lift up your voice and begin to sing to God. Let worship ingrain gratitude within you.

Kneel down

This is a simple one, but if you want to cultivate a lifestyle of gratitude, then you need to get this as well.

Years ago a friend of mine in ministry shared this story with me. We were talking about some of the hardest things we had done in the course of ministry, and he said one of the hardest things he ever had to do was also one of the most glorious moments he had ever been a part of. That got my attention; I asked him to tell me the story.

One night this pastor got a call from a police officer who was a member of his church. The officer gave him some horrible news: the seventeen-year-old daughter of a much-loved and influential man in the church had just been killed in a head-on collision with a drunk driver. When the pastor heard, it just broke his heart. The father of the girl was an incredible man of God and a big part of the church and the community. Above all, he was one of the most grateful people my pastor friend had ever met, and that made him a joy to be around. He was very much loved by everyone around him. The pastor asked to be the one to notify them so that they wouldn't have to hear it in a midnight call from a policeman.

He got off the phone, gathered himself, prayed for a minute, then got in the car and drove over to the house of the family. When he knocked on the door, the man, his wife, and his whole family came to the doorway. The pastor asked if the man could step outside. The man stepped outside, sensing that something was wrong. This friend of mine had to stand there and tell him his daughter had just been killed.

Tears began to flow out of the man's eyes immediately, and they just stood outside together for a little while. After a moment the man said, "Will you please come back inside with me and with my family?" The pastor agreed, and they walked back in together. The father gathered his family together in the living room and proceeded to tell them what happened, and they all began to cry. But then the father said, "Now, wait a minute. Everybody listen to me carefully. Before we begin to ask God why he took her home, let's first thank him for the seventeen years we had together with her." This godly man led his family in an extended period of worship and prayer. They sat there that night, thanking God for the seventeen years they had with their beloved daughter and sister.

Kneel down. We should come to God with our hurts and our pains. God wants us to come to him honestly—not in King James English, not flowery, not beating around the bush. He wants us to be honest and very direct with him. But when we come to him in prayer, we need to remember that prayer is much more than just asking for things. Prayer is primarily designed to be a vehicle for worship and gratitude. That means even in times of difficulty and confusion and pain, our prayers need to be filled with gratitude for God's goodness. We need to train our hearts to filter everything in life through God's goodness.

In 1 Timothy 2:1, Paul says this to Timothy, "I urge, then, first of all, that petitions, prayers, intercession, and thanksgiving be made for all people." Think about your prayer life for a moment. What's the overall makeup of it? Are your prayers top heavy with complaints and requests? Or are they full of thanksgivings to God? Do you thank God for the people around you? Do you thank Him regularly for his goodness? For every passionate request that we bring before God, we should already have given him thanksgivings with just as much passion.

Express gratitude privately and publicly

This one may sound a bit more complicated, but it is not. Here's the main idea for understanding private and public gratitude: we need such a habit pattern of gratitude in our lives that we express gratitude regularly in both private and public situations. We have to have both.

The life of Daniel is a clear example of this kind of gratitude. In Daniel 2, the king of Babylon, Nebuchadnezzar, has a dream that bothers him to no end, but he cannot understand. He rallies all of his wise men and sorcerers to him to explain his dream, but not one of them is able to do it. Nebuchadnezzar is on the verge of putting all of his sorcerers and advisors to death when Daniel runs in and requests time to inquire of the Lord. Nebuchadnezzar grants him time.

Daniel goes and gets alone with God, and God meets him there and reveals the king's dream and its interpretation to Daniel in great detail. Once Daniel receives the revelation, he can't wait. He runs to immediately tell the king everything . . . no, that's not what happens. Even though he is on a ticking clock, he immediately turns to God with prayer and thanksgiving for the revelation. Then, after a private moment of gratitude, he goes and presents his revelation to the king.

Fast forward through Daniel's life many years, or just a few chapters through the book. There has been a change of kings; King Darius is now on the throne and Daniel has risen to be one of his top three advisors. The other two advisors are jealous of Daniel because he has more wisdom and insight and does things with more excellence. The jealous advisors convince King Darius to pass a decree that prevents everyone from praying to or worshipping anyone or anything other than King Darius for thirty days.

Daniel, knowing about the decree, enters his house and opens his windows towards Jerusalem to pray and give thanks to God three times a day as he has always done. He does it with the windows open, for all to see. He gives thanks and praise to God publicly and without shame. Nothing stops him from publicly giving thanks to God.

Daniel is a great example of private and public gratitude. What about us? Can I share one observation with you? We are so quick to share our criticisms, even publicly, but we are often slow to share our gratitude. It shouldn't be like that. Psalm 35:18 says, "I will give you thanks in the great assembly; among the throngs I will praise you." This is gratitude that is not just private, but public. Private gratitude is important because it develops an intimate connection of gratitude between you and the Lord. But you will miss out on the fullness of this truth if you do not take your gratitude to the public realm and remind others of God's goodness.

I have two questions for you: How quick are you to give thanks when nobody is watching? How quick are you to give thanks when everybody is watching? Be careful if you lean towards one or the other because God's goodness, His life, His peace, His joy, and His blessings are given to us both privately and publicly. Therefore, our thanksgivings should be given to Him both privately and publicly.

Psalm 34:1 says, "I will extol the Lord at all times; his praise will always be on my lips." I'm going to think it. I'm going to say it. I'm going to sing it. I'm going to pray it, both privately and publicly. We need to build all of these things into our lives if we want to cultivate true gratitude and change our destinations.

I invite you to declare Psalm 34:1 over your life. Don't just repeat the words powerlessly. Say them to your God. Make a declaration. Make a commitment to living out your life that way. If you are not willing to live it, then don't declare it. But if you want to seek out a lifestyle of gratitude, change your destination, and begin living in the benefits of a grateful life, declare Psalm 34:1 out loud over your life:

"I will extol the Lord at all times; his praise will always be on my lips."

Having God's Heart

I n Ezekiel 36:26, God says, "I will give you a new heart."
God's main purpose for the lives of born-again believers is to conform us into the image of His Son, Jesus Christ. We understand from Scriptures like Romans 8:29. God's overriding, overarching purpose for each and every single one of our lives is to make us more and more like His Son, Jesus. That is the exact same thing as making us more like God because if you've seen the Son, you've seen the Father. He's a chip off the old block. The Son is the exact representation of the Father. That is the gist of the conversation between Jesus and Philip in John 14:8-9. After being with Jesus for three years, Philip says to him, "Lord, show us the father."

Jesus answers, "Don't you know me, Philip, even after I have been among you such a long time?" You can almost hear the disappointment in his voice. "Anyone who has seen me has seen the Father." Jesus and the Father are exactly alike. To be conformed into the image of the Son is the same as being conformed into the image of the Father.

If we are being transformed to be like God, then, above all else, our hearts must become like his heart. That's the biggest factor of becoming like him.

So what does it mean to have God's heart? And, more specifically, what does it mean to have God's heart in the area of giving? Now, you might wonder why I suddenly focused in on giving. It's very simple. I want to zero in on giving because the Bible tells us that God is love, and even with a casual, surface-level reading of the Bible you'll very quickly understand how God spells love: G-I-V-E.

"God so loved . . . that he gave." (John 3:16) When God loves, he gives. That is a natural response. When God loves, it moves him to action. He doesn't just feel something internally and leave it there. It always, always moves him to give. Giving is a big part of who God is. Therefore, if you are very serious about becoming like him, then it is important that your heart become like God's heart and that you become a giver in the same way God is a giver.

We're going to start with a quick heart check by looking at a couple of passages. Ephesians 4:28 says, "Anyone who has been stealing must steal no longer, but must work, doing something useful with their own hands, that they may have something to share with those in need."

Now pause for a moment. What did you just read? Most of the time we read right by that verse and completely miss a big part of the meaning. Most of us just heard Paul tell us to stop stealing. If you're stealing, stop stealing; get a job and have money so that you can live without stealing anymore. But that's not at all what he just said. Look again at what the verse actually says: stop stealing and get a job *so that you can give*. Paul skipped over the whole part about getting a job so that you can have money to live on and make ends meet. He jumped right past that and went straight into giving. Now why would Paul do that? Because Paul had God's heart.

Yeah, yeah, yeah. I know you need money to live on. I understand that. But the main reason why you should get a job is so that you can give. Paul had God's heart; that's why he phrased it that way. The reason that you and I sometimes misread a verse that is so simple and so clear is because our hearts are not yet like God's.

Look at another verse, Acts 20:34-35. This is Paul's writing again. He says, "You yourselves know that these hands of mine have supplied my own needs and the needs of my companions. In everything I did, I showed you that by this kind of hard work we must help the weak."

Now, Paul had a full-time job in ministry—preaching, teaching, doing mission trips, and spreading the gospel. He had a full-time job, but Paul is saying in this passage that he also had a part-time job, which we know from other passages was making tents. He made tents and he sold them. So he had a full-time job in ministry and a part-time job in tentmaking so that he could make money for his needs, for the needs of his companions, and for giving to those in need.

Now, here's a question for you. Do you know someone that has taken a second job or a part-time job on top of a full-time job? Maybe yourself, a family member, a friend, or an acquaintance. Most of us know at least one person like that. Most of them took it on so that they could make ends meet, catch up on some bills, buy a car, take a family vacation, or something like that. All those things are good, but here's the question I have for you: Do you know anyone who has taken an extra job in order to give more to the Kingdom of God? Why is that?

"Well, Pastor Myles, you just don't understand."

I understand better than you think I do. My parents didn't have the money to put me through college, so I had to figure out a way to pay for it myself. I got a job as a security guard working midnight to eight o'clock in the morning.

My roommate and I had a tiny apartment, and we ate peanut butter and jelly sandwiches for breakfast, lunch, and dinner for a whole year. That is not an exaggeration. Peanut butter and jelly for two whole semesters, from September all the way through to the end of May. That's why, to this day, I do not eat peanut butter. I'm sixty years old, and I still won't do it. I mean breakfast, lunch, and dinner. I've eaten peanut butter with every kind of jam and jelly you could think of. Fair warning, never use jalapeño jelly. It doesn't work. Sounded like a good idea at the time, but it didn't pan out.

Our big, big treat came maybe once every two weeks or so. We would take little odd jobs on top of the ones we had and make a little extra money. With that extra money, we would go down to Taco Bell and order the bean and cheese burrito for thirty-nine cents. Flour and beans and a little bit of cheese, but not much cheese. We'd each get two of them—red sauce in one and green sauce in the other. We thought we were in hog heaven.

At the time I was a young Christian who had grown up in an ungodly, non-Christian home. When I got saved at seventeen years old, I was the first one out of all my relatives to do so. None of them were saved. They ridiculed me for it. So there I was, a baby Christian without a good church or a spiritual mentor of any kind. But I read my Bible, and I understood very clearly that I needed to tithe and give. So during all of that time I spent struggling to make ends meet, I tithed. Jalapeño jelly and Taco Bell. But I gave.

After talking about his second job, Paul says, "Remembering the words the Lord Jesus himself said: 'It is more blessed to give than to receive,'" (Acts 20:35). If you've been in church for any length of time, then you are probably familiar with that passage. But I really wonder how many Christians worldwide actually believe Jesus' words are true. I am not saying those who don't believe them are bad, malicious people. It's just that their hearts have not yet become like God's. The human heart doesn't naturally want to give; by default, it wants to receive and take.

Most Christians give not because their heart has become like God's heart, but because they go to church and are persuaded to give. In church they are taught and persuaded into pulling out their wallets. Usually that happens in one of three ways.

Here's the first way Christians are persuaded to give: they are taught that giving is legally required. The Bible very clearly teaches that we should tithe, which means we should give the first 10 percent of all of our increase to God. That is very clear in the Word; there's no real debate about that. The principle is all through the Old Testament, and Jesus himself confirms it in the New Testament.

A lot of people today, especially in America, try to say that tithing is based in the Law, and since we are set free from the Law under the New Covenant, we do not need to tithe. That's just not true. Jesus Himself confirms in the New Testament that tithing is something God desires. Not only did Jesus talk about it, but also tithing precedes the Law. Over four hundred years before God gave the Law to man, Jacob tithed to God. Where on earth did Jacob learn how to tithe to God? From his father, Isaac, who also tithed. Where on earth did Isaac learn to tithe? From his father, Abraham, who did the same thing. We can trace that all the way back to the story of Cain and Abel in Genesis 4. Cain brought an offering to God just in the course of time, but Abel brought the firstfruits of his work. He brought his first 10 percent to God. Where did he learn that from? From Adam and Eve. Where did they learn it from? From God Himself. Tithing is not just under the Law; God still wants us to tithe.

Some churches with good Bible teaching persuade Christians to give because it is legally required. The problem is that's very similar to paying your income taxes.

I usually do my taxes early, but one year I did a lot of traveling and didn't finish them until the last minute. That year I was one of those that you see sometimes on the news, lined up in their cars at the post office on April 15 trying to get their taxes in there and stamped before midnight. I drove to the post office at about 10:30 that night, and in little-bitty Wharton, Texas there was a traffic jam for a block and a half in either direction. I had no idea things happened like that! The people who worked at the post office were running back and forth, trying to keep the mailboxes from overflowing. Cars were coming from all directions; everybody just wanted to drop in their income taxes.

You know what really struck me that night? Out of all of the people I was in line with and passing, I did not see one smile. That's what it's like when you and I are persuaded to give only because of a requirement. If that is your only reason to give, you are missing something.

Here's the second way Christians are persuaded to give: they are made to understand that if they don't give, it limits their blessings. The Bible teaches that if we do not tithe, we're robbing God. Malachi 3:8-12 states this most clearly.

'Will a mere mortal rob God? Yet you rob me.

'But you ask, "How are we robbing you?"

'In tithes and offerings. You are under a curse—your whole nation—because you are robbing me. Bring the whole tithe into the storehouse, that there may be food in my house. Test me in this,' says the Lord Almighty, 'and see if I will not throw open the floodgates of heaven and pour out so much blessing that there will not be room enough to store it. I will prevent pests from devouring your crops, and the vines in your fields will not drop their fruit before it is ripe,' says the Lord Almighty. 'Then all the nations will call you blessed, for yours will be a delightful land,' says the Lord Almighty.

With this verse and others, Christians are often persuaded that they will miss God's blessings if they don't get this area of life right.

Look in the Old Testament at the story of the people of God crossing the Jordan River, entering the Promised Land, and laying siege to Jericho. The Bible tells us in Hebrews 3-4 that the taking of the Promised Land was a natural, historical event, but it is also a picture that contains spiritual truths for you and I, as Christians in the New Covenant.

Here's the story. The Israelites crossed the Jordan River and laid siege to the city of Jericho. God told them not to take a single thing out of the city, but what happened? One man took some things for himself. As a result, the Israelites didn't get any more wins. They started getting beat. In the next battle, a little, tiny town called Ai knocked them out. The leaders of Israel were scratching their heads, wondering what on earth was going on. God said, "You're not going to get any more of the Promised Land until you get this right. You've got something that's mine."

Jericho is a picture of the tithe. If you study the book of Joshua, you'll find that the people of God laid siege to and sacked ten cities. Jericho was the first of the ten—the first 10 percent. Ai shows us the results of withholding the full tithe. You and I can get saved and start coming into the promises of God, but we're not going to get very far into those promises without getting this area of our life right.

"Well, I don't really believe that, Myles. I hear what you're saying, but I just don't agree with that."

You know what? That's fine. You don't have to believe it, but I'll tell you this: a man with experience is never at the mercy of a man with an argument. You have an argument; that's fine and wonderful. But I'm living it, and I can tell you what exactly happens.

"Oh, you pastors, you're all alike. Always fleecing the sheep."

I don't keep any of your wool in my house. I used to work for American Express. The annual bonuses I received working for them were more than twice as much as my annual salary as a pastor. That's a fact. And if your argument is that pastors are all about getting and receiving, let me tell you that there is no way what I receive will ever catch up with what I have given into the Kingdom of God. If you say that I am all about getting, then you don't know me. And if other pastors are a little bit too successful for your taste, maybe they're just blessed because they have been walking in the promises of God for their lives. Honestly, if you don't think that most pastors and associate pastors couldn't go out into the business world and make three or four or five times what they get paid working in ministry, then you need to pay more attention.

A lot of pastors around the world hate preaching on giving. I love to preach on giving. I really do. I love to preach and teach on giving because my hands and my heart are clean, and I want you to walk in the same blessings and benefits and promises that Sallie and I have walked in all these years.

Your church doesn't need money. God will take care of that. God has always provided for everything that He wanted His churches to do, and He always will. You're not going to give? God will just raise up somebody else. It's just like when Mordecai told Esther it was time for her to step up and fulfill God's will for her life. He told her this: "For if you remain silent at this time, relief and deliverance for the Jews will arise from another place, but you and your father's family will perish," (Esther 4:14). Here's the Myles Sweeney translation of that verse: "Honey, this is your opportunity. This is a God-ordained time period for you. But if you don't do it, guess what. God will raise up somebody else in your place." God makes sure His stuff gets taken care of. If you don't give, you'll be the one that loses, not God.

This is not just stuff that I preach and teach. This is stuff that I live personally, or else I wouldn't preach and teach about it. There has been so many different times in my life where God has showed me something powerful, and then this little conversation happens:

I say, "I can't wait to preach that."

Then God says, "No, don't preach that."

"What?"

"Don't preach it."

"But God, this is an incredible revelation."

"You're right, but you're not preaching that right now. Come back to me in five or six years."

God always leads me to live things out before I preach them. He made me live some things for about fifteen years before He finally told me that I could preach them.

As for my family and I, we are walking in so much blessing because we give. And I am not just talking about financial blessings. That's the small stuff, the least of them. We have all kinds of blessings in our lives because we got this right. We lived this out through the good times and the tough times. The tough times are when you prove what's really in your heart.

Giving is not just something for individuals, either. Successful, blessed churches live out this value, too. I have seen churches and church campuses on the verge of having a gorgeous new building, or a brand new property. It's such an exciting time, but it's never about the building. It's about lives. It's always about lives. It's about more people being touched, changed, and transformed by God.

I remember when the church I was leading in Wharton was saving for a new building, the church leaders had an inside joke for many years. They used to say that we were never going to get a new building because every time we got our building fund up to $200,000 or $250,000 I would give it all away. And they were right! They joked about it, but they understood exactly why. They knew that giving like that was how we were going to get a building in the first place. Every time we found another church out there trying to build a building, we would just give them $100,000. That is how we built our own building. We gave corporately because we knew the truth of God's Word, not because we were persuaded to.

There is one more way Christians are persuaded to give: they are made to understand that giving is a good investment. This one is simple and short. Luke 6:38 says, "Give, and it will be given to you. A good measure, pressed down, shaken together and running over, will be poured into your lap."

"What a good investment plan! You mean I put a little in, and I get a whole lot out?"

That's correct.

"Oh man, this is a good deal. We're making deals with God today. I put it in. I get it out."

Do you know that you cannot out give God? My wife and I have always heard people say that, but years ago we decided to try to do it. We took care of bills and everything, but we used anything extra to try to out give God. It did not work. We've tried to do that for more than forty years now, and it has never worked. You cannot out give God. Just try it. Give it a run. I'm telling you, you're not going to be able to. It's not possible. God will never be proved a liar in anything that He says, and He says that He will always give back to you in greater measure. So giving *is* a good investment, but this shouldn't be our only reason to give. If it is, giving becomes nothing more than a business deal with God.

Please, please listen to me right now. Every single one of the three ways Christians are often persuaded to give has a biblical basis. They are all biblically accurate, but, at the same time, they miss God's heart. It's a different thing to have His heart for giving inside of us.

To see God's heart for giving, just look at the story in Mark 12:41-44.

Jesus sat down opposite the place where the offerings were put and watched the crowd putting their money into the temple treasury. Many rich people threw in large amounts. But a poor widow came and put in two very small copper coins, worth only a few cents.

Calling his disciples to him, Jesus said, "Truly I tell you."

When Jesus said, "Truly I tell you," He was telling His disciples to really, really, *really* listen to what He was about to say. That's the meaning of the Greek phrase He used.

Anytime Jesus speaks, it ought to be like that old commercial for EF Hutton, the stock brokerage firm. In the commercial a bunch of businessmen are sitting in a restaurant having lunch. Two of them are talking about investments and the advice of their brokers. Then one of them says, "Well, my broker is EF Hutton, and he says—" Immediately everybody in the restaurant stops to listen, including the waiter. Then the narrator says, "When EF Hutton talks, people listen."

When Jesus speaks, we should all listen very intently. Everything He says is incredibly important. But when Jesus Himself says, "Truly I tell you," before He says something, we really, really, *really* need to listen to it. Our ears should perk up.

What did He say after that phrase in Mark 12?

> *Calling his disciples to him, Jesus said, "Truly I tell you, this poor widow has put more into the treasury than all the others. They all gave out of their wealth; but she, out of her poverty, put in everything—all she had to live on."*

God is not concerned with the amount. He is concerned with the heart. A number of people gave out of abundance. They showed up in their Versace robes, pulled out their wads of hundreds, peeled off twenty of them, and dropped them in there, Jesus yawning the entire time. Then this little widow showed up and dropped in her two pennies. Jesus jumped up and said, "WOW! Did you see that?"

Can I let you in on a secret? God is loaded. It's not about the money because God doesn't need your money. Please hear me in this. Giving isn't for God. Giving is for you. We really don't understand that in the Church.

When my three oldest kids—Kate, Matt, and Susanna—were young and still growing up in our household, we had a family ritual we liked to periodically observe. It was a very important ritual involving Oreos and ice-cold glasses of milk. You might be tracking with me here. We would fill up four glasses of ice cold milk, and then I would have the kids sit at the table with the milk and pick one of them, a different one each time, to come with me into the kitchen.

Let's imagine a specific instance of this. I say, "Matt, come with me." Matt and I go into the kitchen while his two sisters sit at the table. We get in there, open the pantry, and take out the package of Oreo cookies. Then I count out three of them for Kate, three of them for Susanna, three of them for Matt, and three of them for me. Then I give the cookies to Matt and tell him to go to the table and pass them out.

Now, I did not give Matt those cookies for Kate's and Susanna's benefit. If it were just about the girls, I could have handed the cookies directly to them and saved myself a little hassle, trouble, and time. And I certainly did not give my three cookies to Matt for my benefit. I could have just gotten them myself. In fact, I could have gotten ten instead of three. A lot of times I went back to the pantry after they had gone to bed and did get ten for myself, but that's a different story.

Why did I give all the cookies to Matt? I did that for Matt's benefit. I wanted him to experience the joy of giving. I wanted him to learn what a joy it is to give to others so that he could develop a heart like mine. God had already changed my heart to the point where I loved to give. I had Matt give the cookies to his sisters and to me because of what it would do for him.

I hope you're connecting these dots because this is powerful. In the story we looked at a moment ago, Jesus came to the Temple to teach. Then He stopped to show His disciples something about people's hearts. He stopped to show them something about people's love. To do this, He gathered all twelve disciples and took them over to Solomon's Colonnade.

"Where all the teaching was done?"

No.

"You mean He didn't take them to the people who were writing the most notes and saying, 'Amen!' the most? Those are the ones who love God the most, right?"

Nope.

"Then He must have been taking them over to the worship area, with all the people who jump the highest and sing the loudest. Those are the ones who really love God."

No, that isn't where He took them. He brought them straight to the treasury box, where people came to put their tithes and offerings. He said, "Come with me. Let's stand right over here and watch. I'm going teach you something about people's hearts, about their love. Here comes one. Watch what he does. Oh, here comes another one."

I'm telling you, some members of my congregation would have a cow—more like a herd—if they came up on Sunday morning to give and I was standing over to the side watching. But that's exactly what Jesus did. He went to the treasury box because He wanted to teach His disciples about people's hearts. He was showing them how to tell if a person had a heart like His.

I have two books that are records of love. The first one is my Bible. That is a record of God's love for me and for us. But I have a second book that is another record of love. It's my checkbook. My checkbook is a record of what I love. You know what you would see if you looked at mine?

"Ok, yeah. Bills, bills, bills. Ooh, Chili's. More bills, more bills. Chili's again. Mm hmm, yeah, Chili's again. A couple of donut shops in there, but we'll skip those. Huh, Chili's again. I think this guy really loves Chili's."

If your heart hasn't yet become like God's in this area, this idea may be offensive to you. If you don't like where I'm going with this right now, then let me tell you something. God's record book is clear about His love for us. Is your record book clear about your love for Him? Come on. That's fair. God is a realist. He is clear with you about what is really going on; He has showed you His record book, and it tells you something. What does your record book tell Him?

Look at what Paul wrote in 2 Corinthians 8:1-4.

"And now, brothers and sisters, we want you to know about the grace that God has given the Macedonian churches. In the midst of a very severe trial, their overflowing joy and their extreme poverty welled up in rich generosity. For I testify that they gave as much as they were able and even beyond their ability entirely on their own. They urgently pleaded with us for the privilege of sharing in this service to the Lord's people."

One quick note here. Paul was talking about Macedonia and Achaea, which were two different provinces in the Roman Empire. Macedonia in that day was made up of what is now Macedonia and the very northern part of Greece. Achaea was all of the rest of Greece. Macedonia was one of the poorest areas in the whole Roman Empire, but Achaea was the wealthiest province in all of the Roman Empire. Achaea was wealthier than Rome itself. Now let's look back at what Paul is saying in this passage, this time in The Message translation.

"I want to report on the surprising and generous ways in which God is working in the churches in Macedonia province. Fierce troubles have come down on the people of those churches, pushing them to the very limit. The trial exposed their true colors. They were incredibly happy, though desperately poor. The pressure triggered something totally unexpected—an outpouring of pure and generous gifts. I was there and saw it for myself."

These verses have a little more impact when you know about Macedonia's situation, don't they?

Let me just pause for a moment to tell you about something that happened to me and to our churches in the Houston area. In 2017, Hurricane Harvey caused massive flooding all over South Texas where a lot of our GMI churches are located. Not long after that, a pastor that we had connections with visited from Ukraine. We had gone to Ukraine many times before on mission trips, so we had a relationship with this pastor. Do you know what he handed me when he arrived in Houston? He handed me an envelope from scores of churches in Ukraine that all took up an offering for flood relief for people in our churches. I was so humbled. I just sat there and wept in my office.

The people of Ukraine were economically destitute. The churches that gave couldn't afford to pay their pastors more than $100 or $200 a month, and many of them couldn't even afford to rent a place for two hours on a Sunday. When they heard about the floods going on in Houston, scores of them called two-hour and three-hour prayer meetings several nights that week. They were praying for our churches and for the people in our churches. I knew about the prayer meetings, and I was already so grateful. But then that pastor came and handed me the envelope. I just sat there and cried because I knew I couldn't refuse it, but it was so hard to receive. When I expressed to him how hard it was, he just said, "But Myles, they gave with such joy." The passage from 2 Corinthians 8 came to my mind immediately.

Paul said, "I was there and saw for myself," (2 Cor. 8:1-4, MSG). The Macedonians gave offerings of whatever they had and far more than they could afford, pleading for the privilege of helping the Achaeans. Paul goes on in 2 Corinthians 8:8, "I am not commanding you, but I want to test the sincerity of your love by comparing it with the earnestness of others." In the context, Paul was talking about giving. When he said earnestness, he meant giving. He was saying that he wanted to test the sincerity of their love by comparing it to the giving of others.

You don't like that? Doesn't really matter. I don't know about you, but I didn't get a vote. Maybe you got a survey form in the mail from God, but I didn't. He just gave us His Word. It doesn't matter whether we like it or not. You and I are simply to bow our knees to it and say, "Yes, God. You are right."

Don't give unless you really want to. God doesn't want you to give unless you really want to. Let's be honest and real and straightforward about giving. God loves a joyful, a cheerful, and a hilarious giver. Somebody who loves to give. God likes it when people like that give money. But for the rest of you, just keep your money until your heart changes.

2 Corinthians 8:7 says, "But since you excel in everything—in faith, in speech, in knowledge, in complete earnestness and in the love we have kindled in you—see that you also excel in this grace of giving."

I have already told you a story about the pastor's conference I spoke at in New Delhi, India, but I want to tell you another. This was the eight-day conference I did with only one other pastor, who was a powerful, powerful man of God and a legend around the world. This man, in his early seventies at the time, was an incredible pastor and speaker who had planted hundreds of churches in many different places.

There were 1,400 pastors and their wives at this conference, and we worked together to do four teachings every day. That was one of the most phenomenal times of ministry I've ever experienced in my life. It was incredible. The meetings were very powerful, but, looking back on it, the most powerful parts of the whole thing were the evenings after the long days of teaching and ministry. The other pastor and I were staying in an Indian pastor's home, sharing a small bedroom together. They had put two makeshift beds and two little tables in there. Every night we would come in tired, but we always wanted to look over our messages for the next day so that we could tinker with, rewrite, change, and read over them. We had some wonderful conversations, both sitting there at those little tables in that room. We did that every night. One of those nights we were talking, and I said, "Can I ask you a question?"

"Sure, anything," he said.

"I know this is a horrible question, but if you had to pick one thing that most changed your life and your ministry, what would that thing be?"

He said, "Actually, I've been asked that question a number of times, and I always answer it the same way. It's a little bit of a story."

"Will you please tell me?"

"Well, after we had been in the mission field for almost twenty years, my wife and I were told by the mission organization we were a part of that we needed to take eighteen months on furlough. They told us we needed to take a break and forced us to take eighteen months away from the mission field. So we took a ship back home to England. The day we left port I was in the room praying and seeking God, and God spoke very, very clearly to me. It was one of the clearest times that I've heard God in my life. He said to me, 'I don't want you to take a job.'

"I said, 'Well, God, I'm married. I've got two young children. I have to . . . How am I—'

"'I'm going to teach you about faith. And I'm going to teach you about something even more important,' God said.

"I was wondering what could be more important than faith, but it was clear. I struggled with it. Of course my family and my in-laws were asking me what job I was going to do. I told them I wasn't going to get one. They called me a bum. They called me a lazy jerk. It all started coming in.

"So we're there in England, and we don't know what's going to happen. But one of the brothers from a church we were connected with came and met us on the dock while we were unloading. We had never met him before, but he said, 'I have a house. Do you have a place to live? I'll give it to you free. You can use it the whole eighteen months that you're here.' At that moment I thanked God for provision, thinking that it was going to be a glorious time.

"But, Myles, it didn't end up like that at all. We would spend days on forced fast. We fasted because we didn't have a choice. It was one thing if it was just happening to me or even just happening to my wife and I, but our children. It was awful. We had young children that we couldn't buy diapers for. Then God would show up with the most amazing things. Every artist always says that God shows up at the 11th hour, but that isn't the way God works at all. God is always on *his* time. It's not our time, but it's his.

"One time, for example, we didn't have any food. We had been on a fast for a couple of days. Then this guy knocks on our door. He was a vegetable farmer who was taking his crop into the city to sell in the market. He told us that he had driven by our house hundreds of times, but this time the Lord spoke to him and told him to turn around, go back, and give us everything we wanted out of the back of his truck. We got all these fresh fruits and vegetables that we stored up. It was just like that; I could tell you one story after another after another.

"Another time we were in the middle of another one of those times where we hadn't had anything. I was crying out to God, saying 'Why are you making us go through this? I don't understand what's going on.' Then the phone rang and I got a call from a pastor that I know from a big church there in London asking me to preach. I got so excited, and I was looking forward to preaching. But, truthfully, I was mainly excited because it was a big church, and I knew that they were going to give a big offering that we desperately needed. My only concern was that we had hardly any gas in the car, and I wasn't sure if we'd be able to make it to the service that morning. So we started praying the day before that God would multiply the gas in the tank so that we could get to the service. We were afraid that we would run out of gas, not get there, and not get the offering. The whole way there I was driving the car, sweating and praying. God, let us get there. We would get to a stoplight, and I'd hear a chug and say, 'No, no, no, Lord!' But I kept looking in the rear view mirror, and my wife was in the back with the children praying away. I told her, 'That's it, honey. Pray!'

"'No, no, no,' she said. 'You don't understand what I'm doing.'

"'What are you doing?' I said.

"'I'm praying for money,' she said.

"'Yes, that's it!'

"'No. We're going to church and I have nothing give.'

"Myles, I looked back and literally thought she had lost her mind. I thought it was gone. But we got to the church and pull in the parking lot. I was thanking God we made it there. We got out of the car and started walking across the parking lot. Then a man we didn't know walked straight over to my wife, handed her an envelope that was over-flowing with bills, and said, 'Here. God spoke to me this week and told me to go get some of my savings out of the bank, put it in an envelope, and wait until he told me what to do with it. I was walking into church and God turned me around, pointed you out to me, and said that I'm supposed to give this to you.'

"I don't know how much money it was, but it was a bunch because he couldn't even close the envelope. My wife and I were both thanking God. Then the man walked off, and I said, 'Honey, hand that enve-lope to me.'

"'No, I won't,' she said.

"'What?'

"'No, I won't.'

"'Honey, give that to me.'

"'No, I won't. I'm going to put it in the collection plate. I'm going to give this.'

"'You've gone crazy. Give me that envelope,' I said.

"'No. I prayed. I asked God for this, and the man said God told him to give it to me, not you.'

"Myles, there we were, my wife and I, having a heated argument there in the parking lot of the church that I was about to preach in. People starting to walk by and look at us, and I gave in. But I was fuming. I was mad. I had steam coming out of my ears. We got in the church, but I was praying the whole time that God would bring her to her senses before they took up the offering. I couldn't enter into worship or think about my message because I was so worried about the money. We desperately needed that money.

"Then they started the offering. I looked over at her, and she was just all fidgety and happy. I started praying they would start the offering plate on her side so that when she put the money in, I could take it out. Of course, God had it planned better than that. They came to my side, and I handed the plate to her with the hardest, meanest look I could give. She never even looked at me. She took that whole envelope, set it down in the plate, and passed it on.

"I was so mad. It was all I could do to stay quiet. I sat there, breathing heavily. Then I looked back over at her, and, Myles, she had such a glow and a joy on her face. She was so happy that she had given. Then something in me just woke me up, and I realized that she had something that I didn't have. She had something that I desperately needed. I managed to muddle my way through the sermon that morning, and God blessed us with the offering. But that was a turning point in my life and my ministry. I was never the same after that Sunday."

Do you want that? Is there something in you that wants to have God's heart in this area of giving? This is who God is. It's not just some sideline aspect of who He is. This is at His core. Do you want to be like Him? There is no greater joy than the joy in giving your money, your time, your talent, and your entire life away to the people around you and to God's Kingdom.

RIGHT SONG, WRONG SIDE

Worship is a huge topic. We engage in worship in church services every Sunday. It is not just the preliminaries before we get to the "real ministry" of preaching the Word; that's nonsense. Worship is powerful and important in the lives of believers and in the life of the Church. Most of us know that worship is important, but not all of us know that worship ties directly into our trust in God.

Many of you know the story in Exodus of God delivering the Israelites from Egypt. For those of you that do not, let me give you a quick recap. The people of God have just been rescued from four hundred years of slavery. It is easy to just gloss over a fact like that, but pause for a minute and think about how long that was. Four hundred years of slavery. That is ten generations. For ten generations, all the Israelites have known is slavery. At this point it is built into who they are. Four hundred years of horrendous slavery. Then God sets them free.

These people literally dance out of Egypt. And they are not just leaving with their freedom. The Egyptian people were desperate for God's plagues to end, so they showered the Israelites with their gold, silver, and jewels on the way out. God's people dance out of there with the goods.

The Israelites then travel for a few days before they run into the Red Sea and camp there. While they are camping there, Pharaoh has a sudden change of heart and decides to send his whole army to wipe them out. So the Egyptian army rolls up to the Red Sea, and the Israelite people go into a panic with a capital *P*. They begin to cry out, and they are not crying out with things like, "Oh God, we trust You!" They are crying out with things like, "What on earth have you done to us, Moses? You and your God did this! Why didn't we just stay in Egypt? You brought us out here to be slaughtered!" So they are throwing a fit.

God steps in, quiets them down, and gives Moses directions. Moses lifts his staff over the water of the Red Sea, and it parts so that they can walk through on dry ground. Then, after they are on the other side, the Egyptian army tries to follow them through, and God covers them with the sea. He wipes them out.

A lot of people today, even people who are supposedly believers, want to discount the miracles of the Bible. The virgin birth? That didn't really happen. Water to wine? Nah, man. Walking on water? That is just kind of symbolism. They try to take all of the miracles out of the Bible because they do not believe in miracles. The parting of the Red Sea is a miracle that people like this attack very frequently. This is their battle strategy: the Israelites did not cross the Red Sea at all. They crossed a different sea called the Reed Sea. That sea got its name from the reeds coming up out of the water, which is only about two feet deep. That is why the Israelites were able to cross it.

My response to this is like the response of the little boy whose mom was a believer, but whose dad was not. Maybe you have heard this story before. This little boy's dad did not go to church because he did not want to listen to all that hokey stuff and nonsense, all the lies and myths and legends. He was not going there. But the mom took the little boy with her to church one Sunday. They came home afterwards, and the little boy came running into the house all ecstatic. He said, "Dad! Dad! Church was incredible! You should have been there! We heard about this amazing miracle!"

His dad said, "Oh, miracle? Whoa, whoa, whoa, stop. There is no such thing as miracles."

"No, dad," he said, "There was!" The little boy told his dad the story of the Israelites walking through the parted Red Sea.

"No, no, no. Sit down here for a minute, son. Let me explain this to you. That is all nonsense. Some smart people have discovered that it was not the Red Sea that the Israelites crossed. It was the Reed Sea. The water was only two feet tall, so it was no big deal."

The little boy sat there for a minute and looked at his dad, downcast. Then all of a sudden his eyes brightened up. He looked at his dad and said, "That is a miracle! It's an incredible miracle!"

"Are you not listening to me?" his dad said.

"Oh, I heard you, Dad. But it's still a miracle," he said.

"What are you talking about? I told you it was the Reed Sea. It was only two feet deep. That's it."

"I know, Dad, but it was a miracle. God drowned the whole Egyptian army in two feet of water!"

One way or the other, it was a miracle. Of course we know it wasn't the Reed Sea. It was the Red Sea. Here is an interesting truth about the Red Sea: it is over one mile deep. Think about that for a minute. Some of us have seen a rendering of the parting of the Red Sea in pictures or in the movies—the old classic with Charlton Heston or maybe something newer. It is pretty impressive to see someone's idea of the parting of the Red Sea play out, but none of those adaptations really capture the scope and magnitude of the actual event. One mile deep. Think about how far one straight, uninterrupted mile truly is. Measure one out if you have to. Think about what it would be like to walk through the middle of the Red Sea on dry ground with walls of water one mile high on either side of you. What would that have been like?

The Israelites pass through the sea. The Egyptian army tries to follow. The water collapses on them and wipes them out completely. Not a single Egyptian soldier lives. All of this happens in Exodus 14; we are going to pick up the story with the response of God's people in Exodus 15:1-5.

Then Moses and the Israelites sang this song to the Lord:

"I will sing to the Lord,
for he is highly exalted.
Both horse and driver
he has hurled into the sea.

"The Lord is my strength and my defense;
he has become my salvation.
He is my God, and I will praise him,
my father's God, and I will exalt him.
The Lord is a warrior;
the Lord is his name.
Pharaoh's chariots and his army
he has hurled into the sea.
The best of Pharaoh's officers
are drowned in the Red Sea.
The deep waters have covered them;
they sank to the depths like a stone."

Would you like to see that happen to your enemies? I am not talking about your neighbors and your in-laws. I am talking about your real enemies. We don't fight against flesh and blood, but there are spiritual things coming against us. Would you like to see those enemies completely wiped out? The Israelites saw that. It was an incredible victory. But, in a very real sense, it was also a shallow, empty, and short-lived victory.

On God's part, obviously, it was complete. And the people of God sang a great song afterwards. I just quoted the first five verses; the song goes on through most of the chapter. They sang about God's faithfulness and His goodness. They sang about God's might and His power. They sang about how He is a warrior who watches over them and cares for them. They sang all of these wonderful things about God. It is a great song, but there is one problem. They sang it on the wrong side. They sang it after they had already crossed the Red Sea instead of on the original side. It was the right song, but it was the wrong side.

There are always two sides. Every single trial or difficulty we go through has two sides. There is the testing side, and there is the victory side. The testing side is where you are in the mix, wondering if there is any way out. You don't know how what you are going through is ever going to get resolved. You don't see the light at the end of the tunnel. You don't know how long it is going to last. Then the day comes when God intervenes and things change. He moves, and all of a sudden you come through to the other side. That is the victory side. God is good. Hallelujah. You rejoice. You can look back and see what God was doing.

There will always be both—testing side and victory side. God wants us, His children, to come to a place where we worship Him and praise Him whole-heartedly not only on the victory side, but also on the testing side. God deserves our worship even in the darkest moments of our lives. God deserves our worship *especially* when we are in those dark times—when things don't make sense and don't look like they are ever going to get any better.

Anybody can praise God on the victory side. Even unbelieving believers can praise Him then. Even heathens, who don't really believe in God, sometimes light a candle or ring a bell or something for an unnamed "higher power" when they are on the victory side. Thank you, whoever you are up there. Anybody can praise when everything gets resolved, when the goodness and life are showing forth. But can you praise in the difficult times? Because that is when you find out what is really in your heart.

Do you want to know what is really in your heart? Do you want to know what you really believe about God? Do you want to know what you really believe about what God thinks of you and who you are in Him? Evaluate yourself. Take a dip stick and stick it down into your heart. But don't stick it in there when everything is good and life is wonderful. That will give you a false reading. Everybody registers as full when life is good. Instead, take that dip stick and stick it down into your heart when you are going through a really difficult time. What is the measure? That is what you really believe about who God is and who you are in Him.

I know I said this earlier, but I am going to say it again because it needs to be said. Christians are a lot like tea bags. You have no idea what is inside of them until you drop them in hot water. Then what is really inside their hearts comes streaming out. It doesn't really matter what I look like when everything is going well. It doesn't matter how often I say, "Hallelujah! Praise God! Life is good!" What happens when things are in a bad spot? Do I worship God then? Do I praise Him then?

This may not be the typical message on praise and worship, but this is a very, very important part of worship. We, as Christians, need to get this in our lives. We need to come to a place where we really are a faith-filled people. We need to know who God is. We need to be absolutely and completely assured that He loves us, He cares for us, and He is watching over us. The Word says He knows the exact number of hairs on your head! That might be easier for some people than it is for others, I know, but it is still meaningful.

Isaiah 29:13 says this: "The Lord says: 'These people come near to me with their mouth and honor me with their lips, but their hearts are far from me. Their worship of me is based on merely human rules they have been taught.'" That sounds a lot like Christians today who sing songs about God's goodness, faithfulness, and love for them, then, when they experience difficult situations, turn around and tell God, "I thought you loved me! I can't believe you just—" Really? I want to be a person who doesn't just *lip* it, but *lives* it. Don't just be a lipper. Be a liver. Don't just have God's praise on your lips. Live them out in your life, especially in the difficult times.

Think about how the Israelites responded when the Egyptian army showed up behind them at the Red Sea. It is really amazing when you think about it. How many days? Not weeks. Not months. How many *days* had it been since God delivered them from Egypt? How many days since they saw the Nile River turn into blood? How many days since they watched hail fall from a clear sky and turn into fire when it hit the ground?

But then the Egyptian army showed up on the scene. The chariots came over the crest of the hill, and the Israelites saw them. You know what they should have done? After what they had just went through, they should have burst forth in song.

"Hey, hand me a tambourine. Come on, pass them out. These Egyptian guys are fools; they are going down. Do they still not understand who God is? Don't they get that we are God's people and that His favor is on us? They don't get it, but I do. Sword? No, I don't need a sword. Just give me that tambourine. Oh God, you are good. You are faithful. I get to be on the front row and watch another one of these go down. Wow. Tambourine in one hand, popcorn in the other. This is going to be fun to watch."

If they had understood, deep down in their hearts, who God was and who they were to God, they could have marched straight into Canaan and taken the Promised Land. They could have waltzed right in there and taken it all.

"What are all these 'ites doing hanging around on our property? Amalekites, Hittites, Jebusites. What are you 'ites doing? You guys need to clear out. Giants? Whatever. Fortified cities? Whatever. Let's start singing. Let's start praising God."

They could have taken it, singing songs.

"God, you are so faithful and so good. Oh, give thanks to the Lord for His love endures forever. We are His people. Oh yeah. His favor and blessing are on us. We are more than conquerors. We are overcomers.

This is the day. This is the time. This is the place. We are the people, and this is our day. It's our time to take what's ours."

Oh, the songs they could have sung and the victories they could have seen.

Instead, the Israelites responded out of a heart issue. They did not trust God or worship Him in advance through faith. They accused God of neglecting them. That's not a pretty way to say it, but that's what really went down here. They never came out and said it, they accused Him with their behavior. They did not learn the lesson, so they were destined to repeat the test.

This is truth. This is life. If you don't learn a lesson, you are destined to repeat it. If you don't pass the test, you get to take it over again. That is not God getting after you for not passing the test. That is God's love and favor on you. God loves you enough to hang in there with you and develop character in you—the character of His own nature and the nature of His Son. So having to take a test again is really not bad news. It is good news. It means God doesn't expel you. He doesn't kick you out when you flunk the test. He just says, "It's fine that you flunked the test. Here's what we're going to do. We're going to walk together for a while longer. Hopefully you'll understand more of who I am and who you are to Me. Then you get to take the test again. And if you fail it again, it won't stop me. I love you. I'm persevering with you. I'm long-suffering with you. I'm patient with you because I want this character in you. We're just going to keep walking together and taking this test until you pass it." That is the way God works. You have to keep taking the test until you pass it because He is very serious about you becoming who you say you want to become.

God wants you to live a good life. God wants you to have pleasant things, but He is more interested in your character than your pleasure because He is a good dad and a good parent. If you are a good parent, are you not more concerned with your child's character than you are with your child's pleasure in the moment? God doesn't mind us having stuff. He is a good dad who like to bless us with things. But He is more interested in your character. Sometimes you might have to take a step back from stuff until you get the character you need in your life. Character is worth a whole lot more than any stuff or any pleasure you could ever have.

When you face tests and trials in your life, you are going to keep taking them over and over and over until you finally pass them. That is life. That is God's goodness. Don't whine. Don't complain about it. Don't say God is being bad to you. God is being good to you. He is trying to develop you and bring you forward into something bigger and better and more wonderful.

The Israelites did not pass their test, so they had to take it again just three days later. Exodus 15:23-24 gives us the story, "When they came to Marah, they could not drink its water because it was bitter. . . . So the people grumbled against Moses, saying [in their whiniest of whiny voices], 'What are we going to drink?'"

God just delivered these people from four hundred years of slavery. They watched as He worked a bunch of miracles just so they could walk off with a bunch of Egyptian goodies. God delivered them at the Red Sea. They saw Him wipe out their enemies behind them. And now they are all complaining because the water tastes a little bitter.

What does God do? He is not like me, and that is a good thing for the Israelites. God is long-suffering, merciful, kind, and good to them. He sweetens the water for them. Surely now they've learned the lesson. They didn't pass the test this time, but they've got it next time for sure, right? Nope. The test comes again less than a month and a half later. Exodus 16:2-3 says, "In the desert the whole community grumbled against Moses and Aaron. The Israelites said to them, 'If only we had died by the Lord's hand in Egypt! There we sat around pots of meat and ate all the food we wanted, but you have brought us out into this desert to starve this entire assembly to death.'"

"Really? Are they serious? Are these the same guys we've been reading about?"

Yeah.

"These are the same ones that saw, that went through all that?"

Yeah.

"And we're doing this again?"

Yeah.

What's the deal? It's a heart issue. So what does God do in His mercy and goodness and graciousness? He just postpones the test, extends it out a little further. In the meantime, manna in the morning, quail in the evening. That's not a bad deal. I have never had manna, but I have had quail, and it's awfully good. So every morning the Israelites go out and pick up the manna on the ground. Every evening quail just drops into the camp. No shotguns needed; they fall in to be picked up. What a deal.

Surely now they have learned their lesson. For a few weeks they have rolled along and picked up the manna in the morning and quail in the evening. God has provided for them, and they haven't had to do a thing other than pick up the provision. Surely now they have learned their lesson. Surely now they can pass the test.

Nope. Just look at the next chapter, Exodus 17:1-3.

> *They camped at Rephidim, but there was no water for the people to drink. So they quarreled with Moses and said, "Give us water to drink."*
>
> *Moses replied, "Why do you quarrel with me? Why do you put the Lord to the test?"*
>
> *But the people were thirsty for water there, and they grumbled against Moses. They said, "Why did you bring*

us up out of Egypt to make us and our children and live-stock die of thirst?"

What is going on here? Why does this keep happening again and again and again? In fact, it is going to keep happening. They never pass the test, so this generation of Israelites ends up dying before they ever get to the Promised Land. They just die out there in the desert. Why? What is their deal? Here is the deal: they never ever really got it. They never understood. These were people who always sang of God's goodness and God's favor on the victory side, but never on the testing side. They always praised God on the victory side of the trials, but not once did they ever praise God on the testing side.

Here is a good question to ask yourself: When do I praise God?

God is the same yesterday, today, and forever. Do you believe that? It is from the Word, in Hebrews 13. That means God was the same last week, last month, and last year as He is today. That means He was the same last year, when you were in the middle of that mess, as He is today, when you are out of it and rejoicing over how good God is. He was good back then too. He was just as faithful, just as loving, just as compassionate, and just as caring when you were in the mess.

I got into an interesting conversation one Sunday morning when I was first developing this message. After the service was over, I started talking with a guy I didn't know. He was a fairly new member of the church. I was just visiting with him, but he said these exact words to me, "Myles, God was good this week." Then he started to tell me a story from his week, but I said, "Whoa, whoa, whoa, stop. I want to hear the story; I imagine it's a good one. But I can't let you say that and just move on. I'm sorry. I just can't. You've got to understand something. God was just as good the week before this one and the week before that and the week before that."

"Oh, yeah. Of course," he said.

Yeah nothing. This is something we cannot just accept with a "yeah" or an "of course." We have to really understand this and be firmly convinced of it. We can fall into "God was good this week" thinking so easily. But God is just as good and just as faithful when we are in the midst of a mess and it doesn't look like there is any change coming. If we are genuinely people of faith—people who believe in God and believe we are who He says we are—then we worship him *now*.

Can I be honest with you? Is it okay for a pastor to be honest? I might fall off somebody's pedestal after saying this, but that's a good thing. There are Sunday mornings when I do not feel like worshipping God. Do you know what that means? It means I'm human.

"Well, I just thought your life was so perfect and you just never—" You need to get educated. That's not what life is like.

"Are you talking about like two times in the last year?"

No, no, no. I don't feel like worshipping more times than that. You know what I do when I feel like that? I sit down and fold my arms because I am not going to be a hypocrite.

Not really. That would be foolish.

You know what I really do? I worship. And my worship is not out of hypocrisy, it is out of obedience to God's Word despite my circumstances and my feelings. I put on "the garment of praise for the spirit of heaviness," which is what the Bible tells us to do (Isaiah 61:3). Worship is a choice. It is a decision. If I get up and don't feel like worshipping, I tell God, "It doesn't matter. I am going to worship You because you are worthy. I am going to worship you because you were the same yesterday as you are today and will be when this thing gets resolved in my life."

We have to learn how to do that. We have to learn how to handle the moments when we don't want to worship. When those moments come, praise God and thank Him. Do it by faith. Do it because you know God is who He says He is. Do it because you know He loves you despite anything that might be going on. You know what will happen when you do that? All of a sudden—Bang!—you will start worshipping. Sometimes it might take a little while. It might be in the second or third song, but usually it will be within the first minutes of the first song. The heaviness will leave. The cloudy vision you did not want to admit you had will clear up. Circumstances will no longer dictate how you think and feel. You will worship. Make the decision. The feelings will follow.

I have discovered a powerful truth through the years of my life. When things are really bad and you are going through difficult circumstances, praising God is not just a good thing to do. In those times, praising God is not even just a good opportunity to measure and evaluate your faith in God. It is that, but it is not just that. There is something else here that is really important to understand. In difficult circumstances, praise is the pathway to victory in your life. Praise is the way you get from where you are to where God wants you to be.

For young believers, God will be gracious to you like He was to the Israelites. He will walk with you for a while as you learn about Him and who you are in Him. But there comes a time and a place where He says, "Okay. Time for you to grow up. Take the diaper off and put on some big boy pants. Come on, let's do this thing." There comes a time and a place where we need to start worshipping God in advance. When that time comes, you will not experience victory in your life until you start praising God. That is the only way it is going to happen.

Paul and Silas discovered this principle when they were in a Philippian jail. They went to Philippi because God told them to go, so they were walking in complete obedience to God. The people in Philippi greeted Paul and Silas warmly and showed them their nice Philippian shiny sticks. Then they introduced the pair to their nicest bed and breakfast.

Did I get that right? I meant that the Philippians beat Paul and Silas, put them in chains, and threw them in jail.

To all appearances, this was an awful situation. They spent the entire afternoon and evening of the day in this jail. Evening turned into night, which turned into late night. But even at midnight, Paul and Silas were still singing praises to God. God broke the chains. Praise was the pathway to their victory.

The same was true for Jonah. A lot of people don't know that about Jonah. You will miss it in the story unless you read carefully. Jonah decided to disobey God, so he got on a ship. When the ship hit a storm and almost went down, the crew just tossed Jonah overboard. He was swallowed by a whale. What happened inside the whale? Jonah 2:9 happened: "But I, with shouts of grateful praise, will sacrifice to you. What I have vowed I will make good. I will say, 'Salvation comes from the LORD.'" In the next verse, God commanded the fish to vomit Jonah up on the shore.

Praise is the pathway to victory in any situation. Sometimes the situation is thrust upon you, like it was for Paul and Silas. Sometimes the situation is of our own doing, like it was for Jonah. But either way, praise is the pathway to victory.

What about Jehoshaphat, the king of Judah? He had three massive armies gathered together against him and his limited forces. It looked like those enemies were going to annihilate the armies of Judah. Then God gave Jehoshaphat a word, and the king obeyed. He sent the musicians and singers to the front of the army. As they sang and worshipped, God wiped out the enemy (2 Chron. 20). God brought them victory in response to their praise.

My wife and I have discovered this to be true in our own lives as well. We discovered this truth years ago, and we began to walk it out in our life together. We have seen it happen over and over, time and time again. Something bad happens. Maybe it is a health or financial emergency. Maybe someone made up a terrible story about us that is spreading like wildfire. We have faced many bad situations, most of them not from our own actions. Do you know what I usually catch myself doing? Whining. I don't like to admit it, but it's true.

"I can't believe this. I've been faithful to you, God. I mean—"

Whoa, whoa, whoa. That is just whining. Whining is phase one. Here is phase two:

"OK, God. I accept this. You are going to do something good through this in my life, so I accept it. I don't like it. I'm not happy about it one bit, but I will accept it."

That is at least a victory over whining. Then comes phase three:

"You know what, God? I'm not just keeping a stiff upper lip anymore. I'm not just accepting this. I really see what You're doing in me through it. You're changing me. I still don't really like it a lot. It's still unpleasant. But I'm beginning to see that this is really a good thing here."

That is a victory over phase two. Then all of a sudden you graduate. It's time for phase four:

"God, you are so good. I never would have signed up for this course on my own, but I am so glad You signed me up for it. Wonderful things are happening in my life through this. I'm a different person than I was just a few months ago. I worship you, I praise you, and I thank you that in Your sovereignty and wisdom You are taking me through this."

For my wife and I, life always changed as soon as we finally got to a place where we were praising God in the midst of the situation. Not just praise because we knew we were supposed to praise, but real praise. We saw what God was doing in our lives through the situation, and we were thankful for it. Every time we got to that place, God moved very quickly, and the situation completely changed.

Somebody asked me a crazy question about this years ago at a pastors' conference. Another thing I learned long ago: if you speak at pastors' conferences, you will get a lot of crazy questions. Some of them will be kind of crazy, some of them will be very crazy, and some of them will be very good. This question was great. A young pastor came up to me and said, "Can I ask you a question?"

"Sure."

"Give me the two biggest faith lessons you've learned in your life," he said.

"You're going to have to give me a minute to think about that one," I said.

A part of me loves questions like that, but another part of me hates them. It is just hard to narrow things down that much. But I sat there and thought through all the lessons I had learned for a minute, and then I said, "Oh, I know what they are."

"Really?" he said.

"Oh yeah. I've got a bunch of them. But if you want me to narrow it down to two, I'll give them you give them to you real simple and real easy. Here's the first one: I learned how to give my way into prosperity. I learned how to give my way into blessing from a place of need. That's number one. Here's number two: I learned how to praise my way into victory."

If you get just those two things down in your life and in your walk with God, you are going to go along a long, long way. Just these two things have been life-changing for me and my wife and our family. They have changed where we are, where we have been, and what we have experienced in a very, very good way.

Take one more look back at Exodus 14, when the Egyptian army showed up at the Red Sea. The Israelites began to whine. Well, the Bible actually says they "cried out to the Lord," (Exod. 14:10). When you are in a mess, is it all right to cry out God? Yes, of course. But make sure that your cry is not a whine. Make sure it is a cry of faith. Don't cry out to Him with things like, "Why would You do this to me? How could You do that? Why are You letting this happen to me?" That's a whine.

So the Israelite people began to whine. What did God say to them in response?

"There, there, little ones. Gather 'round, little children. You just don't understand. Let me explain to you. Everything's gonna be okay. Don't be ruffled. Don't be bothered."

That's not at all what He said. In fact, He was pretty harsh. What did He say to them?

"Stop whining! Why are you crying out to me? Stop your whining. Get yourself together and move forward!"

I am paraphrasing, but that was the essence of God's message to the Israelites. Above everything else, God wanted them to move forward. That is what I want for you today, and I promise it is what the pastors, elders, and leaders of your church want for you. We want you to move forward into victory in your life. We want you to experience victory in your life, in your marriage, in your family, in your work, and in everything else your life touches. We want you to get this truth about worship, live it out, and experience it so you can develop your own life stories out of these things and use those stories to teach this principle to others. We want you to worship your way to victory again and again and again. We want you to be a person who moves forward with a song in your heart and on your lips, praising God all the way to where you are going.

A lot of times church services start with a worship leader excitedly asking something like, "Hey, how many of you had a great week this week? Been blessed this week? That's great! Well, why don't you just worship with me this morning? Let's worship God!"

What about when the opposite is true? We never hear that one.

"How many of you had an awful week this week? Horrible, terrible? How many of you are going through a really, really difficult season right now? Doesn't look like there's a light at the end of the tunnel? Well, we are going to worship for that today. Let's worship God!"

If you are battling something in your life right now, take this as your opportunity. Look that situation or that problem dead in the eye. Then worship God over it. Thank and praise God, staring straight at what you are struggling with. Take this opportunity to start applying these principles of worship in your life. Put on some worship music. Begin to praise the Lord in the midst of your situation. Step up and worship over whatever issue is before you right now. Whether it is a health issue, a financial issue, a job situation, a relationship problem, or something else, worship on the right side today.

LOVE THE HOUSE

I t is important for all of us to love the house of God. But before I can talk about doing that, I need to back up and make sure you understand what I mean when I use the word *love*.

Love is a decision. You have to make a decision to love. It's not something we can put on autopilot. Unfortunately, because of the fallen nature we inherited from Adam and Eve, human beings don't default to love. God defaults to love. We don't. We have to make a decision to love. So love is a decision, not an emotion. If you wait to feel loving before you love people, then your love is going to ebb and flow.

If you are married, then you know what I'm talking about, right? Sallie and I have been doing marriage counseling for many, many years. I can give you example after example after example of married couples who came to us for counseling and said something like this right off the bat: "I just don't feel any love for him/her anymore." That doesn't make any difference. Here's why: feelings follow actions, which follow decisions. If you don't feel love for your spouse anymore, then make a decision to love. Start doing the things a loving person would do; do the actions of love. Some people think that's hypocritical, but it's not. It's a decision of your will. You decide to love. As your actions follow that decision, the feelings will come.

I tell these things to all of the couples who come to Sallie and I for counseling, and I can't remember a single time one of those couples ever responded with, "Oh, what a great idea!" Nope. They all think it's crazy. But I have seen couples who listened to this advice go from not being able to sit on the same couch together to not being able to keep their hands off each other in just a few weeks.

Feelings follow actions, and actions follow decisions. Love is a decision.

As it is in a marriage, so it is in the Church, the house of God. I have never seen anyone withdraw from their marriage and end up loving their spouse more because of it. In the same way, I have never seen anyone withdraw from involvement in their church and end up loving the house more as a result. It just doesn't happen that way. If you're waiting to feel like loving the house before you love the house, your love for the house is going to ebb and flow.

When the disciples looked at Jesus' life, they saw His love for God. They also saw His love for God's house. At that time God's house was the Temple. When they saw Jesus' love for God's house, they all remembered the same passage in the Old Testament—Psalm 69:9, which says, "Zeal for your house consumes me." Wow. What a statement.

Zeal for the Lord's house didn't interest Jesus; it consumed Him. We are talking about a passion, a burning love, and a love put into action. That is God's ideal for us. God calls us all to become more Christ-like, and you can't say that you're becoming more like Christ without a consuming love for the church.

Some Christians think they can get away with just saying they love God, and that's it. Just me and God, doing our own little thing over here. That's not the truth. To love God is to love His house. We need to grow in our Christ-likeness until our passion for the house is so strong and unwavering that we never have to decide to love the church again. It needs to be a decision we have already made, a course we have already set.

I want to get into the heart of this truth by going over several Psalms written by David. These verses come from different times in David's life, and all of them indicate his love and passion for God's house, the thing that we now call the church. Psalm 26:8 says, "Lord, I love the house where you live, the place where your glory dwells."

Psalm 27:4 says, "One thing I ask from the Lord, this only do I seek: that I may dwell in the house of the Lord all the days of my life, to gaze on the beauty of the Lord and to seek him in his temple." David said, "One thing I ask." That's like rubbing the genie lamp for one wish. That's the one thing David wanted more than anything else: to dwell in God's house.

Psalm 36:7-9 says, "How priceless is your unfailing love, O God! People take refuge in the shadow of your wings. They feast on the abundance of your house; you give them drink from your river of delight. For with you is the fountain of life in your light, we see light."

Psalm 52:8 says, "But I am like an olive tree flourishing in the house of God; I trust in God's unfailing love for ever and ever. For what you have done I will always praise you in the presence of your faithful people."

Psalm 84:10 says, "Better is one day in your courts than a thousand elsewhere; I would rather be a doorkeeper in the house of my God than dwell in the tents of the wicked."

Psalm 92:12-13 says, "The righteous will flourish like a palm tree, they will grow like a cedar of Lebanon; planted in the house of the Lord, they will flourish in the courts of our God."

We could go on and on and on. It only took me about twenty minutes to pull these verses. It was very simple, very easy. There's a lot to pick from. And this is not just from the psalms or just in the Old Testament. You can see this same theme throughout all of Scripture. To love God is to love God's house. This is a big issue. It has been a big issue since the beginning of the Church, and it will continue to be one until the end of time.

But loving God's house is a key issue right now because so many Christians are entirely disillusioned with the idea of church. They are disillusioned with because they think it isn't what it should be, isn't what it could be, and isn't what it was designed by God to be. It has all these messed-up people in it. It is led by all these imperfect leaders.

At the heart of it, these Christians have been hurt and offended by some part of the church. Somewhere along the way they weren't treated the way they wanted to be. Maybe they weren't greeted properly one day, or maybe they weren't given enough recognition for their efforts. Whatever it was, something gave them enough motivation to cut themselves off. The Word of God is clear, saints. It is not just important to love God. It is important to love God's house. It is important to love the church.

To go deeper into this, let me back up and tell you a little bit about my background, my history, and my early church life. I got saved at the age of seventeen back in 1975. At that time I began to love God. Out of that love for God, I began to love God's house.

During the early years of my Christian life, I went off to school, graduated, got married, got a job in San Antonio, and then moved to California. Sallie and I spent time in a lot of different churches in that time. We weren't church-hopping, we would just move to a new place and have to find a new church.

As I look back at those churches, I would have to say they were pretty much nonspiritual houses. God's presence was not completely absent from them, but they all had a very natural, nonspiritual approach to church and the Christian life as a whole.

You might be thinking, "Poor you, Myles. It's such a shame you spent those early years of your Christian life in churches that didn't have much of God's presence and his power." You know what? I am very, very grateful for that time in my life. God led me down that path for a reason.

"Myles, can you work on this?"

"I need your help painting that."

"Myles, can you come over here and do this?"

I did a lot of different things in those churches. I didn't do them because of some great calling I had; I did them because they needed to be done. Maybe you are still thinking, "Poor you. You had to do all those things." Listen, those things were good for me. Through them I developed a love for the house of God.

That love was not dependent on my feelings. It was not dependent on me sensing or feeling God's call into a certain area. It was not dependent on me fulfilling my destiny because I didn't have a clue what that meant back then. It was not even dependent on me praying about everything I was asked to do or hearing a clear word from God. I just loved God, and I loved His house, and I loved the people in His house. That's what God's house is really made of—the people. I loved serving the people. I also loved the church leaders. I loved serving those God had put me under, and I loved doing things that went beyond their expectations.

Fast forward to 1991. Grace Community Fellowship in Wharton began. You may have heard some of the stories about that. God grew up a church underneath us, and we didn't even know what was going on. Once we picked up on what was happening, we started looking around, trying to figure out who was supposed to lead this new thing. Fingers kept pointing my way, and I kept saying no. Once I began to understand what God was doing in our midst and my part in it, I began to cry out to God. "God, I don't know what I'm doing here." Then He spoke to me so clearly.

On this day, God interrupted what I was thinking about. My mind was on something miles and miles away, but His word just came to me in that moment. He said this to me: "Myles, don't build Me a Christian theater. Build Me a house." I had never thought about it that way. The Lord kept speaking to me, saying, "My people, they love a show. They love to be entertained. Don't build Me a Christian theater. Build Me a house. Build it strong. Build it with foundation. Build it so that it will last. Build it generationally. Build it well, take your time, and do it right."

I said, "God, I don't know how to do that. I don't have a clue what to do."

"That's fine. I will teach you as we go. Along the way I will bring to you people who will fill the different gaps. They will fill the gaps in your knowledge, the gaps in your gifting, and the gaps in your ability to see things. I'll bring the right people in the right times to step up, take an area, and run with it."

It has been one of the great joys of my life to partner with God and to partner with so many incredible people in building that amazing house. It's not a perfect house, but it's an amazing house. What a glorious privilege it has been to build it. I have seen so many lives transformed in that first church in Wharton, in the other GMI network churches that sprang out of it, and even in other churches all over the world that we've had major influence on. It's amazing to think about the many lives we have had the ability and opportunity to touch, both here and abroad. I really believe that thousands upon thousands upon thousands more lives will be touched by what we do at Grace Ministries International. I believe that with all my heart. It's a glorious privilege and a glorious honor, and I count it as such.

This is what we tell visitors in our church, our house. First of all, welcome. We're glad you're here. We really are. We hope you feel welcome in our house, but we especially want this for you: find a house. Find a place where you can belong. Find a place where you can sit down, kick your shoes off, and get comfortable. Find a place where you can plug in and commit yourself. Find a place where you can put your shoulder to the wheel and help drive things forward. Why? Because your Christian growth—not just the growth of the church or the Kingdom of God—is tied up in committing to do that. We just looked at Psalm 92:13 a moment ago. When you are "planted in the house of God, you will flourish in the courts of your God." That's a wonderful promise. Everybody wants to flourish! We want to flourish in every area of life. In this verse God is promising that we will flourish, but there is a condition. Before you can flourish, you need to be planted in the house of the Lord.

"Oh, Myles, I love God's house."

That's an easy thing to say. In order for it to be true, you've got to love God's house *somewhere*. Saying you love God's house means nothing unless you find a local house, plant yourself there, and commit to it. Otherwise it's like saying you believe in generosity without ever giving any money. You've got to decide to love a house somewhere. It's a decision. Maybe you can bring your love to the house you are in right now. Maybe you can love that house into something bigger and better than it is today. That's great. But if you can't love the house you're in, then you've got to find another house, plant yourself there, and love that house. This is the question for you today: will you be one of those who love the house?

Let me be clear about something right now. Some people love the house. Others love their function in the house. Loving your ministry in the church is not the same thing as loving your church. Through the years, I have seen so many people step out of a position, a ministry, or a function and very quickly just fade into the woodwork. Sometimes they fade completely out of the church. Loving a position or a ministry is not the same thing as loving the house. If it's just about loving that position, then it's all about you. You don't love the house; you love yourself.

Imagine you are serving somewhere in the church, doing something that you really like doing. Then a greater need rises up in another ministry, and a pastor asks you to drop what you're doing and go serve in the other ministry. If your love for the house decreases because you are moved from one thing to another, then you don't really love the house. You love your ministry, and you love yourself.

What if a ministry you are serving in gets shut down? That happens. Some ministries are good for a season, but need to end so that time, energy, and resources can be reallocated to something different. If your response to that is to withdraw from involvement or leave the church, then you were never there for the house. You were there for yourself. Who will love the house?

At the end of Jesus' life, we see that He formed two unique relationships with two different men. He had many, many followers, but He chose to form deeper relationships with only two of them. Those two men were John and Peter.

John refers to himself in Scripture as "the disciple that Jesus loved." Jesus loved all of His disciples. We know and understand that, but He clearly had a unique connection with John. You probably get what that's like. We all have people we love, but then we also have people who share with us what seem to be near-supernatural connections. Sometimes they still take a little while to build, but something always just clicks, and it is clear there is something really special going on. That creates a really one-of-a-kind relationship, and I think that's what Scripture is talking about here. It's not that Jesus didn't love the other disciples, it's just that John was the disciple Jesus especially loved. In John 13, the Bible says John laid his head on Jesus' chest. They were close. When Jesus told the disciples one of them would betray him, Peter was dying to know who it would be, but he didn't dare ask Jesus directly. He leaned over and told John to ask Jesus.

The disciple that Jesus loved. Wow. How about that for a title? I'm the disciple that Jesus loved. That's something I think all of us would want. It's a pretty amazing statement.

Look at what happens later on in the book of John, in John 21. Jesus has already been crucified and resurrected, and the disciples are going fishing. They're in a kind of limbo period, if you will, because Jesus has been resurrected, they've seen Him twice, but they still don't have a clear picture of what to do now. They're not really sure. There is a big transition going on in their lives, and so they do what most all of us do when we are in transition—they go back to the last thing they knew. For them it was fishing. For you it would probably be something else, but the pattern is the same. We have that tendency when we're in transition or when we're facing the unknown. We go back to where we are comfortable and do what we know we are good at. That's what the disciples are doing here. They have been fishing all night long without catching a thing. The sun rises, light comes across the water, and suddenly there's a guy on the beach hollering out to them. "Hey, have you guys caught anything?"

"No, not a thing," they yell back.

"Put your nets in on the other side."

They haven't caught anything, so it's kind of hard to argue with the guy. They drop their nets on the other side of the boat and pull in a massive catch of fish. At this point, light bulbs are beginning to turn on. This scene is eerily familiar to them, and they begin to recognize who it is on the shore. John 21:7 says, "So then the disciple whom Jesus loved [John] said to Peter, 'It is the Lord!' As soon as Simon Peter heard him . . . he wrapped his outer garment around him (for he had taken it off) and jumped into the water." He doesn't stick around to pull in the catch of fish. He doesn't take the boat ride over to the shore; that would have taken just a little while longer, but it would have been much, much drier. He just jumps over the side of the boat and swims to shore. He gets to the shore and finds Jesus already cooking some fish over a fire.

Now, I don't know if you stop and think about these things when you read your Bible, but I do. This is a pretty mind-boggling story. We are talking about the resurrected Christ, the Son of the Living God, who has been exalted to the place at God's right hand and given all authority in heaven and on earth. And here He is, cooking breakfast for His friends. I like that. It's mind boggling, but I like it. It tells us something about who Jesus is, and it tells us something about who God is. It tells us that He loves us and He cares about the details of our lives. It also tells us this: God loves to serve. He loves it. He gets a real joy, a real kick out of serving you and me.

So the disciples bring their fish in and add them to the fish Jesus already has. They all have a nice breakfast. At some point, Jesus pulls Peter off to the side a bit and asks him a question.

When they had finished eating, Jesus said to Simon Peter, "Simon son of John, do you love me more than these?"

"Yes, Lord," he said, "you know that I love you," (John 21:15).

What a question. He's not asking whether or not Peter loves him. He's asking whether or not Peter loves him *more*. More than the world? No. More than all the people who love and follow Christ? No. More than the other disciples. And how does Peter answer?

"Yes, Lord," he said, "you know that I love you."

Jesus said, "Feed my lambs."

Again Jesus said, "Simon son of John, do you love me?"

He answered, "Yes, Lord, you know that I love you."

Jesus said, "Take care of my sheep."

The third time he said to him, "Simon son of John, do you love me?"

Peter was hurt because Jesus asked him the third time, "Do you love me?" He said, "Lord, you know all things; you know that I love you."

Jesus said, "Feed my sheep," (John 21:15-17).

I have really pondered this passage because it's a really odd moment. When you stop and think about this thing, it's a bit strange. You would think Jesus would have chosen the disciple whom He loved to feed, grow, and lead the Church. You would think He would have commissioned the disciple whom He loved to be the pillar of the Church Peter was soon to become. But Jesus didn't choose the disciple that He loved. He chose the disciple that loved him. That's who He picked out from the rest.

The most sustainable, lasting, and productive relationships in life are not the ones you have with the people you love. They are the ones you have with the people who love you. If you are a parent, then you probably understand this. When your kids grow up and leave the house, this is going to become even more evident to you. As the years go by, the child you maintain the closest relationship with won't be the one you love the most. It will be the one who loves you the most.

If it is only your love that's sustaining something, then your love is always going to have to sustain that thing. If you have a relationship that is built on your love and your love only, then it is going to have to stay that way. There is nothing else sustaining that relationship. When you relax your love or go through difficult circumstances, it will be very easy for the other person to pull away.

Do you still want to be the disciple that Jesus loved? What about the disciple who loved Jesus? Jesus didn't entrust the keys of the Church to the disciple whom He loved. He entrusted the keys of His Church to the disciple who loved Him.

Let me say this to you right now. Spiritual growth is not about how much the church loves you. Spiritual growth is about how much you love the church. I wouldn't expect a big amen on that one, but it's the truth. It's not about how much the church loves you. It's about how much you love the church.

Through my years in ministry, I have seen many people continue to grow rapidly and become more and more like Christ. Those were not the people whom the church loved really well. They were the people who loved the church with all their heart. When you love the church, it opens up your life to God's blessings and gives you the ability to affect many, many people for the Kingdom of God.

How much do you love the house of God? How much do you think about it? How deeply do you feel about it? In John 21, there were two guys standing side by side in the same boat. The disciple Jesus loved stayed in the boat. The disciple who loved Jesus jumped overboard.

"Do you love me more than these?"

"Yes, Lord, . . . you know that I love you," (John 21:15).

I think Jesus recognized a depth of love in Peter that was not in the other disciples. But some people, reading this story, could be a little bothered by Peter's answer. I mean, who did Peter think he was? How could he say that? It seems problematic and prideful. But you know what? Peter knew it was true. Peter knew it because he had just come through a very dark, difficult time in his life. He had just denied Jesus three times. He went through the fire. Listen, when you go through something like that, you come out on the other end understanding something very important. You understand what is holding you.

What is holding you? A lot of Christians would say it's Jesus' love for them. Jesus' love will hold you. Praise God for that. But if His love is the only thing holding you, then you aren't going to make it very far. Past a certain point, you must be held by your love for Him.

What helps you survive bitter, difficult, and painful circumstances is not who loves you. What helps you survive is whom you love. That's the telling factor. Peter emerged from his dark hour with a huge love for Jesus. Peter knew he loved Jesus and could not live without Him. He was totally sold out for Jesus.

Here's the question for us today: Do you love Jesus? Everybody says yes. Then Jesus says to us, like he said to Peter, "Love My Church. Feed them, serve them, work with them, put up with them. Hang in there with them, imperfections and all, on the good days and the bad days. Love them. Love My Church."

Are you in the church primarily for what the house can do for you? To some degree, we are all in the church because of what the house does for us. That's good. That's healthy. That's natural. I don't want to be a part of a church that's dead and does nothing for me.

I heard a church leader address the problem of dead churches really well one time. They put this guy on a stage and asked him what he believed about new Christians in struggling churches. They were hoping he would answer by saying it was fine for baby Christians to stay in dead houses until they become spiritually mature enough to decide where to go for themselves. He responded by telling them he didn't believe in putting live chicks under a dead hen.[1]

He cut straight to the point there, but it's true. I have never seen anything in Scripture that indicates church is supposed to be a mission field. Church is there to help build us up, cause us to grow, strengthen us, stretch us, and help us become all that God wants us to be so that we can have a big impact on the world around us. So, in one sense, we're all in the church because of what we're getting from it. We all love the teaching, the worship, the fellowship, the encouragement, and the prayer support. Church is great! But are you in the church primarily for what the house can do for you? Or are you in the church primarily for what you can do for the house?

John F. Kennedy said something similar to this about the country. You might have already connected those dots. "Ask not what your country can do for you, but what you can do for your country." I think that's a good question. Who will love the house?

In the book of Psalms, King David says over and over how much he loves the house of the Lord. In Psalm 84:10 he says he would rather be a doorkeeper in the house of God than dwell in the tents of the wicked. Let me give you an equivalent that we might be more familiar with. King David would rather be on the greeting team for the house of God than skip church and watch TV. He's talking about a deep sense of satisfaction and joy coming out of serving in the house of God. We should get more satisfaction and joy out of serving in the Lord's house than we get from all the other fun and exciting things that go on in our lives. It's great to love all of those other things and enjoy them, but we were made for the deep sense of satisfaction and joy that comes out of showing our love for the house. That's what David is talking about.

Zeal for God's house consumed Jesus. Christ-likeness is God's amazing plan for our lives. He desires for us to grow into the person of Jesus Christ, becoming more and more like Him. That's His overriding purpose for each and every one of us. Romans 8:29 says we are to be "conformed to the image of his Son." What does that mean? I'll tell you. It means there are many areas that I need to grow in, and there is much change that needs to take place in my life. I have a long way to go, but I'm having a good time getting there. It hasn't all been sunshine, but all sunshine makes for a desert anyway. I'm in the process. How about you?

If you looked through the pages of Scripture, I'm not sure you could find anyone who got a bigger fresh start than Peter did. I'm not even sure you could find someone with a bigger fresh start if you looked through all of history. Maybe Paul could rival him, but Peter denied the Lord three times. Then Jesus asked him the same question three times. Do you love me? Do you love me? Do you love me?

The meaning there was not lost on Peter. I mean, he may have been a little slow to get it because he was slow. That's not a knock. I like that about Peter because I really identify with it. Sometimes it just takes me a while. Sometimes God has to kind of knock and say, "Hello, is there anybody there?" But then I finally get it, and I get lost in it. It becomes hard to move me off of the revelation God had for me. I see that in Peter's life, and I love that about him. He was slow, but he always got it.

I don't think the nuances of the situation were lost on him. Early on in the whole process, as he jumped out of the boat and swam ashore, he was probably excited. But, somewhere in there, the scene started getting a look and a feel that was just a little bit too familiar. There was a bonfire, and it was just him and Jesus. I imagine he was thinking something like, "Ooh, the last time I was with the Lord there was a bonfire going. Jesus was standing off in the distance, and I denied him three times." Then Jesus pulled him aside.

"Do you love me?"

"Yes, Lord, . . . you know that I love you," (*John 21:15*).

What about you? Do you need a fresh start in life? Maybe you need a fresh start in loving the house of God. Maybe you, like so many others, have gone through things in the house of God that were disappointing, painful, or hurtful. It grieves my heart that you may have faced that in the church, but things like that happen because people are people. Not one of us is perfect. We say and do the wrong things. We don't always make the best decisions.

Maybe you looked at the church and decided we were all just a bunch of hypocrites, a bunch of people who don't live up to what we preach. Welcome to the club. Nobody complains when a hospital is filled with patients. The hospital is a smart place to go when you're sick. If you're a hypocrite, welcome. You came to the right place. We'll help you.

Wherever you have been hurt or disillusioned with the church, this day can be a fresh start for you. It can be a fresh start in your love for God's house. Reaching the full measure of transformation will take time, but this could be the beginning of that process. Open your heart to receive the freshness and newness God wants to restore to you today. Let Him fill your heart with love for His house.

Part 5

Finish Strong

THE POWER AND
GOODNESS OF GOD

I t is very, very difficult for any of us living today to fully appreciate
the things the Apostle Paul endured and how horrible they really
were. The reason for that is very simple. When we read about his life
today, we know that we are reading about the life of the Apostle Paul.
We know Paul's history, we know all the things he did in life, and we
know where he ended up in the end. Because we know those things,
it is extremely hard for us to truly appreciate what he went through.
He describes some of the most horrible things he experienced in 2
Corinthians 11:23-28.

> *I have worked much harder, been in prison more fre-*
> *quently, been flogged more severely, and been exposed*
> *to death again and again. Five times I received from the*
> *Jews the forty lashes minus one. Three times I was beaten*
> *with rods, once I was pelted with stones, three times I was*
> *shipwrecked, I spent a night and a day in the open sea, I*
> *have been constantly on the move. I have been in danger*
> *from rivers, in danger from bandits, in danger from my*
> *fellow Jews, in danger from Gentiles; in danger in the*
> *city, in danger in the country, in danger at sea; and in*
> *danger from false believers. I have labored and toiled*

*and have often gone without sleep; I have known hunger
and thirst and have often gone without food; I have been
cold and naked.*

Imagine you had never read that passage of Scripture before. Imagine also that you did not know who the Apostle Paul was; you had never heard of him. Imagine that someone printed those verses in 2 Corinthians out by themselves on a piece of copy paper for you. Can you imagine reading those verses without any knowledge of who they were about? Most people would immediately conclude that the person who wrote them was a criminal.

"Wow. What a messed-up dude. That guy must have lived a bad life and done some shady deals to end up in those kinds of predicaments all the time."

Probably the best any of us would do is assume that, for that person, the circumstances were all BC—before Christ entered his or her life. Maybe the things in this list were the things that actually brought the person to Christ. That would make sense, but it's not the truth.

You and I know that we are actually reading a list of the trials and sufferings experienced by the Apostle Paul. This was a great man of God who wrote two-thirds of the New Testament and had more insight than any other person who walked Planet Earth other than Jesus himself. That is who we are reading about.

We know Paul was saved in his early thirties, and we know he was beheaded in Rome in his mid-to-late fifties. That means that all of the things he listed took place in his life in a span of less than twenty-five years. And that list is just a short summary of all the things Paul went through. He just gave us the highlight reel.

Think about that for a minute. Let's be honest here. If even one of those things on that list happened to you in the course of your entire life, you would say it was extreme.

"Wait, what? You were shipwrecked? Oh my God! You mean you spent a day and a night out on the open sea? That's extreme."

Look at the list. Don't just read past it. Look at the list of things in there. In those days, people died on a regular basis from taking just one round of the thirty-nine lashes. Paul was flogged with the thirty-nine lashes on five different occasions. Past that, Paul says that he was "pelted with stones," (11:25). That is just the translation. Do you know what that was? It was a good, old-fashioned stoning. Remember, stoning was not for punishment; it was for execution.

Let me tell you this about myself: I am not afraid of death. I'm really not. People ask me, "Are you afraid of dying?" Not at all. There are just some ways of going out that don't exactly jazz me. Eaten by lions. Burned alive. Those two make the top ten, but being stoned makes the top three.

Paul was stoned. That was a death sentence, but somehow he miraculously survived. Later in the New Testament he writes, "I bear on my body the marks," (Galatians 6:17). Have you ever thought about that? His body probably looked like he had been a gladiator for twenty-five years. He would have had marks and scars all over.

Paul said he was also shipwrecked three different times. We know from Scripture that one of those times he spent weeks prior to the shipwreck going through massive, horrible storms and being blown around the Mediterranean Sea. Every day for weeks it seemed like the ship was going to go down. Finally it did, and all the crew and passengers washed up on the island of Malta. Paul and the other survivors were very cold and very wet, so they started doing what cold, wet people do—look for wood to make a fire.

As they were gathering wood, the people who lived on the island came to see what was going on. The survivors welcomed the islanders and began to tell them about the storm and the shipwreck and how they got washed up on the island. Then, as they were hearing the whole story, the islanders watched Paul get bit by a poisonous snake as he reached for some wood on the ground. Do you know what they concluded? They thought that Paul must have been an evil man. Because of the storm, the shipwreck, and the snake, it was clear to them that God must have been trying to take Paul out. Let's not be too hard on the islanders; some of us would conclude the same thing.

But then Paul didn't die. In a storm for three weeks—didn't die. Shipwrecked and washed up—didn't die. Bit by a poisonous snake—didn't die. The islanders watched and watched and watched, but Paul did not succumb to the poison. So they changed their minds and concluded that he was a god.

There are two important truths here, especially for leaders and future leaders. If you are going to lead, you have got to understand these two things. Number one: the people around you are so fickle. One minute you are the G.O.A.T. (greatest of all time), the next minute you are the goat *cabrito* (barbecue time, baby). That is the way it works.

Here is the second powerful truth: when bad things happen, it does not necessarily mean you need to change what you are doing. That is a powerful truth. Horrible, horrible things happened to Paul throughout his Christian life. The moment he got saved, people started trying to track him down to murder him. He had to be lowered down from the top of a city wall in a basket so he could run for his life. Bad things started from the very get-go. But Paul did not decide that he was outside of God's will for his life. He did not decide to regret and rethink committing his life to Christ. When something bad happened, he didn't come to the conclusion that he was on the wrong track. Because of that he did not quit his calling or his purpose in life.

I wanted to start with that first passage, Paul's list of tribulations, before moving to this second passage because I want to spend a little more time with this one. This is a very, very familiar passage. Romans 8:28 says, "And we know that all things work together for good to those that love God, to those who are called according to his purpose."

All things. This verse should floor us. The same man who listed out all of his extreme sufferings just turned around and told us all things work together for good.

Now, "all" is a very small word. But I want you to understand this: there is nothing that is not covered by the word "all." Nothing. Do you believe that all things work together for good? You might be going through some things right now that make you unsure. Can that really be included in all things? Or maybe your mind jumped back through your life and landed on a few horrible things that you experienced. Could those things have worked for your good?

Paul knew something very, very important. This is something that every Christian needs to know: everything in this life is either God-sent or God-used.

Not everything that comes into our lives is God-sent. The devil loves to mess with us. We understand that. We get that. We live in a fallen world, so not everything that comes our way will be from God. But let me tell you this: God uses all things, whether they came from him or not.

It is easy to agree with that when you read it in a book. It is easy to hear someone quote Romans 8:28 and say, "Oh yeah, oh yeah. Amen." But there are times when every single one of us wants to change the wording of that verse. We know that *some* things work together for good. We know good things work together for good in our lives. We know things that make sense to us work together for good in our lives.

Paul could have added other words if he had wanted to qualify what he said. He could have added a few more words to the sentence; it wouldn't have made your Bible that much heavier. But he didn't add any qualifiers. He didn't add any other words. He gave it to us—pure, unadulterated, full-strength, and all-encompassing. All things work together for good.

When somebody tells us something, we attach more value or less value to what that person said based on what he or she has gone through in life. We either enlarge what they said or shrink it based on the speaker's life experience. Take somebody like Nelson Mandela. He spent twenty-eight years wrongfully imprisoned. He did not do a single thing to deserve it; the authorities just put him in prison and left him there to rot. Twenty-eight years passed before he walked out. He didn't come out bitter. He didn't come out angry. He didn't come out seeking vengeance. He walked out of prison with a message of forgiveness that he spread to anyone who would listen. When a man like that, who was so wrongfully treated, preaches about forgiveness, we want to tune in. We value what he says.

I have always loved the song "Amazing Grace." I loved that song when I first heard it as a new believer in Christ. I still love that song today. It is a gorgeous song. I don't care if it is the old hymn version or some modern update; I love it. I sang it for many years without wondering much about it, but one day someone asked me who wrote the song. I didn't know, so I looked it up. A man by the name of John Newton wrote "Amazing Grace." Big deal. Good for John, right? Then I learned John Newton's background. He was a slave trader who met Jesus, renounced his profession, and became a prominent abolitionist, actively fighting against the slave trade in all its forms. The first time I went back and sang that song after I knew the story of John Newton, it impacted my life. The song was already wonderful, but it increased tenfold in its meaning.

The Apostle Paul speaks to us from the pages of Scripture in Romans 8:28. This is a man who went through hell on this earth for almost twenty-five years saying to us, "All things work together for good." All things. All those beatings, all those trials, all those imprisonments, all those betrayals. When somebody like the Apostle Paul, who has experienced the things that he experienced in life, says that all things work together for good, that is powerful.

All the bad things this world can serve up to you and all the bad things the devil could possibly do unto you are working together for good in your life. All the bad things! God is weaving together all the horrible things in your life—even the worst things that you have gone through—into a pattern of progress, a pattern of blessing, and a pattern of success. All things. Do you believe that?

Imagine an auditorium full of hundreds of people. If I spoke to those people and asked them to stand up and two-thirds of the people in the room stood up, did *all* the people stand? No. If I asked them to stand and everybody except for one person stood up, did *all* the people stand? No.

"But it was only one, Myles. In a group that big, it is hardly worth mentioning that one person didn't stand. I think it's close enough. We can go ahead and say it's all."

Here's the problem: I think many Christians think that is the way Paul meant this verse. They think Paul didn't really mean all. Do you know why people think this way? Because they have something in their lives they think cannot be included. So when they read Romans 8:28, they have exceptions because there are some things in their lives they believe don't quite count.

When Paul used the word *all*, he had no exceptions in mind. Please hear me right now. If there is one thing in your life that God cannot use, then God cannot use all things. If there is just one thing—one thing in your history, one thing in your background, one thing that you went through, one thing that was done unto you, one stupid thing that you did—that God cannot use, then God cannot use all things. That one thing, if He really cannot use it, disproves the Word of God and makes God a liar. If you believe that even one thing in your life defies God's power and ability, that thing will haunt you for the rest of your life.

All is a very small word. Maybe that is why we don't focus on it enough. We use it often, but we don't really mean it.

"He does that *all* the time."

"I hate *all* of this."

So the word *all* doesn't mean all to all of us all the time in all situations. But Paul picked this word specifically. Under the leadership of the Holy Spirit, he picked this word, and he meant it. His life was full of things that are hard to include in the things God uses for good, but he meant all.

What an incredible promise, saints. All things. Good things, bad things, beautiful things, ugly things. Things that you know about and things that you don't know about. That's a big one. Do you realize God is doing more behind your back than He is out in front of you? Have you figured that out? If you are going to make it any distance down the road of building God's Kingdom, you need to know that. Most of us have a tendency to trace God in our lives only through the things that we perceive as Him. If you start doing that, you will end up basing your faith on your own ability to trace God and his fingerprints in your life. The real test of faith, the real test of your walk with God is the ability and the commitment to trust Him when you cannot trace Him at all.

They are so many times in our lives when we have no idea what God is doing behind the scenes. We spend most of our lives this way. We see the things that are happening to us clearly, right out in front. We know what is going on, and it looks like a mess. It looks like a disaster. This is horrible. I don't deserve this. How could this happen? We see what is out in front of us, but we cannot see what God is doing behind our backs.

There are and will be many times for all of us when it seems like God doesn't even know we exist. Our prayers seem to go unanswered. Things go from bad to worse. We go from shipwreck to snake bite. Then comes Romans 8:28, and we want to agree with it. There is something inside of us that knows, kind of intuitively, that it is right. But at the same time there is a nagging doubt because the verse just doesn't add up when we consider all the bad things we have gone through. Maybe our experiences are some of those unusual, outside-the-Bible exceptions. Yeah, right.

Don't ever try to trace God in your life by the stuff that you know. Don't do it. That is incredibly dangerous.

You and I need to allow for the fact that if God is God, then there is a lot of stuff we don't know about working for our good right now. We can't see it. But if God is God, then we can know it is true. He is doing things you don't see right now to make even the worst of your experiences work out for good in your life. Good things. Bad things. All things.

God is using friends for good in your life. Well, that's an easy one. Of course God is bringing wonderful friendships into your life. Of course those friends are there to help make your life richer and fuller. But listen, God is also using enemies for your good. God can take somebody who hates your guts and use that person for good in your life. He can cause people who want nothing more than to see you go down to do things that bless you and your life incredibly. Sometimes those people know it, but other times they don't even know they are blessing you.

God can use all things. He can use people that mean you good, and he can use people that mean you harm. He can use things that you did well, and he can use things that you did not do well. He can use things that were your fault, and he can use things that were not your fault. He can use good decisions, and he can use bad decisions. He uses all of it for good in our lives.

God will sometimes even cause things to operate outside of their natural, created order to work for good in our lives. Did you know that? God so loves you and so loves me that He sometimes yanks things outside of their natural, created order and has them do the impossible.

Have you read the story of Balaam in the Bible? This man was on his way to do something he knew was wrong, and it was going to cause an angel of the Lord to kill him. What did God do? God had mercy, even though Balaam was obstinately headed toward sin. He was on his donkey, headed straight for an invisible angel with sword drawn, ready to kill. The donkey was able to see the angel, and he stopped in the middle of the road. Balaam began to beat the donkey and yell at him. So God said to the donkey, "Ok, this guy's not getting it. Go ahead and talk to him."

"What have I done to you to make you beat me these three times?" said the donkey (Num. 22:28). The donkey spoke. That was outside of his natural, created order.

What about the prophet named Jonah, who went AWOL on God? God called a whale.

"Hello, Whale Uber? This is God. Yes. Yes. Yeah, one-way trip to Nineveh. Party of one."

In the New Testament, Peter comes to Jesus and says, "Hey, I've got taxes to pay."

"Go fishing," Jesus said.

Can you imagine what Peter is thinking? "I just feel like Jesus is insensitive to my needs. He's not listening to me. I've got taxes to pay. I've got real, practical needs."

Then Jesus said, "Oh, and when you catch the first fish, check in its mouth."

That didn't make any sense. But Peter went, caught a fish, and popped its mouth open. He probably felt stupid when he was doing it. But there, in the mouth of the fish, was a coin valuable enough to pay the taxes.

I've got questions I want to ask certain people when I get to heaven. This is one of them: "Peter, did you eat that fish?" If he did, that was all kinds of wrong.

God can use all things. Do you believe that? He can use natural things, supernatural things, and even nonsensical things. God uses whatever, whenever, and however for good in our lives. If God can make a donkey and a whale and a fish do his bidding, then he can make anything and everything work for good in our lives.

Let me tell you what I believe. I believe the Apostle Paul had some foundational beliefs that allowed him and caused him to write the words of Romans 8:28. I believe there were foundational truths established and solidified in him that led him to write what he did. And these things were not just thoughts he wanted to believe. They were not just ideas that would be nice if they were true. They were not just concepts that he believed were theologically correct. These were absolute truths that were settled in him so deeply that everything in his life filtered through them. I believe he had those kinds of foundational truths established in him.

I want to look at two of those truths here. As I studied this, I actually found about five or six of them. But here are the two best and most important foundational truths that allowed Paul to say—unequivocally, without wavering, full-on, full-strength—that all things work together for our good.

1. God is sovereign.

Paul writes a lot of different things. In Romans 8:31, he says, "If God is for us, who can be against us?" Why even bother? What are y'all doing? You are so stupid, stacking up against me. I've got God on my side! If God is for me, who can be against me? They are wasting their time.

You can't write stuff like that unless you believe God is sovereign. You can't live the life Paul lived unless you believe that God is sovereign. Sovereign means supreme power and authority. Absolute power, absolute authority.

"Yeah, I got that. I understand that. I got that in Sunday school years ago."

I'm talking about something different than the mentality you got from Sunday School. Please hear me. I'm talking about filtering everything in life through this fact. God is sovereign. God is sovereign.

God is sovereign. God either did it, or He is using it. We have to see everything that way. I am not talking about stopping, catching ourselves, and remembering that fact after living in a funk for a week. I am talking about living life and filtering everything through a settled, established belief that God is sovereign. He is the supreme power. He is the supreme authority.

You can see this throughout Scripture, but one of my favorite examples is the book of Esther. That is an amazing book. One of the things that is so amazing about the book of Esther is this: God's name is not said one single time in the entire book. Not one single time is the name of God mentioned. Yet I challenge you to find another book of the Bible where God is more involved behind the scenes. He is in there, amazingly so.

According to the book of Esther, one night the king woke up and couldn't get back to sleep. He kept turning the pillow and changing positions, but nothing seemed to work. He finally got up and went to get some reading material. The book of Esther says that he picked up the book of annals of the king, which was basically a bunch of governmental, legal documents. Clearly the guy was just using a different strategy to try to go back to sleep; this was boring, official mumbo-jumbo. So he was reading through the annals, and he came across the report of a guy named Mordecai, who found out about an assassination attempt and warned the king's guards of it so they could put it down before it happened. When the king read of this, he did not remember ever hearing about it. He called in some of his servants.

"Hey, tell me about this guy Mordecai. Did anybody ever do anything for him?"

"No one ever did anything," the servants answered.

"Well, we need to fix that." Then the king called in one of his top henchmen, a man by the name of Haman. Haman hated Mordecai's guts. He had been planning to kill Mordecai for some time, but he was trying to figure out the most diabolical, painful way to take him down. So the king called Haman into the room and said, "I've got a very important task for you, Haman."

"Oh, I can't wait. Whatever it is, my king, I'm happy to do it."

"I want you to go get this guy named Mordecai, and I want you to do a big parade for him. Put him in my chariot and have everybody bow down to him. We are going to honor this guy like nobody has ever been honored in this kingdom before other than me."

How do you think Haman felt about that?

God is like a conductor. He waves his wand over there. "No, no. You're not going to sleep tonight. Wake up. Doesn't matter which way you turn, you're not going to sleep. Wake up. All right, now let's go over here. Over here. Pick up that book. Yeah. Find some reading that you think will put you to sleep. That's good. Turn to page 285. There you go."

"Well, God just did that for Mordecai."

No, he does things like that for you and for me. God is sovereign. Paul had this foundational truth locked up inside of him.

2. God is omniscient.

God knows everything. His knowledge is infinite and unlimited. That means a lot of different things in a lot of different areas. But when it comes to you and I and our lives, one of the things it means is this: when God wrote the book of your life, he didn't start with page one. God always starts with the last page and works backwards.

Psalm 139:16 says, "All the days ordained for me were written in your book before one of them came to be." God has already lived your life. Do you understand that? There is not one single thing that has happened or ever will happen in your life that catches God off guard.

"Oh no! Joey, I am so sorry. I was busy over here doing these other things, and I looked over to see that thing happen in your life, and now everything is just a mess. Let me see if we can fix it."

No, God always knows everything. It's all the same to Him. Please hear me. Please get this. When God enters your life, he does so from the future. That is how he walks into your life and into the situations you get in. He doesn't enter it saying, "Oh, let me catch up and see what's happening here." He comes into your life and into the situations in your life from the future.

I have had a lot of different Christians, new believers and veterans of the faith alike, come to me and say the same thing.

"I know what Scripture says, but I'll tell you this, Myles. I am going through this horrible thing, and I just have this feeling inside of me that I just can't shake. I feel like God is not really empathetic with my situation."

Do you know what the standard, traditional answer to that is?

"Oh no, no. He understands. Don't worry. That's just what you're feeling right now. God is empathetic. He feels what you feel."

You know what? I don't think that is true at all. I think there are lots and lots of times in our lives where God is not empathetic at all. Do you think God is just not feeling how you are feeling about this mess in your life? He's not. Why? Because He knows what you are crying about, and He knows six months from now you are going to be rejoicing over that same thing. He entered your life from the future, so He passed by all the great results from that thing on his way in.

God is omniscient. That is more than just a lofty theological concept. It has practical, real, and powerful implications for our lives. God has been in your future, and he is not panicked.

I have walked with God for over forty years now, and I have been in ministry for over thirty of them. In that time, God has walked me through and taught me a bunch of different things. He tends to teach me those things slowly and in pieces. As I walk with him, He allows me to understand little bits of something, just around the edges. I keep walking with Him, I keep reading His Word, I keep praying, and I keep listening. Then, all at once, God just solidifies a whole bunch of those pieces into one incredible theological insight.

That happened to me recently, and I want to share the insight that God gave me with you. Here it is. Are you ready for it?

God is like GPS.

It may not make sense right now, but hang with me here. God is like GPS in two ways.

Here is the first: God is like GPS when you are on course. When you are driving on course down a long, straight road, your GPS doesn't say a single thing. Not a blessed word. That can get a little unnerving if you are not confident that you are going the right way. You might thump the GPS a few times. What's up? Is it still working? It doesn't come on and say, "Keep going just like that." In fact, someday I want to make it do just that. I think I am going to get together with one of these young guys who can build apps. I want to build a reassurance app that you can add to your GPS. The app will make the GPS voice come on every few minutes with a nice reassuring message.

"Great job."

"You are doing so well."

"Yes. Stay right here in this lane."

But until I make that app, your GPS is not going to do that. It just leaves you alone because you are on course. If you get off course, it will tell you. But if doesn't say anything, it means you are on course.

God is like that. That is what I have experienced in my life. When I am on track with God, I don't hear a lot. You might think I should, but I don't. I had to learn that if my heart is right and I am not hearing a lot from God, most of the time it just means I am on track.

Years ago something very dramatic happened in my life, and I became afraid of something. I understand that Christians are not supposed to be afraid of things, but this fear has been a wonderful thing for me. I am so thankful for the day that I became afraid of getting my way. I don't want my way because I know that God's way is always better. If you are not going your own way and your heart is in the right place, you can trust God even if you don't always hear from Him. You are on track.

Here is the second: God is like GPS when you are off course. When you make a wrong turn, your GPS does not come on and say, "I am so ticked at you. That is the third wrong turn today. You know what? I am not speaking to you anymore. Goodbye." That is not what GPS does. It simply comes on and says, "Recalculating."

Can I tell you something? God is the same way with you. God loves you. God is in love with you—mistakes, mess-ups, failures, weaknesses, and all. He does not quit talking to you. He does not hang up on you. Bad decision? Recalculating. He doesn't get in a tizzy or a panic. He looks out ahead and sees the turns you are going to make, and He prepares the way for you. He loves you that much. His power and his goodness override everything else in our lives.

Perseverance

S ome time ago all of the pastors of the Grace church network came together to develop a sermon series. That sermon series was called "Turning Point." We planned it to be full of key teachings that catalyzed dramatic change in our own lives. So each of us had to take the fifty, eighty, one hundred powerful, life-changing truths that we had received and pare that number down until we had just two or three, the best of the best.

When I thought back on my life, I chose perseverance. Without perseverance, there is no way I would be the man I am today. If God had not gotten that truth into my life years ago and continued to build on it, there is no way I would be doing the things that I am doing. Not even close. Perseverance is huge. It is massively important for anyone who wants to be successful in life.

God wants you to be successful. Do you understand that? That is very clear throughout the Word of God. Jesus said, "I came that they might have life and have it abundantly," (John 10:10, ESV). What is abundant life? It is successful life. You cannot have abundance without success. Jesus wants you to be successful.

He also wants you to be successful in all areas of your life. If you haven't picked that up from the words of Jesus in the Gospels, then you can find it in 3 John 1:2, which says, "Beloved, I pray that in all respects you may prosper . . . just as your soul prospers," (NASB). That is a Spirit-inspired prayer, showing God's heart for us. He wants us to prosper and be successful in all areas of our lives, even as our souls prosper and are successful.

We need to understand this. God wants us to be successful. Or you can say it this way: God wants us to win. He wants us to win and win and win again. He wants us to be winners in life.

Vince Lombardi said it very well years ago when he said this, "Winning is a habit. Unfortunately, so is losing."[1] Winners succeed consistently. Losers succeed every now and then. What is the difference? Why do winners succeed again and again? Because winners consistently do the right thing. To be successful, you have to consistently—daily, many times each day—make the right choices, the right decisions. That is how you get to success in life.

Another word for this is character. When we talk about being successful and consistently doing the right thing, we are really talking about character. If you want to be successful, you have to have character. If you want to experience success in your marriage, your family, your career, your job, your walk with God, or any other area of your life, then you have to have character.

Christians should be the most successful people on the planet. They *should* be, but in church after church around the world, there are countless Christians not walking in the success God Himself wants them to walk in because they don't build godly character in their lives. Many of them are caught up in charismania and being filled with the Spirit, thinking that is what will make them successful. But success is more than just being tapped into the power source. You must have character to be successful in life. That might not get very many amens, but it's true.

Let me explain with an illustration. There are two neighbors, Neighbor A and Neighbor B. These neighbors have identical backyards, and in those yards each of them has a big garden of the exact same size and shape. Spring comes around, and both neighbors plant the exact same things in their gardens on the exact same days. Everything is the same except for the fact that Neighbor A does not have a watering hose. All he has is a little watering can, so he has to fill it up at the spigot, walk all the way across the yard to the garden, pour out the little bit of water, and go back for more. He has to go back and forth over and over again in order to water his garden. Meanwhile, Neighbor B has a brand-new, fifty-foot hose with the fanciest spray nozzle you have ever seen.

Which neighbor should end up with the best garden? Well, Neighbor B; he has the advantage, doesn't he? He is tapped directly into the source, and he has a spray nozzle with fifteen different settings. How could he not end up with the best garden?

Let me add to the story a little bit here and tell you something I left out. You see, Neighbor A has tremendous character. He is diligent. He is faithful. He works as unto the Lord. Meanwhile Neighbor B is lazy, even though he has the setup and the advantage. He starts things and doesn't finish them. Now which neighbor do you think will have the best garden? Who is going to produce the most fruit? Neighbor A will because of his character.

Character drives success in life. It is not enough for you and I to have all the advantages we have in Christ. We must also have God's character. There is a lack of character in the world today. This is even true among Christians; so many of them lack godly character, and, therefore, they miss the success that God wants them to have.

Right now we are going to take a specific look at one specific character quality: perseverance. Perseverance is huge. It is incredibly important for us to get if we want to be successful.

Hebrews 6:11-12 says this: "We want each of you to show this same diligence to the very end, so that what you hope for may be fully realized. We do not want you to become lazy, but to imitate those who through faith and patience inherit what has been promised." Most translations say "faith and patience." A few translations say "faith and perseverance." The Greek word translated here as *patience* or *perseverance* was once more commonly translated *long-suffering*, which is a better, more direct translation of the original Greek word.

There are two different ways you can suffer for a long period of time. One of them is when suffering is pretty much thrust upon you. Circumstances and situations happen, and you have to hang in there despite the obstacles and problems that pop up. This kind of long-suffering does require patience. But there is one other way you can suffer for a long period of time. That is when you suffer on a path you chose for yourself. Sometimes we choose certain paths of suffering because of the payoff at the end.

Think about an athlete who suffers through all kinds of training. Why does he put up with all that suffering? So he can get the prize at the end. Think about a student in school who suffers through algebra. Maybe it doesn't even have to be a hypothetical student; I know a lot of people can relate. All of the studying, all of the extra work, all of the "suffering" is for the payoff of a good grade at the end. It is the same with many different things in life.

So we can have long-suffering through things that happen to us, which is patience. We can also have long-suffering through things that we choose, which is perseverance. That is why a number of translations use the word *perseverance* instead of *patience*. *Long-suffering* can mean either, and the context lends itself more to perseverance when it says, "Show this same diligence to the end, so that what you hope for may be fully realized," (Heb. 6:11). That verse is talking about hanging in there so that you receive what God has promised to you. It is talking about perseverance.

Perseverance is so important because success is a journey. We do not get to take one big step into success. There are no three simple steps to do this week that will magically rocket you into a successful life. It doesn't work that way. We have to take little step after little step after little step after little step. Success is a journey that is taken one step at a time.

"Well, Pastor Myles, life is just so hard. When is the journey going to end?"

Read my lips: when you die and go to heaven. That is not a happy thought, but it is the truth. I could tell you something happy, but it wouldn't be true. The hard and long-suffering journey towards success ends when you die and go to heaven because we live in a fallen world where bad things happen to good people. The Bible says it rains on the just and the unjust (Matthew 5:45). We live in an unpleasant world; there are problems, trials, sorrows, and pains. Those things are not going to end prematurely when you reach success; those things are just life.

This was taught to us by none other than the great philosopher Doc Holliday. Have you seen the movie Tombstone? If you have not, then repent. Go get it and watch it. Tombstone is one of my favorite movies; in our household we watch it at least once a year. It is full of incredible quotes. In one of scene, Doc Holliday is talking to his buddy, Wyatt Earp. Wyatt is unhappy because his life has been so difficult, and he is realizing that he will have to face more unpleasant things soon. At one point Doc asks Wyatt, "What'd you want?"

"Just to live a normal life," Wyatt says.

Doc Holliday kind of looks over at him and says, "There's no normal life, Wyatt. There's just life. Now get on with it."[2]

Do you want just a normal life? Do you want an easy life? There's no such thing as a normal life. There's just life.

Jesus demonstrated for us how to live this life successfully. Look at how He lived through the Gospel accounts; it is obvious again and again. His life shouts out to us. Perseverance, perseverance, perseverance. Then flip some pages and go further into the New Testament. Look at Paul's life and acts through his letters. What do you see? Perseverance, perseverance, perseverance. Study the lives of all the great men and women of God who went before us. What do their lives preach to us? Perseverance, perseverance, perseverance. This is how you live successfully: perseverance.

Unfortunately, we live in a culture where people around us want things quick, they want them cheap, and they want them now. In other words, they want things without any work or sacrifice. If we are not careful, brothers and sisters, we can get sucked into thinking like they do without even realizing it. From microwaves to performance-enhancing drugs, everything around us shouts, "I want it, and I want it now." Instant this. Instant that. Instant fame. Instant riches. Instant success. This attitude is permeating culture in a way it never has before.

We have to be careful because there is something inside each of us that wants to take the shortcut. It is part of the old human nature. It is like the sign on the door of the woodworking shop: "Antiques manufactured while you wait." That is crazy, but there is something in us that believes it would be nice if that sign were true.

That is why we have to understand the incredible importance of perseverance. There comes a time in every single marriage, in every single family, in every single job, and in every single life where quitting looks pretty doggone good. There comes a time when problems seem undefeatable, when mountains seem unmovable, when defeat seems absolutely inescapable, and when retreat seems like the only logical option. So let me define perseverance in one simple way.

It is always too soon to quit.

I have always loved taking things that resonate with me and taping them to my bathroom mirror. When God speaks to me or makes something stand out to me, I put that word or that thing up on my bathroom mirror. Maybe it is a Bible verse. Maybe it is a quote. Maybe it is a picture with a quote.

Whatever it is, sometimes it stays there for a few months. Other times it comes down after a few weeks. But every once in a while, when it is something really important, God will not let me take it down. There is one thing that stayed on my bathroom mirror for about ten years; that is much, much longer than any other quote or picture I ever put up there. I cannot tell you how many times I tried to take it off because I was so tired of looking at the thing. I had the image and the words seared in my mind, so I didn't think I needed to look at them anymore. But every time I started to think about taking it down, the Lord would just come over, tap me on the shoulder, and say, "Don't take that down yet. Not yet. You have got to get this."

This was the quote: "Perseverance is hanging on after others have let go." When everybody around you has let go, perseverance says, "I'm not letting go. I'm hanging in there. If God called me to this, then I'm not letting go of it. I'm not moving."

God's commands to us are standing orders. If you have been in the military, you know what that means. Standing orders are commands that are meant to be obeyed indefinitely. It means you are given a command to do something, and you continue to do that something until you are given a new command. If an army officer were to tell a private to stand at attention in front of a door, the officer can leave, but the private will still be standing at attention in front of the door. It doesn't matter if the officer forgets about the private and leaves him there for eight hours; it was a standing order. You don't move off of that order until you receive fresh orders.

So many people are constantly trying to jump around and change things. They want something new. They want something different. There is a restlessness that comes from the Holy Spirit, but there is also a restlessness that comes from the old sin nature.

"I need a new job. I need to change. I need to move."

Whoa, whoa, whoa. That is not of God. If He called you to the place and the job that you are in right now, then stay there until He calls you to something else. God's commands are standing orders; keep following them until He gives you new ones.

Perseverance is all about the three *p*'s: promise, problems, and possession.

Perseverance begins when God gives you a promise. Yahoo! You got a promise from God. Everybody says amen. Then you start walking towards that promise. In almost every single case, you will encounter a problem or problems.

You understand the devil hates your guts, right? You are a child of God. It is only natural for him to resist you. This world is also filled with the enemy's nature, so that will be pushing against you as well. When you got that promise from God, did you think you would just walk over and take it easily? That doesn't happen very often. When you receive a promise from God and start walking towards it, there is almost always opposition and pushback. You are going to encounter problems that are meant to make you stop and turn back. How you respond to those problems will determine how quickly you possess the promise.

I get a promise from God. I move towards it. I encounter a problem or problems. I respond to those problems. I eventually possess that promise as a reality in my life. That is the process, but where does perseverance come into play? Perseverance is enjoying the journey between the promise and the possession.

"Now wait a minute, Pastor Myles. I was paying attention, and there's a problem here. You said I am going to encounter problems and unpleasant things as I move towards the promise in my life. But now you are saying that I need to enjoy the journey between the promise and the possession."

Yeah, absolutely.

"Well, that doesn't sound possible."

It is. Do you really believe the promise is true? If you believe that and know that you are walking in God's ordained path towards the promise, then hitting problems just means you are one step closer to the possession of the promise.

Imagine that I set a man in front of you; we'll call him Matt. Then imagine that I bring in another person to stand next to him; we'll call this new guy Chris. I give each of them instructions. Matt, stand here and don't do anything. Chris, slap Matt on the face as hard as you can ten times.

That would be crazy. And wrong. But hang with me.

Imagine that Chris really does it. He hauls off and slaps Matt right in the face. Matt's cheek turns red. You cringe. Matt smiles. What's the smile about? Go ahead, Chris; we're waiting on you. Chris smacks him again. And again. And a fourth time. Anything humorous about the situation is completely gone. But Matt is still smiling. In fact, his smile is even bigger. Why? Why is he—

Five, six, seven.

You are no longer just uncomfortable; now you are a bit horrified. Matt is not smiling anymore. Instead, he has started to laugh.

If you were actually watching that scenario play out, you would probably be wondering what on earth was wrong with Matt. How many of his screws are loose? But let me change the whole story for you here. I sat down with Matt before this whole thing and told him after Chris slaps him ten times I would give him $2,000.

Now it makes a lot more sense, doesn't it? No wonder he was laughing. It was absolutely painful, but he knew every one of those slaps got him one step closer to the fulfillment of the promise I gave him. As long as he believed I had the goods, then every slap just brought him closer to receiving the promise. Knowing that allowed him to be joyful even though it was unpleasant.

Can you translate this into your life? If you really believe God's promises for you are true, then every step through pain, setbacks, problems, and trials is just one step closer to the fulfillment of the promise. All you have to do is keep moving forward. If you believe the promise is good, then you can even move forward with joy. Do you have a Bible? Have you read it? Your promises are good. God's promises to you *are* good.

Never ever has anything great been accomplished without perseverance. Look around you. Find anyone who is really successful in any field—business, education, art, whatever. Look closely at that person's life. You will find perseverance as a main characteristic every time. Look at any man or woman of God who impacted the world in a big way. Every single one of them had perseverance as a key characteristic in life. Every single person in the Bible who did anything great for God was a person of perseverance.

Sometimes we read stories in the Bible and totally miss the truth in them. Do you know the story of Moses? He finally got wind of who he was as a young man; he discovered that he was supposed to be the deliverer of God's people. So he went out on his own, in his own wisdom and knowledge and strength, and he tried to make it happen. Guess what—it was a total disaster. In fact, he ended up killing a man and fleeing for his life. He spent forty years in the wilderness before God showed up in the form of a burning bush and said, "Go back to Egypt and be the deliverer I have called you to be."

"Do what? Say what?"

"Go back to Egypt and be the deliverer I have called you to be."

"Egypt? Deliverer? God, have you forgotten? Been there, done that, and it didn't work out well at all. It was an unmitigated disaster. I killed a man."

But God said to him, "Go back and try again in your place of failure."

Listen to me right now. Perseverance is going back to your place of failure and trying again. That may not be geographically; it usually isn't. It may not be the exact same job or situation, but it will be something very similar. A lot of Christians miss opportunities like this. When bad things and failures happen, they think the path to healing lies is putting as much distance as possible between themselves and any situation that could be considered even remotely close to what they went through. But they are wrong. The fulfillment and completion of healing comes when we walk in a place so similar to the original place of failure that it makes us nervous and uncomfortable. But walking through it allows us to experience the fullness of healing.

"Well, I was hurt by church leaders years ago, so I'll never trust another church leader again."

That sounds like a wound God has mostly healed, but as long as you have that problem of trust you have not been healed completely. How is God going to bring complete healing? He will bring you into a similar situation. He will put you under godly leaders who have your best interest at heart. And as you walk in that similar situation, you will understand and finally be healed.

It is often the same in relationships, marriages, and many other areas of life. God brings healing by leading you into a similar place. Go back to your place of failure and try again.

How about the story of Noah? Most people know that one. God told him to go build an ark for his family and all the different kinds of animals. He stayed at that single task for 120 years. That speaks clearly of his faithfulness in a big, big way. One project. 120 years. He endured people laughing at him and mocking him because, according to the Bible, rain had not yet fallen from the sky. For 120 years he prepared for a flood, surrounded the entire time by people who did not know what rain was.

"What are you building that ark for?"

"Well, it's going to rain. It's going to flood."

"Oh, come on. What a nutcase."

Noah persevered through the ridicule. His perseverance saved not only his family, but the entire human race. That includes you and me.

As the story of Noah demonstrates, perseverance is doing what God tells you to do regardless of the words and opinions of others. It is not budging, not coming off of what God commanded you to do even when it doesn't look successful and doesn't look like you are getting anywhere. Stay the course.

John Wesley was a very, very powerful man of God who founded the Methodist Church and brought revival to Western Europe and all of America. Literally tens of thousands were swept into the Kingdom of God under his ministry. When he first felt God call him to preach and teach, he was part of the Anglican Church, which is what we know today as the Episcopal Church. He grew up in that denomination. Then he felt God's call, and he started asking to preach. At first a church would let him, so he would preach. Then they would kick him out and say, "Never again." They thought he was too crazy, too wild, and too strong. So he would move on to the next church. Churches everywhere were kicking him out, one after another.

Wesley kept a daily diary, and I want to pull some passages from it. These are widely quoted paraphrases from words Wesley wrote at the beginning of his preaching and teaching.

> *May 7, 1738, Sunday morning:* "Preached in Saint Lawrence's. Was asked not to come back anymore."

> *May 7, 1738, Sunday evening:* "Preached in Saint Katherine Cree's church. Deacons said, 'Get out and stay out.'"

> *May 14, 1738. Sunday morning:* "Preached in Saint Ann's. Can't go back there either."

> *May 21, 1738, Sunday afternoon:* "Preached in Saint John's. Deacons called special meeting and said I couldn't return."

> *May 21, 1738, Sunday evening.* "Preached at St. Bennet's. Was quickly informed I won't be preaching there anymore."

Not going to well, is it? Now let me give you a few direct quotes from just a year later.

> *May 8, 1739, Sunday morning:* *"Went to Bath, but was not suffered to be in the meadow where I was before, which occasioned the offer of a much more convenient place, where I preached Christ to about a thousand souls."*

> *September 9, 1739, Sunday morning:* *"Declared to about ten thousand, in Moorfields, what they must do to be saved."*

> *September 16, 1739, Sunday morning:* *"Preached at Moorfields to about ten thousand, and at Kennington Common to, I believe, nearly twenty thousand."*[3]

Stay the course. What has God told you to do? Keep doing it. Stay the course. Persevering people stay the course. They are not controlled by circumstances. They are not controlled or manipulated by the people around them. They stay the course. That is perseverance.

How about Shadrach, Meshach, and Abednego? You know those guys. Remember the story about them? The king called them in and told them to bow down to a golden idol, and he threatened to throw them into a fiery furnace if they did not. What was their reply? We will not bow. We will not bend. And by the way, we won't burn either.

Perseverance is a passion in your soul that will carry you through fear and intimidation. It will hold you. You will not move. You will persevere. You will keep going forward.

In one of his letters, the Apostle Paul refers to the "light and momentary troubles" in his life (2 Corinthians 4:17). What troubles is he talking about? Did he have a hangnail? Back up and read about the life he lived up until he wrote those words. He was shipwrecked in the open sea three separate times. Three other times he was beaten with rods and thrown in jail. One time he was actually stoned and left for dead. We don't know whether he actually died and God resurrected him, or they just thought he was dead. Either way, he got back up and walked right back into the city that stoned him to preach. That is perseverance.

There are Christians in churches today who want to walk away from God. Why? Because He hasn't given them all the blessings they expected. They didn't get the promotion at work. They didn't get this. They didn't get that. Can I tell you something? I am okay with that if you are a baby Christian. But if you have been serving God for ten years, then it is time for you to trade in your diaper for a suit of armor. Come on, Christian. Cowboy up and get this thing done.

Perseverance stands in the face of loss. It doesn't wilt. It doesn't back up. It doesn't run away. It stands in the face of loss. It stands in the face of rejection. It doesn't need public approval. It doesn't need a pat on the back, and it definitely doesn't give one whit about political correctness. Perseverance tells mountains to get out of the way. Perseverance declares, "If God is for us, who can be against us?" (Romans 8:31). Perseverance declares, "I can do all things through Christ who strengthens me," (Philippians 4:13). Simply put, perseverance gets the job done. It doesn't just start well; it finishes well.

Paul, at the end of his life, wrote, "For I am already being poured out like a drink offering, and the time for my departure is near. I have fought the good fight, I have finished the race, I have kept the faith. Now there is in store for me the crown of righteousness, which the Lord, the righteous Judge, will award to me on that day." (2 Timothy 4:6-8). What race is he talking about? He is talking about the race that God has marked out for us that he wrote about in Hebrews 12:1. Every one of us has a race to run, a life course God Himself has marked out for us. He made us for specific purposes. He made us to do specific things.

God marked that race out for us, and we are to run that race and run it well—with perseverance.

For just a moment I would like to take you back in time to October 20, 1968. I want us to go together to the Olympic Stadium in Mexico City. The high altitude and thin air of Mexico City were very, very good for sprinters, long jumpers, throwers, and athletes like that. It really helped them. But those same conditions were absolutely brutal for athletes that ran long distances, especially the marathon runners. Almost seventy runners came to run the marathon; they were the best runners in the world from many different nations. About 25 percent of them didn't even finish the race. The conditions were that difficult.

That year, Mexico City elected to schedule the marathon as the last event of the Olympics right before the closing ceremonies, which was a common practice.

Picture this with me. They start the marathon on time. The runners run their 26.2 miles. The winners come into the stadium and cross the finish line. The other runners trickle in over the next little while. They have a medal ceremony for the top three—gold, silver, and bronze. Then, immediately following the medal ceremony, they do the closing ceremonies of the Olympics. Once that is done, everybody leaves. After a short time, the stands are practically empty. Everyone has left.

But then, more than an hour after the official end of the race, a runner enters the stadium. Here comes John Stephen Akhwari, a runner from Tanzania who wouldn't quit. Earlier in the race, Akhwari had tangled with some other runners, fallen, and broken his knee. He had it taped up and continued on. He would run a little bit. Then he would walk. Then he would stop, grimacing in pain the entire time. You could see the pain on his face as he ran.

But he makes it to the stadium. The Olympics have already been over for some time, but word goes out that there is another runner. They quickly get the PA system back on. Hold on, clear the track. We've got another runner coming in. Akhwari finishes the lap of the stadium. He finishes the race.

Afterwards it was written about Akhwhari:

Today, we have seen a young African who symbolizes the finest of the human spirit. A performance that gives true dignity to sport. A performance that lifts sport out of the category of grown men playing at games. A performance that gives meaning to the word courage.[4]

When asked why he did not quit in front of television cameras the day after the race, Akhwhari said simply, "My country did not send me five thousand miles to start the race. They sent me five thousand miles to finish the race." Brothers and sisters, beloved of God, that is the way to finish. Jesus did not save you and send you into this world to start the race. He saved you and sent you into this world to finish the race. That's why we absolutely must run this race with perseverance.

LIVING A LEGACY

D uring the reign of King David, God gave Israel prosperity and victory over all their enemies. He blessed them in every single way, but something began to burn in David's heart.

David's heart was burning because he was living in a gorgeous palace while God's dwelling was still just a tent, the Tabernacle. David had it in his heart to build God a magnificent temple. He told his desire to the prophet, Nathan, who said, "Whatever you have in mind, go ahead and do it, for the Lord is with you," (2 Sam. 7:3).

Later that night, God spoke to Nathan. The prophet returned to David the next day to say no, God did not want David to build a temple after all. God had something He wanted to give David. Then, in 2 Samuel 7:11-13, Nathan gives King David a word from God.

> *The Lord declares to you that the Lord himself will establish a house for you. When your days are over and you rest with your ancestors, I will raise up your offspring to succeed you, your own flesh and blood, and I will establish his kingdom. He is the one who will build a house for my Name, and I will establish the throne of his kingdom forever.*

This is a very beautiful and powerful promise from the Word. And this is not just a promise to King David. It is a promise to you and I.

This is a word from God that comes to us, saints and beloved children of God. After your days on this earth are over, your dreams in God can continue. Long after your physical life is finished, your influence can live on through succeeding generations.

So many people have talked for so many years about what it means to leave a legacy. Let's look away from *leaving* a legacy because right now I want to teach you about *living* a legacy. I want you to know what it means to live a life that is so big in God it transcends your lifetime on this earth. You can live in such a way that, after you are buried and gone, your life will continue to echo on and on through succeeding generations. That is living a legacy.

In order to get the concept of living a legacy, you need to understand one thing up front. Very simply, there are three stages to life.

The first stage of life is the survival stage. A lot of people live their whole lives in the survival stage. What do I mean by that? I mean they're just living on Barely-Get-Along Street. They're just hanging in there, making it month-to-month or maybe even week-to-week. Am I talking about their finances? Yes I am, but I'm also talking about much, much more. They are barely hanging onto their marriage, their family life, their own lives, and their relationships with God. They are living in survival mode.

"I made it this week. Oh, that was a great message my pastor preached this Sunday. Wasn't the worship good? It just charged up my batteries. You know what? I think I'll be able to make it all the way to next Sunday."

By Thursday or Friday, they can't wait for Sunday. Sunday arrives just in time to charge up and make it again for another week. That's living in the survival stage. When we are living in the survival stage, we are powerless. Other people don't need us. We need other people. Because of that we have no power or influence in the world.

In Ecclesiastes 9, the Bible says no one listens to a poor man. You may not like that. I may not like that. But that doesn't change the truth. The Bible is not even saying that it's proper, that it's right, or that it should be that way. The writer of Ecclesiastes was just making an observation. That is the reality of the world we live in. Nobody listens to a poor man!

Again, are we talking about finances? Yes. Only finances? No. We are talking about finances and more. You can be poor in different areas of your life just like you can live in survival mode in different areas of your life.

If my marriage is being held together by scotch tape and Elmer's glue, are you going to come to me for help with your marriage? Probably not. If you do, then you have some problems. The cheese has fallen off of your cracker. The elevator isn't going all the way to the top floor. There is no reason to come to me for marriage counseling if my marriage is a disaster. I am poor in that area. Why would you want to listen to me?

God wants to deliver us from survival mode. He does not want us to live in poorness in any area of our lives. God wants us to prosper, to be blessed, and to be successful in every way. He wants to deliver us out of the survival stage and bring us into the second stage of life.

The second stage of life is the success stage. This is the beginning of what God wants for us. When we come into success in God, then we become empowered. For some empowerment means a healed marriage. For others empowerment means a family life that has come into God's order and blessing and flow. It could mean a career breakthrough or an educational accomplishment. There are different areas in our lives that empowerment can apply to.

The important thing about this stage is once you have come to success in an area, you are able to influence others. When you come to a place of success, others will look up and say, "How did you get there?" God wants us to be influencers. That's in the Word of God. Jesus said that we are the salt of the earth (Matt. 5:13). What does salt do? It influences. It changes. God intends for you and I to be people who are successful in areas where the world around us is struggling so that the world will want what we have in God.

Step one is to get delivered out of survival mode. Step two is to enter into success. Once we reach success, it is time to step into the third stage of life.

The third stage of life is the significance stage. Once we are in a place of success in life, we can cross the line of success and enter into significance. We have the potential to influence other people in the success stage, but we won't enter the third phase until we actually take up that potential and begin to influence other people.

When we move out of survival and into success, we then have the opportunity to step up to a whole different level by living a life of significance. God wants to bring us out of survival mode and into success mode. He wants us to be successful in every area of our lives, but once we reach a place of success, God's prayer is that we will not be satisfied simply with being successful. He desires for us to take that success and impart it to others. He wants us to influence the world around us. That's in our workplaces, in our homes, and in every other area of our lives. God wants you to become significant.

I've known a lot of people who were very, very successful but not the least bit significant. I've seen marriages that were incredibly successful but not touching any other marriages. I've seen dynamic businesspeople that had incredible success with their finances, but they refused to pass that success on to anyone else. These people were successful, but they had no influence or impact. They were successful, but not significant. Let me tell you, it won't take long after they are dead for people to completely forget about them. Do you know why? Because they did not live a big life. They didn't live a legacy.

I have also known some wonderful examples of people living a life full of significance. You can look back through the history of the Church and see many, many good examples. One example that you may not be familiar with is a man named Milton Hershey. Americans will recognize that last name immediately; Hershey's is one of the widest-selling chocolate brands in the United States. The chocolate is very well-known, but most don't realize that Hershey himself was an incredible Christian man. He was a very, very godly man who lived a legacy.

Years ago I went to a business conference in Corpus Christi, Texas. At that point in time, The Hershey Company owned some real estate and hotels, and they had a hotel there in Corpus Christi. That's where this conference was. When I got there, I looked at the schedule and noticed that, for the first session, the hotel manager was going to be given forty-five minutes to greet all of us and welcome us to the hotel. I thought that had to be a misprint. I mean, maybe they meant forty-five seconds. When was the last time you went to a business conference where they gave the hotel manager forty-five minutes to an hour at the beginning of it? I thought something had to be wrong.

But it wasn't wrong. It was exactly right. He talked to us for the full forty-five minutes, and it was incredible. It was powerful. He went beyond just welcoming us to the hotel; he told us about the life of Milton Hershey with pictures and illustrations to explain the whole story.

Did you know that, in the last years of his life, Hershey gave away over 95 percent of all of the money that he made to the Kingdom of God? This man also, over the course of his lifetime, built many, many orphanages. These orphanages didn't just take kids off the street to feed and clothe them. Hershey brought in some of the best and brightest teachers he could find to train the orphans and prepare them to go out and impact the world. His life was full of stuff like this. It was a phenomenal story.

During that time, one thing really caught my attention. As the hotel manager told Hershey's story, he broke down and started crying probably three or four times. I was thinking the guy must really love his job. There was no telling how many hundreds of times he had done this same speech and told this same story. But there he was, crying again.

At the end of his presentation, he thanked the audience. Everybody applauded. But, as the applause died down, he said, "Oh, I'm sorry. Let me share just one more thing. I apologize for breaking down in the middle of that. I've told this story hundreds and hundreds of times, but I can never get through it without crying. I was one of those boys that went through Hershey's orphanages. Over 80 percent of the children who went through those orphanages are now serving in upper management positions at the Hershey Corporation." That's living a legacy. That's what God wants for us in our lives.

There are five keys to living a legacy.

1. Serve the purpose of God.

We have to connect the success of God in our lives with God's purposes for our lives. This is really important.

If you go to 2 Chronicles 12, you'll find a really interesting story. In this chapter there are many stories about the great and mighty men of David. When David was establishing his kingdom, which is a type and shadow of the Messianic Kingdom under the Lord Jesus Christ, many great and mighty warriors began to gather around him. It's fascinating to hear about these great guys doing incredible exploits.

One group of mighty men, called the Gadites, came to David and said, "David, we're with you. We're throwing everything in with you." Now, what's so significant about that? The Bible says these Gadites could use every weapon of warfare. They could shoot the bow right-handed and left-handed. They were as swift as gazelles, and their faces were like the faces of lions. These guys were some stout warriors. They were big-time dudes that you did not want to find across the line from you on the battlefield. The Bible says the least of them was a match for one hundred men. The least! Can you imagine a guy getting into a fight, looking around, and going "Ok, ten, twenty, thirty, forty, fifty, sixty, seventy, eighty, ninety, one-hundred. One hundred to one. That's a fair fight. Bring it on." And that's the wimp of the bunch! The greatest of them was a match for a thousand; he's counting them off in hundreds!

These guys, obviously, could have built their own little kingdom. They could have had their own little fiefdom, but they understood something. Somehow they learned that there was something bigger going on in their world. They understood that there was something more that they had to do with their lives, so they chose not to just do their own little deal. They took their success and connected it with the purpose of God for their lives and for their generation.

Ecclesiastes tells us that a life lived outside of the purposes of God doesn't have any real significance or meaning beyond its days. It says a life like that is just a breath on a mirror—it shows up, then it's gone. That's it. That life is over.

We need to take our lives and hook them up like wagons to the eternal purposes of God. God's purposes are eternal. When we connect our lives to them, they give our lives eternal purpose as well. Can you see that? That's the way we live a legacy.

Yet we have this so backwards so much of the time. I teach a lot on family issues and child training, and sometimes I get asked to speak about that at conferences. At those conferences, this is something that I hear all the time: God first, family second, and church third. That sounds very good, very smart, very religious, and just plain stupid. The Bible says that deep calls to deep, but if you stick around for long enough, you'll learn that stupid also calls to stupid. And there's a lot of people out there answering when stupid calls.

People get defensive about this topic.

"Well, I'm not going to put my church in front of family!"

That's crazy. That's unbiblical. God says to seek first the Kingdom of God, then other things will be added to you. Sometimes seeking the Kingdom means staying home and investing in your family. Sometimes seeking the Kingdom means sacrificing time with your family to serve God.

Now, I will not deny that it is also possible to abuse this truth. You can get into the ditch on either side of this road, but the Kingdom should always come first. If we're going to live a big life, then we have to prioritize serving the purposes of God in our generation.

I love this story about a man and his eight-year-old son. The man is reading his paper one morning, and one whole page of it has a map of the world on it. This man gets a clever idea. He takes some scissors and cuts the map up into a bunch of pieces. Then he calls his son in from the other room and says, "Son, I know you're beginning to study geography in school. Why don't you take these pieces, go to the other room, and see if you can put the world together. Do the best you can, and then call me. I'll help you finish it." The son takes the pieces of newspaper and runs into the other room. The father sits down, thinking he has at least another forty-five minutes to finish the paper. About five minutes later the eight-year-old runs back in and says, "Dad, Dad! Come look! I got it all put together."

"There's no way. Let me come fix it," the father says.

When he walks into the other room, though, the world is put together perfectly. He's amazed, and he tells the boy, "This is unbelievable. Who helped you?"

"Nobody, Dad. I put it together."

"How on earth did you do that? How could you put this all together?"

"Oh, Dad, it was real simple. You see, on the back of the world there was this picture of a man. I put the man together, and the world came out perfectly!"

If you put the man together first, the world will come out perfectly. If you put the purposes of God first, then your world will come out perfectly.

2. Be ambitious.

If you want to live a life so big it echoes down through generations to come, you're going to have to be ambitious.

"Did he really just say that?"

Yes, I did.

"Ambition? That's bad, isn't it?"

No, no, no. Edmund Burke had it right when he said this: "Ambition can creep as well as soar."[1] Ambition in God can soar like an eagle. Ambition in selfishness and pride can creep like a snake on the ground. Ambition can be good, and ambition can be bad.

But let me ask you this: When is the last time you heard of a church preaching on ambition? Never. That's part of the problem! We have so many lazy, unambitious Christians sitting in pews all across America. They sit there, wondering why this nation is in such bad shape and why the Church is so ineffective at having any influence on it. I can tell you why. Because of all the lazy, unambitious Christians. They have been sitting on the pier, waiting for their ships to come in. Except they have been waiting so long, the pier collapsed underneath them, and they didn't even notice!

We need to understand what the Bible actually teaches about ambition. Look at the parable of the talents in Matthew 25.

"Is ambition in the parable of talents?"

Yes, it is. You might have missed it, but it's in there. A man, representing Jesus, gives a different number of talents to different servants, then leaves on a journey. Servant number one gets five, servant number two gets two, and servant number three gets one. When the man comes back, he goes to his servants. What has servant number one done? He's multiplied his five to ten, and the man says, "Well done, good and faithful servant!" (25:21). And servant number two? He has multiplied his two to four, and the man again says, "Well done, good and faithful servant!" (25:23).

So everything is going really wonderful in this parable until we get to servant number three. What's the story there? What's the problem? Oh, servant number three woke up every morning and went to work at eight o'clock. Then, at five o'clock every afternoon, he got home from work, sat down, ate his dinner, and spent the rest of the night sitting in his recliner, changing channels, scratching, and burping. He lived that same day over and over again. The man, who represents Jesus, comes to him and says, "You wicked, lazy servant!" (25:26).

Let me paraphrase for you: "You wretched, lazy, unfaithful slob. Give me back that talent I gave to you. You are a bad investment." I see this over and over again in church after church and Christian after Christian.

"Oh, Myles. You don't understand. If I had more talents and gifting, I would do more."

If you're not using the one you have, what makes you think you're going to do well with ten? If you're not using the one you have, what makes you think God is going to give you ten? In fact, God tells us in His Word that He won't.

There's got to be something stirring inside each and every one of us in this day and in this hour. There's got to be something in us that cries out and says, "I'm not willing to stay in this place anymore. I'm not willing to stay in a place of comfort and complacency." There's got to be a passion in our hearts that drives us to rise up from where we are and go to where God wants us to be.

I believe that our lives are gifts from God. I also believe one of the ways we repay those gifts is by living significant lives. You are called to repay God's gift to you by living a life that impacts the world around you. Repay Him by living a legacy.

Have you seen the movie "Saving Private Ryan"? Fantastic movie. It's a bit gory and a bit bloody; I understand that. But it's a very powerful movie. If you haven't seen it, let me give you a quick synopsis. On D-day, the first day American forces entered mainland Europe in

World War II, American soldiers hit the beaches near Normandy and all along the coast of France. Those soldiers got mowed down by the thousands. Death letters for all those soldiers had to be typed up in Washington D.C. and sent to parents and family.

The plot of the movie starts with a lady in the office where those letters are typed up noticing three letters with similar names going to the same address. Thinking they must have been brothers, she takes the letters to one of the commanding officers. The general looks at the letters and realizes the terrible situation—three brothers, all dead, and all at once. He begins to research and finds out there is a fourth brother who was also in the war, but he was still alive. This general makes a decision. He doesn't want the parents to lose all four sons, so he decides to send a special detachment of troops to Normandy to find and save Private Ryan.

Captain Miller, played by Tom Hanks, is the leader of this detachment of troops. They wind their way through German territory, trying to find Private Ryan. One by one they get killed. They're getting shot; they're getting stabbed; they're getting blown up by mines. They're dying right and left. Towards the end of the movie, they finally find Private Ryan. But just as they find him, a big battle breaks out, and they all get caught up in it. Fighting is fierce on both sides until the very end of the battle, when the Americans turn the tide and begin to win. The Germans retreat, but keep firing as they go. Right then, Captain Miller takes a bullet in the chest and falls, fatally wounded. He's lying there, bleeding out; he knows that he's not going to make it. With all the strength left in him, he begins to yell out, "Ryan! Ryan!" The soldiers around Miller go, find Private Ryan, and bring him over. Then Captain Miller reaches up, grabs Ryan by the shirt, and says, "Earn it. *Earn* it."

What was Captain Miller saying to Private Ryan? He was saying this: "Listen! We laid our lives down for you! We bled and died to save your life. You better do something significant with your life."

When I first watched this movie, tears started running down my face as I watched that scene play out. I wasn't just crying because Tom Hanks was dying. As those words were coming out of his mouth, all I could hear were the words of Jesus: "Myles, I laid down my life for you! I bled and died for you! Your life better count for something. Your life better be significant."

We need to live a life that is *full* of ambition. It brings pleasure to God. For us to squander our lives would be just a smack in His face. Get a life! If you aren't already living a life, then get one! I think young people say that a lot these days. Get a life. That's a good phrase. We need to say that every Sunday in church. Get a life! Get out of that recliner, put those greasy Twinkies down, get up, and get a life. Do something significant. Be successful, then start impacting and influencing other people. Live a legacy.

Many years ago, I was reading in a life insurance journal, and I found something very fascinating. It really ministered to me. That goes to show that you can find something from God in just about any place. A life insurance journal. It was just a short poem by an anonymous author, but it stuck with me, and I wrote it down.

> *There once was a very cautious man who never laughed or played.*
> *He never risked. He never tried. He never sang or prayed.*
> *And when, one day, he passed away, his insurance was denied.*
> *For since he never really lived, they claimed he never died.*

The sad truth is we could say the same thing about so many individual Christians and even whole Christian churches. Come on, get a life. You say you laid your life down for Jesus. What life? You didn't have a life! What sacrifice? Zero from zero still equals zero. You can't lay your life down until you get one.

Have you seen the movie "Braveheart"? I know, another bloody, gory movie reference. But it's a great movie, with powerful stuff and powerful pictures in it. God spoke to me through that movie as well.

One of the most powerful scenes in the movie is right towards the end. William Wallace is in captivity, and he knows he's about to be executed. This girl who is in love with him is in his cell, crying and telling him how much she doesn't want him to die. He just reassures her, saying, "All men die. Some men never truly live."

Truly live. Get a life. Live a big life. Live a legacy. Don't settle for anything less.

3. Don't get distracted by the small things.

If you want to live a life that transcends your days on this earth, you cannot get distracted by small, petty stuff. To live a life that impacts the world around you, you can't get bogged down with every minute detail of what's going on. All the people around you are getting caught up in the small things. Don't let yourself go there.

There's an old Indian proverb that goes like this: when hunting for rabbits in tiger country, watch out for tigers. When hunting for tigers in rabbit country, don't worry about the rabbits. Are you a rabbit hunter? Or are you after the big things in life? If you have been a rabbit hunter, then get delivered from that!

In order to live a significant life, you cannot get hung up on all of the petty stuff. This one is easy to understand, but there is a problem. We are all surrounded by rabbit hunters. Sometimes they're in our own family! People all around us get caught up and excited about hunting all these rabbits. If we are not careful, we'll get caught up in it with them.

There is another problem. We don't like this one, but it's true. All of us have a little bit of rabbit hunter in us, don't we?

Several years back, I was watching the news, and I saw one of the saddest things I have ever seen. It was an account of something that had happened in Houston, Texas. The night before that news report, a bunch of teens had been out riding in a car, and another car cut them off in traffic. They decided to use the air guns they happened to have with them in the car to scare the other driver. They pulled up beside the car, rolled down the windows, and stuck out their air guns. They didn't realize the other car was full of teenagers that did have real guns. As soon as the other teenagers saw guns pointed at them, they rolled down their windows and opened fire. The gunfire killed one and put two or three others in critical condition.

This was obviously a tragic, tragic story. But it stayed with me for days, and I didn't know why it kept coming up in my mind. I would be in my prayer time or studying the Bible, and this story would keep coming up. I just wanted to get it out of my mind. I was asking God to help me stop thinking about it. Then it finally dawned on me. Sometimes I'm a little slow, but I usually get there. I finally realized the Lord was trying to speak to me. I asked him why he kept bringing it back up in my mind. He said, "Because that's just like you."

"Lord, not me. Surely that's not me. I mean, I have never gotten in a car, driven up beside somebody, and held an air gun out. I have never done that," I said.

"No, you haven't. But you have some rabbit hunter in you," he said.

"Lord, where?" I said.

"Well, let me give you a quick example, Myles. How about when you're driving and the speed limit is fifty, but somebody in front of you is going thirty."

"Well, Lord . . . yeah, that's true. There's a bit of a problem there."

Then he brought back to my memory something that had happened just a couple of weeks before. I had been driving somewhere with my whole family in the car, and the car in front of us was driving real slow. Man, I was really frustrated. I was having this whole conversation with the other driver in my head, and not a nice one. You know how that is. *What's going on? Why won't you move? It's the skinny one right next to the break; step on it and the car will go!* But I hadn't said a word out loud yet. Then I heard my twelve-year-old daughter, who had been sitting quietly in the backseat, burst out, "Park it or drive it!"

I didn't turn. I just cringed at the steering wheel with my eyes straight ahead; I was afraid to look. When I finally mustered up the courage, I glanced over at my wife. She was looking right at me with a look that said so clearly, "Yeah, you know where she got that from, don't you?"

God said to me, "Come on, Myles. That's a rabbit. You're going to have a stroke one of these days just worrying about somebody driving slower than the speed limit."

Let me make this point in a different way. Imagine driving down Houston's Southwest Freeway in rush hour traffic. If you haven't been in Houston traffic, then this won't make sense to you. I promise you have no idea how bad it gets. It's wild. It matches anything I've seen anywhere in the world. Imagine you're in the midst of that on a Friday afternoon, 4:30 p.m. Cars weaving in and out of lanes. People cutting people off. If you're in the middle of rush hour traffic in Houston and there is a fly buzzing around in your car, can I give you some great advice? Don't worry about the fly. Especially not if I'm in the car next to you! That's a recipe for a ten-car pileup. Some poor guy is going to be driving home from work one day, and the next thing he knows he'll be standing before God in heaven. "Hey, what happened?"

"Well, it was a fly."

"A FLY?! You mean I died and came to heaven just because of a fly?"

Come on, don't sweat the small stuff. Don't get hung up or bogged down on small, petty, unimportant stuff. You will not live a legacy if you do that.

4. Respect the mentors and protégés God brings into your life.

Respect those that God brings over your life. Respect them; receive from them. Don't disrespect them. Don't dishonor them. Listen to what they have to say. If they tell you to do something, even if you don't agree with it, do it. Unless it's unbiblical or you have an awfully good reason not to do it, then do it. Respect them. Respond to them, engage with them, and pursue them. Don't make them pursue you; you pursue them. Respect the mentors God brings into your life.

If God has grown you to a place where protégés are now approaching you and learning from you, respect those proteges. Treat them with love and take the responsibility God has given you seriously.

One of the most beautiful passages in the Bible that you can find about this is the story of Esther in the Old Testament. She starts life with a tough row to hoe. She is an orphan and a refugee; that's two big strikes against her right out of the gate. She has no mom or dad, no one to provide for her. On top of that, her home country has been totally wiped out, and she's living in a foreign country.

Her uncle, Mordecai, takes her in. He trains her, develops her, teaches her, and imparts all sorts of things to her. We only know that because later, when she comes into the palace, she knows exactly what to do in different situations. So he did more than just teach her reading, writing, and arithmetic. Mordecai mentored her. He taught her social graces and how to handle herself in all kinds of circumstances. Mothers and fathers, I hope you pay attention to that.

Then one day the king is searching for a new queen, and he decides, in his wisdom, that the best way for him to find a new queen is to have a beauty pageant. Yes, that's right—a beauty pageant. Mordecai, the mentor of Esther, tells her, "Look, honey, this is from God. You sign up. You're going to get in that beauty pageant."

"Me? A beauty pageant?" she says.

"Yes. Get your bathing suit on, go down there, and enter that beauty pageant."

Now I know a lot of fundamentalist Christians here in America today that would have a major problem with that. Let me ask you something. This gal saved an entire nation. What have you saved lately? Come on. God used this beauty pageant to bring her to a place where she could save an entire nation. So obviously God didn't have near as much of a problem with it as some of our brethren today.

She enters the beauty pageant. She wins the beauty pageant and becomes what? Ms. Persia! She gets the banner and a crown on her head. She's the new queen.

After Esther is queen for only a short while, Haman, the king's right-hand man, starts plotting to wipe out all of the Jews. Mordecai, her uncle and mentor, lets Esther know about it. He tells her, "Honey, this is why God brought you to this place. It's your time to shine. It's your time to step up to the plate and bring deliverance to your people. Use your favor with the king to save our nation."

"Well, I can't do that. If I go before the king without a summons from him, then it's curtains for me. They would kill me. He has to ask for you. You don't get to come," she says.

"Let me tell you something," Mordecai says. "If you don't do it, then God will raise up someone else who will."

Now we know the story. She went in and did it. She saved a nation. But there's a powerful truth in this story that we don't need to miss. Mordecai tells Esther that if she doesn't do it, then God will raise up somebody else. If she had not listened to her mentor, do you know what would have happened? We wouldn't have the book of Esther today. We'd have the book of Betty or the book of Donna or the book of somebody else. God would have raised up someone else, and that person would have stepped onto a larger stage in life. That person would have lived the legacy, and it would be that person's life continuing to echo down through generations, impacting people today. We need to respect the mentors and respect the protégés that God brings into our lives.

I've heard so many messages through the years spoken by so many preachers and teachers about how this Christian life is not a sprint, it's a marathon. Now, there is some value to that teaching because it does impress on our minds that the Christian life is not a short dash but a long race run over many weeks, months, and years. But I want to make sure one thing is clear. The Christian life, properly understood from Scripture, is not a marathon. It is a relay race. We are meant to run, as fast and hard as we can, the race God marked out for us. As we go, we are to raise up and mentor those around us so that we can hand the baton off to them. Then they can take the baton and run with it.

When we originally bought the land on which Grace Community Fellowship in Wharton now sits, we bought twelve acres. I still remember the many conversations we had when I first told the elders I felt God was calling us to buy those twelve acres. One issue just kept coming up: twelve acres is an awful lot of land. None of them thought we needed twelve acres, but I told them I believed the direction was from God. They finally agreed to buy all twelve acres because we got such a great deal on the land.

Less than a year later, we found out that three acres adjacent to our property were going up for sale. I went back to the elders and told them we needed to buy those acres too. They were pretty surprised since we were still not sure what to do with the twelve acres we already had. They asked me why we needed that much, and I told them the truth, "I don't know."

They were even more surprised, but then I told them this: "I don't have a clue, but you know what? I think the generations after us are going to figure out what to do with it, and we're not going to short-change what they are going to be able to do. Let's sacrifice now. Let's buy the land now and set them up for the future."

This is God's pattern. When Solomon took over the throne, King David had already prepared all the material he needed to build the Temple. David was the one who got the vision from God to do it. He had the blueprints drawn out. He had all the money stored up. He made peace with all the enemies around Israel so that Solomon could focus attention on building the Temple instead of war. David had it all set up.

That's the way we need to live our lives. That's living a legacy. Proverbs 13:22 says it this way: "A good person leaves an inheritance for their children's children." That's not just speaking about natural children and descendants. I'm not just speaking about your genealogy or living a legacy only within your natural family. I'm talking spiritually. It's important that we leave an inheritance and a legacy to those in our spiritual family, the family of God. We need to leave them an inheritance so that each generation can build and progressively grow the Kingdom of God.

5. Keep running.

Listen to me. If you're going to live a big life, then you have to keep running. Keep running, keep running, and keep running. If you get knocked down, get back up. Keep running. Keep running. Don't quit. Don't get tired. Keep running. If you get knocked off course, then get back on course. Keep running. Keep moving forward. Don't quit. Come on. The race is not always won by the swift; it's won by those who keep running. Don't sit down. Don't get weary. Don't give up. Don't get the feeling that you've arrived. Don't get to a place of success and camp there. Keep running. Keep going forward. Keep running.

Years ago I watched a show on the Discovery Channel about salmon. I know that sounds like a boring show; at first I thought it was boring too. I started to change the channel a couple of times, but I just felt like there was something there. It was kind of fascinating. Then

I began to really watch. It was talking about how these salmon live for years out in the ocean, and then, one day, something clicks inside of them. They turn and begin to swim across the ocean floor by the thousands and thousands, each heading back to the very pond that they were born in. They swim against the tide and up these rivers, jumping over incredible obstacles. Many of them get eaten by bears along the way. You've seen those pictures, right? Some of them go over to the shallow part of the water to rest, and most of those get eaten by bears too. Some of them finally make it. They're ragged, tired, and torn-up, but they are there. Once they finally arrive, they spawn, lay eggs, and die. When those eggs hatch, the decaying bodies of the parent become valuable food and nutrients for the hatchlings.

Does that sound like an awful story to you? It's not! It's a glorious, powerful, wonderful story. It's a great picture. Can I tell you something? I'm going to swim upstream. I'm going all the way there. I'm not going into the shallow area to take a rest and get eaten. I'm going to get all the way there, and I'm going to lay my eggs before it's over with. I'm going to lay my life down and die, and hopefully my life has enough nutrition in it that it will bring sustenance to those who come after me. I want to live a big life. I want to live a legacy.

There was a time when missionaries packed their belongings in pine boxes when they left the country because their life expectancy was so short. They didn't have vaccines back then, and nobody knew how to combat all the myriads of illnesses in foreign countries.

C.T. Studd was called to be a missionary to the Far East during that time. He was one of the world's most renowned athletes; he was a big-time star, but he gave it all up when he got saved. He felt a call to the mission field and left everything, taking his coffin with him. Everyone thought he was crazy, and they let him know. Do you know how he responded? This is what he said: "I will blaze the trail, though my grave may only become a stepping stone that younger men may follow."[2]

Younger men and younger women have followed his life as a stepping stone to the mission field for years and years and years now.

There's another one, Borden of Yale. This is one of my favorites. Borden of Yale was a bright, sharp young man, one of the most prominent students at Yale University. He was from a very wealthy and well-connected family. He had an amazing reputation with the professors at Yale and even the president of the university. They all thought that Borden could do anything he wanted to, speaking of him in absolutely glowing terms.

Then, in his senior year, he got saved and felt a call to the mission field. He told his friends he felt called to go to China, and they all told him that he was nuts! They tried to make him understand all the great things he could do with his future in America; they wanted to keep him from throwing all that away. But he said no. He refused to listen to them, and he told them God had called him to the mission field. He sent word home to his parents, but the reception at home was even worse. They were highly upset. They even considered going in, taking him by force, and holding him against his will until he came to his right mind. Borden would have none of it. He wouldn't be dissuaded. He was certain God had called him to China, so he set out for the mission field.

He got as far as Cairo, Egypt, where he contracted a fatal illness and died a very painful, slow death. He spent the last days of his life in a hotel room all by himself, dying in solitude. When the news of his death came back to America, so many of his friends and family thought they were vindicated. They thought about all the ways they had tried to warn him, but he didn't listen. They didn't understand why he threw his life away.

Some months later, his possessions arrived in a trunk. As his parents began to painfully go through some of them, they found his personal Bible and flipped through it. They found six words, written there. They shared the six words with the rest of the family, but soon others heard them, and they began to spread. When a certain newspaper reporter heard the words, he came in and asked the family all about Borden. He wrote and published a story about the man. Then other papers picked up on the story, and it went all across America. Young men and young women from all over the nation stood up and volunteered to take Borden of Yale's place and go to China. Even though Borden never made it, they went by the thousands in his place. What were the six words he wrote in his Bible? "No reserve, no retreat, no regrets."

No reserve. I left nothing in any spare tanks, baby. I burned it all. I didn't put anything aside for a rainy day. I put it all out there. I gave it all I had, all up front. No plan B. No reserve.

No retreat. I'm not backing up one step from what I know God called me to do. I don't care about the cost. I don't care if I die here this day. I have no retreat in me. I'm not backing up, not one inch. No retreat.

No regrets. I never made it. I never set one foot in China, but I have no regrets because I know that I have done what God called me to do. No regrets.

Keep running. Respect the mentors and the protégés that God brings into your life. Don't be distracted by small, petty stuff. Be ambitious, and serve the purpose of God. These five keys will help you live a legacy. They will help you live a life that's larger than your days upon this earth.

NOTES

Prophetic Vision

1. Hudson, Hugh, dir. *Chariots of Fire*. 1981. N.p.: Twentieth Century Fox Film Corporation, Allied Stars Ltd., and Enigma Productions. DVD.

Purpose of Vision

1. Moody, D. L. Quoted in Paul Gericke. *Crucial experiences in the life of D.L. Moody*. New Orleans: Insight Press, 1978.
2. Bright, Bill. *Have You Heard of the Four Spiritual Laws?* Peachtree City, GA: Campus Crusade, 2007.

Quitter, Camper, Climber

1. Stoltz, Paul G., "Do You Know Your AQ?" *Workforce* 77, no. 12 (December 1998), https://www.questia.com/magazine/1P3-36863657/do-you-know-your-aq
2. Whittier, John Greenleaf. "Maud Muller." In *Yale Book of American Verse*, edited by Thomas Raynesford Lounsbury. New Haven: Yale University Press, 1912. https://www.bartleby.com/102/76.html

3. Peabody, Endicott. Quoted in Robert Dallek. *Franklin D. Roosevelt: A Political Life.* New York: Viking, 2017. 25.
4. Muir, John. Quoted in Badè, William Frederic. *The Life and Letters of John Muir.* Boston and New York: Houghton Mifflin Company, 1924. https://vault.sierraclub.org/john_muir_exhibit/life/life_and_letters/chapter_10.aspx

From Simon to Peter

1. Dyer, Frank Lewis and Thomas Commerford Martin. *Edison: His Life and Inventions.* 1910. Project Gutenberg, 2006.
2. Kettering, Charles. Quoted in T. A. Boyd. *Professional Amateur: The Biography of Charles Franklin Kettering.* New York: E.P. Dutton & Co., Inc., 1957.
3. Ford, Henry and Samuel Crowther. *My Life and Work.* Garden City, New York: Garden City Publishing Company, 1922. https://books.google.com/books?id=4K82efXzn10C&vq
4. Watson, Thomas J. Quoted in Dr. Roger von Oech. *A Whack on the Side of the Head.* Warner Books, 1987.
5. Bartleman, Frank. *Azusa Street.* New Kensington, PA: Whitaker House, 2000.

Reaching Your Potential

1. Mason, John. *You're Born an Original Don't Die a Copy.* N.p.: Insight Publishing Group, 1993.
2. Franklin, Benjamin. *Poor Richard's almanack.* Waterloo, Iowa: U.S.C. Publishing Co., 1914. https://archive.org/details/poorrichardsalma00franrich/page/26

3. Kram, Mark, "The Battered Face of a Winner," *Sports Illustrated*, March 15, 1971, 16. https://www.si.com/vault/issue/41004/21

4. Watson, Thomas J. Quoted in Dr. Roger von Oech. *A Whack on the Side of the Head.* Warner Books, 1987.

5. Sanders, Oswald. *Spiritual Leadership: Principles of Excellence for Every Believer.* Chicago: Moody Publishers, 2007. 104.

Being Response-able

1. King, Larry. *Larry King Live.* Unknown episode.

2. Carpenter, Karen and Richard Carpenter. "Rainy Days and Mondays." Writers: Roger Nichols, Paul Williams. A&M Records. 1985.

3. Liberty First News. "Must See Richie Parker Guy With No Arms Of Hendrick Motorsports Inspirational Video." Reporter: Tom Rinaldi. February 11, 2014.

Poverty Spirit

1. McGraw, Dr. Phil. *Dr. Phil.* Unknown episode.

Changing Your Destination

1. "Proven Men Porn Survey." Proven Men Ministries, Ltd. Conducted by Barna Group. 2014. https://www.provenmen.org/2014PornSurvey/

2. Kennedy, Dr. James. "The Christian's Magic Wand." Fort Lauderdale, Florida: Coral Ridge Ministries Media, Inc., November 28, 1996. 4. https://www.djameskennedy.com/full-view-sermon/djk19647x-the-christian's-magic-wand

3. Henry, Matthew. Quoted in Arnold Gingrich. *Coronet,* Vol. 17, 1944.
4. Wurmbrand, Richard. *In God's Underground.* Bartlesville, OK: Living Sacrifice Book Co., 2004.

Love the House

1. Moody, D.L. Quoted by Rick Godwin in a Trinity Broadcasting Network interview.

2. Perseverance

1. Lombardi, Vince. "What It Takes to be Number One." Family of Vince Lombardi c/o Luminary Group LLC, 2019. http://www.vincelombardi.com/number-one.html
2. Cosmatos, George P. and Kevin Jarre, dir. *Tombstone.* December 25, 1993. N.p.: Hollywood Pictures, et al. DVD.
3. Wesley, John. "The Journal of John Wesley." The Revival Library, 2015. http://www.revival-library.org/index.php/catalogues-menu/1725 /the-journal-of-john-wesley
4. Greenspan, Bud, dir. "The Last African Runner." N.p.: Cappy Productions, 1976.

Living a Legacy

1. Burke, Edmund. *Select Works of Edmund Burke: A New Imprint of the Payne Edition.* Vol. 3. Indianapolis: Liberty Fund, 1999. https://oll.libertyfund.org/titles/658
2. Grubb, Norman. *C.T. Studd: Cricketer and Pioneer.* Cambridge: The Lutterworth Press, 2014. 120-121.